FOURTH EDITION

Human Evolution

PROCESSES AND ADAPTATIONS

By Steven J. C. Gaulin

UNIVERSITY OF CALIFORNIA - SANTA BARBARA

cognella® | ACADEMIC PUBLISHING

Bassim Hamadeh, CEO and Publisher
Kassie Graves, Director of Acquisitions
Jamie Giganti, Senior Managing Editor
Jess Estrella, Senior Graphic Designer
Bob Farrell, Senior Field Acquisitions Editor
Natalie Lakosil, Licensing Manager
Kaela Martin, Associate Editor
Kat Ragudos, Interior Designer

Cover image: Original cover design by Jess Estrella.

Printed in the United States of America

ISBN: 978-1-5165-1221-8 (pb) / 978-1-5165-1222-5 (br)

CONTENTS

REPRODUCTION: THE EVOLUTIONARY BOTTOM LINE

ACKNOWLEDGMENTS

It is both gratifying and humbling to thank the many people who helped this book materialize—some without their knowledge, or responsibility. The ideas in any human brain mostly came from other brains. Even our innovations owe a debt to their seeds and triggers. Notably, Darwin and Wallace—whose ideas dominate this book—were separately inspired by Thomas Malthus's *An Essay on the Principle of Population*. I know my intellectual debts are many and large.

Though we never met, George C. Williams has long been my personal guide to the mysterious territory of living matter. His masterful book, *Adaptation and Natural Selection*, is an intellectual touch-stone that should be fully explored by any serious young biologist. Equally influential were four brilliant evolutionists I have had the pleasure of knowing to varying degrees: my graduate advisor and the originator of modern hunter-gatherer and primate studies, Irven DeVore; the flamboyant and influential theorist, Robert L. Trivers; and (from the other side of "the pond") the quintessential synthesist Richard Dawkins; and perhaps the most important evolutionist since Darwin, the enigmatic W. D. Hamilton. These people truly "built the roads" that modern evolutionists now comfortably cruise. Our intellectual landscape would be completely different if any of their contributions were missing, and we'd be stuck in some significant ruts.

Theories can be elegant and powerful; but they're worthless if we can't communicate them to our students. Dawkins is, and DeVore was (miss you, Irv), a brilliant communicator. I try to channel these two masters whenever I write or lecture.

I am fortunate to be a member of a first-rate Anthropology Department at U.C. Santa Barbara. Though we have many strengths, we have an international reputation for evolutionary approaches to the study of human behavior, a perspective which is foregrounded in this book. Two of my Santa Barbara colleagues have had an especially strong influence on my views and presentation: John Tooby, a founder of the dynamic field of evolutionary psychology, and Michael Gurven, one of the most influential anthropologists still lacking grey hair (damn you, Mike).

Two other groups have also contributed significantly to my development as a teacher: your predecessors, and my dedicated crew of Teaching Assistants. Every time I teach this (or any) class, students generously poke holes in what I'm saying. That's a double gift because it lets me clarify the point at hand, but it also teaches me about some ambiguity that needs to be addressed in my writing. Keep asking; we'll all learn more.

My Teaching Assistants have been, and continue to be, true colleagues. In our weekly meetings and more informal discussions, they regularly offer valuable feedback about content, organization, and—most importantly—about which explanations do and don't work. In addition, two of my long-term Head Teaching Assistants—Kate Hanson Sobraske and Anne Pisor—intelligently critiqued portions of this or previous editions of the book. Working with all of these talented and committed people is a daily pleasure.

I also wanted comments from smart people outside the biological sciences, because so many of my students fit that description. Considered suggestions by my muse, Judith Geiger, and by my admired friend and fellow teacher, Diane Siegal, greatly improved the clarity and coherence of my prose. With thoughtful attention to effective visual communication, Judith also created many of the illustrations in this edition. Qinglin Yin carefully proofread the entire manuscript.

At Cognella, my Acquisitions Editors, Marissa Applegate for the first two editions and now Bob Farrell have both been excellent and congenial advisors. Jamie Giganti, Senior Managing Editor, and Kaela Martin knowledgably and amiably guided me through the many phases of publication. Jennifer Bowen Levine, Administrative Program Specialist, and Danielle Menard have cheerfully and efficiently dealt with all my (often naïve) questions. Jess Estrella planned and executed the cover graphics, and Dani Skeen led the marketing efforts.

PREFACE

The fundamental premise of twenty-first century biology is that life as we know it is a product of evolution. There are many separate lines of evidence that support this premise, so many that biologists would comfortably make the same claim about any life form that we might eventually find, anywhere in the universe. Among all known material processes, only evolution could assemble life's intricate precision.

Charles Darwin is often misremembered as having "proved" evolution. He did *not* do that, nor could he have. But putting philosophical issues of proof aside for now, Darwin's actual contribution was to offer a plausible *mechanism* that could cause evolution to happen: natural selection. It's this mechanism that we want to understand as fully as we can, because it is, as far as we can tell, the "designer" of all living things. If you understand a mechanism then you know what it will—and won't—do. Thus, my overarching goal is to help you fully grasp the way this inanimate designer, natural selection, works. Only then will you be in a position to understand its products—ourselves included.

This book is not organized around facts and definitions. Instead I want to help you acquire a new set of conceptual skills; specifically, an evolutionary "tool kit" that you can take with you and apply to any question about any living thing. I'm eager to answer your questions, but sooner or later our paths will diverge. If I can teach you to *think like an evolutionist* during our time together, I will have given you portable tools more powerful than Wikipedia.

Structurally this book is divided into five Sections, each with several chapters. The first Section carefully, but (I hope) approachably, lays out the key mechanisms and processes of evolution, including the genetic system of inheritance on which it critically depends. This is the core of the tool kit; I use as much example and analogy as I think will help you to not merely learn the vocabulary, but to "try on" the various modes of thinking that let evolutionists answer real biological questions.

In the second Section we challenge ourselves by intentionally singling out some the bigger evolutionary puzzles: altruism and homosexuality. I walk you through the various ways that evolutionists have addressed these puzzles to help you sharpen your tools and learn to handle them with precision by solving some hard problems.

The third Section turns our focus on the past, to understand where we came from. We begin by developing methods of determining evolutionary ancestor-descendant relationships. The next two chapters lay out the first two thirds of the human fossil record and explore ways of interpreting it. In the final chapter of Section three I set the fossils temporarily aside to summarize some of the specific evolutionary forces that we believe sculpted our more unique human traits.

Section four provides a temporal sequel to Section three and brings our tour of human evolution right up to the present. It begins with a chapter on the biological diversity of our genus, *Homo*, and details how a single species of that genus eventually came to occupy most of the globe. This is followed by an evolutionary perspective on our most distinctive

trait—language. We next learn some clever methods for identifying traits that natural selection has recently been favoring. The last chapter in this Section explores why natural selection hasn't yet fixed some of our current imperfections.

The last Section turns to reproduction, since it is the evolutionary "bottom line." Like altruism and homosexuality, sexual reproduction is also an evolutionary puzzle because of its multiple disadvantages. We try to solve that puzzle, and then go on to explore why, in some species the sexes are very different, but in others only a surgeon could tell them apart. The book concludes with an evolutionary analysis of male-female bonding and love.

As I wrote this book I tried to strike four simultaneous but different balances. First, for reasons that will soon be clear, adaptive evolution would not work without genes (or something much like them). And genes would not exist except for evolution's designer, natural selection. So any evolutionary tool kit will need some non-trivial genetic components. In addition to providing the essentials of genetics in Chapters 3 and 4, a genetic perspective on evolution is interwoven throughout the book.

The second balance I have tried to strike was between the (sometimes abstract) evolutionary processes that shape organisms and the beautiful adaptive outcomes these processes have created. Neither makes sense without the other, and I show you how to stitch the two together to make testable evolutionary predictions.

My third balancing act was to clearly map the methods used by evolutionists (which I find are often neglected in textbooks) while still giving proper attention the exciting results. Since I want to give you a tool kit, I need to make clear how those tools are used, and the kinds of answers each tool can, and cannot give.

My final attempt at balance was aimed at maintaining both scientific precision and a sense of fun. I truly love these ideas, I love sharing them, and I hope you will hear that in what I have written for you.

Steven J. C. Gaulin
Santa Barbara CA

CHAPTER 1

SOLVING THE CENTRAL PROBLEM OF BIOLOGY

Why is there something rather than nothing? What is the fabric of the universe? What is life? Why do living creatures so precisely match the demands of their environments? How did our species come to be? Such basic questions might seem easy to answer; after all, they concern stuff that is all around us. But, ironically, they are among the most difficult—and most interesting—questions we can ask. In this book our journey begins well after the Big Bang; and we'll take the basic processes of physics and chemistry for granted. On the other hand, we will dig deeply into the nature of living things, with our own species as our special focus. At its core, this book is about you, your family, your friends, and everyone you'll ever know. It is about how we humans came to be; why we are like other animals in so many ways and so unusual in other respects. When we understand the *processes* that design organisms we will have powerful insight into the nature of those organisms. And that is our entirely achievable goal.

The idea that unites all the above questions is that they highlight "the mystery in the common-place." We can negotiate our everyday lives without asking these fundamental questions, accepting things as they are because, after all, they seem to have always been that way. Or we can open our eyes, shift our perspective, and realize that what we have taken for granted desperately needs explanation; none of it *had to* be this way. Why is it this way? The more you ask this question, the more you will learn.

Beginning down this more inquisitive path, the first perspective shift I want to share with you is that life—the millions of teeming, photosynthesizing, breathing, eating, and reproducing species now populating our world, all of it—is wildly improbable. That's because the natural state of matter is chaos, not order. Atoms don't spontaneously jump together and form, say, an octopus. And even if they did—in a spectacularly improbably moment—they would not stay that way for long. Build anything, from a sandcastle to a skyscraper, and the forces of nature will sooner or later tear it down. Things fall apart; molecules eventually distribute themselves randomly. Physics fans will recognize that I'm talking about *entropy*. Unless some force is acting on them, matter and energy both spontaneously proceed to a natural state of disorder, of chaos, of randomness.

But living things are just the opposite; they are highly ordered, highly *non-random*. We use the word "organism" because living things are so *spectacularly organized*. Every organ, every tissue type is a patterned and integrated arrangement of atoms and molecules. And each organ is in its place, coordinating with other body systems and doing specific "jobs" that contribute to survival and reproduction. To understand how very precisely tuned organisms are to the demands of the environment, it's helpful to see how small changes can cause serious problems. Here is one example.

Earth's inhabitants are made of proteins, about 92,000 different proteins in the case of humans. One of these proteins, called hemoglobin, is found in red blood cells and its very important job is to carry oxygen to the tissues and to help dispose of carbon dioxide. Like all proteins, hemoglobin is made up of smaller molecules called amino acids. Counting the so-called alpha and beta chains, there are 574 amino acids in each hemoglobin molecule. Let's see how precisely tuned this molecule is. If there is a substitution—one kind of amino acid for another—at the sixth position on the beta chain, the unfortunate result is sickle-cell disease. Until the development of new therapies in the last few decades, people with sickle-cell disease typically died by the age of 20. A single amino acid change (out of hundreds) in just one of 92,000 proteins was fatal. Of course, changes in other proteins can be similarly harmful. For our bodies to work, a huge number of molecules have to be in exactly the right places! Do you see what I mean when I say that organisms are precisely tuned?

We'll detail more about how these amino acids and proteins are formed in Chapter 4, but the point here is how highly organized each of them is. If we move away from the microscopic level of molecules we continue to see the same kind of ordered complexity. For example, many animals have exquisite camouflage that allows them to blend into their environment. Figure 1-1 shows a stick insect (*Timema poppensis*) among the needles of a redwood tree, its primary food source. Its size, shape, and frosty striped pattern closely match the needles, and if the image were in color you would see that the shade of green is identical. Animals are not alone in meeting the challenges of their environment. Many plants have physical (e.g., thorns) or chemical defenses (toxins) that allow them to discourage herbivores. Here again, any departure from these ordered patterns would compromise the organism's ability to survive and reproduce. Life is massively anti-entropic!

Figure 1-1. Camouflaged insect on its host plant.

At every level it defies the natural physical tendency to disorder and randomness.

And life has one more very fancy trick up its sleeve: It makes extremely reliable copies of its ordered complexity. True, we live in a world of photocopy machines and cameras that can make various kinds of copies. But these devices can't make copies of *themselves*; Xerox machines don't make Xerox machines. (Think about what additional components they would need in order to do that.) We haven't made a machine that can reproduce, nor one that can adapt to its environment with such exquisite sensitivity as even a single-celled organism can. Life is special; the atoms and molecules in living things are organized in ways that cannot be explained by the laws of physics. Something else is going on with life. That's why there is a separate science, biology, to study it.

Take a minute to appreciate the paradox: Matter and energy naturally tend towards disorganization, but in living things—and only in living things—we find complex structural organization, at all levels from the microscopic to the macroscopic. And, via reproduction, living things pass on their structural organization across great expanses of time. Why the difference? How does life, and life alone, *defy entropy?* That is the core problem of biology, mentioned in the first paragraph: How do living things achieve and maintain highly nonrandom states of matter? Why does each type of organism match so exquisitely the various demands of its unique environment? It is the core problem because, as we will see, every other biological question must be framed, analyzed, and answered in terms of how we solve that core problem. So let's get on with it!

LIFTING THE VEIL: NATURAL SELECTION AS THE DESIGNER OF ORGANISMS

Biology was born as a true science about a century and a half ago. Since Aristotle, and probably long before, its early practitioners were avidly assembling observations and doing careful description and cataloguing, but they had no framework for organizing this raw information because they hadn't solved its core puzzle.

In the summer of 1858 London was particularly unpleasant because of unusually hot weather, combined with the death throes of an ageing and inadequate sewer system. Perhaps that's why Charles Darwin was happy to stay at his suburban home in Downe and have his most important paper (Darwin and Wallace, 1858) presented by a colleague. In that 16-page document, read at the July meeting of the Linnaean Society, these two men cracked biology's central problem. They argued that living things matched their environment simply because those that didn't failed to thrive. Their theory, which they called *natural selection*, claims that *nature automatically chooses* which types get to reproduce. "Nature" in the previous sentence is the sum total of factors that might impede survival and reproduction: starvation, predators, parasites and pathogens, competitors, climate and, yes, entropy. Every population consists of unique individuals, each one exhibiting its idiosyncratic pattern of traits. Darwin and Wallace argued that some traits allow an individual to better address the set of challenges posed by its environment. Individuals that have better traits tend to survive and leave more offspring, and thus pass on to succeeding generations the traits that helped them in their "struggle for existence." In this way, traits that help individuals meet the tests of their environment accumulate in the population over time—in the many offspring of the better-fitting individuals, and in their offspring's offspring, and so on. In essence, organisms fit well with their environments because, in each and every generation, those environments are acting as a *filter* that allows only the better-fitting individuals to survive and produce offspring.

Of course environments are not stable. Mountain ranges are built up or eroded down in ways that affect rainfall and temperature regimes; continents merge and break apart; the earth wobbles (technically, precesses) on its axis; our sun's fusion furnace ebbs and flares; comets smash into the earth and volcanoes erupt, both throwing light-blocking debris into the atmosphere; new predators, competitors, or germs can invade. Because of these environmental changes, evolution never stops. Organisms are constantly being remolded to match new environmental challenges. If we could create time-lapse films that spanned not mere days or weeks, but centuries and millennia, we would see organisms morphing like Claymation figures: dinosaurs transforming into birds and hoofed carnivores changing into whales.

By the standards of science, Darwin and Wallace succeeded wildly because they solved multiple problems with a single theory. For example, they not only explained why the traits of each species differ; they also explained why species have changed over time—why fossils reveal animals and plants that are different from those of today. As you move more deeply into this book you will see that their theory solves many other puzzles as well.

ONLY A THEORY?

You will have noticed that I used the word "theory" to describe Darwin and Wallace's idea of evolution by natural selection. Students often ask, "Why just a theory; isn't evolution a fact?" This is important so let's take some time to sort it out.

Philosophers have the unenviable job of policing our understandings of the world. The particular squads of philosophers who inspect our scientific understandings are, unsurprisingly, called philosophers of science. These guardians of scientific thought will tell you directly that there are no facts. In their world view, there are two main categories of information: observations (things we can detect and measure about the world), and there are theories (ideas intended to make sense of those observations). Non-philosophers often use the word "fact" where a philosopher would say "observation." To take a relevant example, we can dig holes in the ground and find fossils that are noticeably different from anything alive today. These fossils, and our measurements of them, would be observations (not facts). How shall we explain such observations? With a theory, of course. One theory might be that organisms have changed over time because of natural selection. That is the theory that we'll be exploring in this book, but to see how science is done you need to understand that it's not the only possible theory that could be proposed to explain our fossil observations.

I'm sure you can think of others, but consider this one. Perhaps every few million years an intergalactic "Noah's ark" arrives and dumps a whole new collection of organisms on earth which typically out-compete the ones that were dumped previously. If that happened, it could potentially explain why there are fossils and why the life forms of today are not the same as those of the past. Oh, you don't like that theory? Why not? How did you decide? What are the rules for evaluating theories?

Every theory attempts to explain one or more existing observations (e.g., fossils), but it must also *make predictions*—it must tell us what specific *new* kinds of evidence to look for. If the "intergalactic repopulation" theory were true, wouldn't we expect to find some trace of those unearthly visits, some kind of interstellar trash, maybe even some old discarded spaceships? Also we should find coordinated waves of biological replacement with a whole set of species disappearing and another set appearing at the same time. Moreover we shouldn't expect to find any "transitional" creatures, intermediate between those of adjacent waves. Instead, each group of organisms should be quite dissimilar from the previous group since they have no common heritage. Indeed, because they could have come from different galaxies, they might

be expected to have wildly different anatomy, physiology, and even chemistry.

To test the theory of intergalactic repopulation and the theory of natural selection against each other, we would evaluate how well their predictions match the available evidence, like the *fossil record*. We've just discussed some of the predictions of the intergalactic repopulation theory. It turns out that the theory of evolution by natural selection would make nearly opposite predictions. For example, it doesn't predict discrete waves, with many species being "switched out" simultaneously; instead each species should change at its own rate, somewhat independently of those around it and in response to particular changes in its environment. It also predicts an abundance of transitional forms that share many features and that differ from each other only by small, incremental degrees. It also predicts an absence of ancient spaceships.

Note that any theory rests on a proposed causal process—in these cases, successive recolonizations or gradual natural selection. And these causal processes automatically generate predictions which can be compared to observations of the real world. Yes, as I imagine you concluded from the outset, the intergalactic repopulation theory doesn't do very well—its predictions are not well supported by real-world observations. Instead, the history of life on earth is chock full of transitions with one form grading into another. The observation that the same hereditary system (see Chapters 3 and 4) is shared by all life on earth is yet another vote for the theory of natural selection. If successive waves of creatures came from disparate places in the universe, why should they all encode their hereditary information with precisely the same molecule?

Thus science has only observations and theories, and any particular theory will stand or fall based on how well it matches its own predictions about new observations. Moreover, any idea that can't be tested in this way—by making predictions—isn't a theory, even if it claims to explain certain existing observations. So, by the standards of science, the "intergalactic repopulation" theory is a theory; but it's a poor one because its predictions do not match our observations. That's why we would reject it.

Here's one more weakness of the intergalactic repopulation theory: How does it explain the precise fit between organisms and their environments? As stated, it can't. There is no reason to expect that creatures delivered from elsewhere in the universe would be well suited to specific conditions on earth. On the other hand, the theory of evolution by natural selection gets bonus points here because it not only explains the fossil record and our shared mode of inheritance; it also explains why organisms match the demands of their environments. Theories that explain multiple kinds of observations are held in higher regard than those with more limited application.

Notice that I did not say "Theories that explain multiple kinds of observations are considered to be proven." It is a cardinal rule of science that *no theory can ever be proved*. A theory can be better and better tested, by forcing it to generate more and more predictions. But, even if every one of those predictions is verified, it is still not proven; it is simply better supported than it was. We can disprove theories when their predictions turn out to be false, but we can never prove them (despite simplistic claims in the popular press). Why? Because theories no one has yet imagined might also fit all the observations and make even more accurate predictions. So, like all other scientific explanations, evolution by natural selection *is just a theory*. But it is a theory that has been rigorously tested for over 150 years and it is still standing, simply because no existing theory does as good a job of explaining so many disparate observations. That's why evolution by natural selection has become the organizing principle of modern biology. It's time to look more carefully at how natural selection works, and to be explicit about what it can and can't do.

THE LATHE OF ADAPTATION

Science isn't just definitions but it needs them, just as everyday speech does. What can be confusing is that science often borrows ordinary words and gives them a special meaning. Consider the word "charm." You would have a reasonable idea what different things were being talked about if a jeweler or movie-critic used this word. And a particle-physicist would mean something else, something quite technical if she used the word. So when you are learning about a science that's new to you, it's very important to notice the specific meanings it attaches to words whose everyday meaning you already know. Failing to notice those technical meanings is a major source of problems for students. I will highlight where the biological meaning of a word is different and more precise than its every-day meaning.

"Adaptation" is an uncommon word in everyday speech. Regardless of any prior ideas you might have about it, for biologists, it has a special meaning. They use the word to refer to the *fit between the organism and its environment*, that core biological puzzle that I highlighted in the first paragraph. It's convenient to have a single word to sum up this idea, as opposed to the bulky phrase I have already repeated many times. Biologists use the word in a general way ("*Adaptation* tends to be quite precise" meaning "The fit between the organism and its environment tends to be quite precise"). And they also use it to refer to specific traits that address particular environmental challenges ("the porcupine's quills are an anti-predator *adaptation*" or "thick dental enamel is an *adaptation* to tough foods"). We also use the word in its various grammatical forms ("Vultures are *adapted* for soaring flight" or "Depending on how rapidly they reproduce, organisms can *adapt* quickly").

In the title of this section I suggest that it can to be useful to think about natural selection as the "lathe of adaptation." A lathe (Figure 1-2) is a machine tool that can be used to shape a wide array of objects.

Figure 1-2. Lathes can be used to shape a wide variety of objects.

Analogies—in this case, comparing natural selection to a lathe—are helpful for illustrating complex or unfamiliar ideas by showing their similarity to something more familiar. But they can also usefully highlight differences, where the analogy doesn't quite fit. Taking the differences first, natural selection is not a tool; it is a process. And it is a process that occurs automatically, without any intervention by sentient beings; no human (or other) operator is needed. That distinction is critical to understanding Darwin and Wallace's idea. Natural selection is an inescapable and spontaneous consequence of biological variation. Individuals differ. Because of those differences, some types will inevitably be better adapted than others, and those better-adapted types will tend to leave more progeny (offspring), thereby spreading their better adaptations to their more numerous descendants.

Now let's look at the similarities. Like a lathe, natural selection is versatile; it can build many different kinds of organisms, from a bacterium to a giraffe. Moreover, natural selection is capable of very precise sculpting; look back at the insect in Figure 1-1. Like a lathe, it can build things that *really fit*—that precisely match some function. Finally, natural selection builds these precise adaptations by editing things out. The lathe carves away material from a shapeless mass to create a coherent design. Natural selection builds adapted organisms by discarding traits that don't match the demands of the environment. Inevitably, by this editing-out process, better adaptations are retained. That's not to say that only perfect adaptations are retained. But, as the automatic editing process repeats, generation-after-generation, natural selection is discriminating among a set of better and better adaptations. As a result, the current winners can fit the environment better than the winners of the past generation, and adaptation is gradually pulled toward perfection. It's as if a lathe operator, instead of beginning with something shapeless, began with the already-pretty-good product of the last generation of lathe operators.

WHAT IS NATURAL SELECTION EDITING?

We have argued that natural selection shapes adaptation because better-adapted individuals tend to have more progeny and worse-adapted individuals tend to have fewer. Combining this with the *assumption that offspring resemble their parents*, then better-adapted traits will tend to accumulate in the population and worse-adapted traits will tend to be weeded out. Of course, assumptions need eventually to be clarified. Darwin and Wallace, like all observant people of their day, knew that offspring *do* resemble their parents. (For a long time people have used that knowledge to create a wide variety of animal and plant breeds, simply by choosing as breeders those individuals that had the traits they liked. This process, now called *artificial selection*, provides us with another useful analogy of natural selection.) But, to return to the main point, neither Darwin nor Wallace nor any of their contemporaries knew *why* offspring resemble their parents.

The nature of the hereditary system was first described by Gregor Mendel in 1865 (see Chapter 3), just seven years after Darwin and Wallace's famous paper on natural selection. But, unfortunately, no one in the 19th century—including Darwin and Wallace!—read and understood what Mendel was saying. From careful breeding experiments Mendel had correctly deduced that parents don't pass their traits directly to their offspring; instead they pass microscopic elements that affect the development of the offspring's traits. To take a common example, a mother would not pass her brown eyes to her son; she would pass a coded "recipe" that carries the instructions for making eyes brown. You're right; these recipes are *genes*, but I'm going to leave the important discussion of what genes *are* (their structure and mechanics) for another occasion. To maintain this chapter's focus on the central problem of biology, I need to emphasize what genes *do*. Genes encode extremely precise self-assembly instructions. The genetic differences between individuals, between you and your friends for example, are differences in your self-assembly programs, your genetic recipes.

Let's combine this very basic understanding of heredity with what we know about natural selection. The raw material that natural selection works with is the differences between individuals, in particular, differences in how well they fit their environments—in how well-adapted they are. We now know that the heritable part of these differences comes about because individuals carry different genetic recipes. So, natural selection edits the pool of genetic recipes by "evaluating" how well the products of those recipes match the demands of their environment. This is not especially strange. It's not much different from the way chefs evaluate a recipe, not by merely reading it but by actually using the recipe to make the dish and see how it tastes.

Each (sexually-produced) individual gets a whole collection of recipes at the moment of conception. Those recipes immediately begin expressing themselves, initiating a developmental process that, if successful, will eventually produce an adult organism. What determines who gets to pass his or her recipes along? The filter of natural selection, and it has just one standard: *Whether the adaptations built by those recipes meet the demands of the current environment.* Because the best-adapted individuals will tend to have more offspring, the recipes that built those highly adapted individuals will get passed on more often. As a consequence, adaptation-building recipes accumulate in the population.

We could profitably return to our cooking analogy. If you could flip through the personal recipe files of a large number of cooks you would find some recipes are very common— for example, many cooks have Julia Child's "Beef Burgundy" recipe. Other recipes may exist in just one or a very few copies. Here's the point: If a recipe produces an especially tasty dish, it will be passed to lots of cooks and end up in a lot of recipe files. If the recipe yields an uninteresting dish, it won't be passed along very often. Can you see a similarity to the way natural selection acts on genes? The genetic recipes that build (not tasty, but) well-adapted organisms will tend to be passed along more often than ones that build poorly-adapted creatures.

To think clearly about evolution, you will need to consider two levels at the same time: individuals and the genetic recipes that build them. Individuals wrestle with the various challenges of their environments and in the process reveal themselves to have better or worse adaptations. Better-adapted individuals get to be parents more often, but they don't directly transmit their adaptive traits to their offspring. Instead parents transmit the recipes that built their adaptations. How about this summary? Genetic recipes audition for the future by building organisms, and the recipes that build the most successful organisms get to stay in the game. This way of thinking captures the reality that individuals are ephemeral; they are born, may produce some offspring, and die. But genes—genetic recipes—are potentially immortal because the good ones can be passed to offspring, and those offspring's offspring... for millions of years... This is a good example of what I meant when I said that our answers to all biological questions would be shaped by the way we answered the core question of why organisms fit so well with their environments. Evolution by natural selection is the lens through which all of biology comes into focus.

CHAPTER SUMMARY

Natural selection is the most important force in biology. Without natural selection living things would not be so stunningly well matched to their circumstances; in fact, there would be no living things! Natural selection can explain why each type of organism so elegantly matches the various risks and rewards present in its environment, and thus *can solve the central problem of biology*. Please be sure that you understand why the persistent bias of natural selection—preferring one type over another—will automatically sculpt adaptations. The perspective I have tried to assemble through logical argument, analogy, and example is that natural selection is the likely architect of everything that is functional and anti-entropic about living things. Whatever feature (of whatever organism) we want to understand, we will make more progress if we base our analysis on these ideas about evolution by natural selection. And that is precisely what we'll do in the rest of this book.

CITED REFERENCES

C. R. Darwin and A. R. Wallace (1858). On the Tendency of Species to form Varieties; and on the Perpetuation of Varieties and Species by Natural Means of Selection. *Journal of the Proceedings of the Linnean Society of London, Zoology, 3*: 45–62.

FIGURE CREDITS

CHAPTER 2

EVOLUTION TODAY

Evolution by natural selection is not something that happened in the dry, dusty past and is now finished. Remember, natural selection is simply a label for the observation that, as a result of fitting better with the local environment, some individuals leave more offspring than others. This "differential reproduction" happens in each and every generation. Thus natural selection is going on constantly in all living things, including our own species. It's true that evolutionary change occurs at the pace of generations, so it's not always easy for us to see evolution happening. We humans have especially long lifespans so it can be challenging to measure evolution in our own species (though see Chapters 5 and 18). But many species reproduce much more rapidly than we do. This means that we can actually watch ongoing evolution in species with significantly shorter generations than ours.

A compelling example of this—and one with dramatic practical implications—is the rapid evolution of antibiotic resistance in bacteria. Antibiotics were not discovered until the 20th century, and scientists have worked diligently to develop a wide range of types. But—think about it—these antibiotics substantially change the environment of bacteria. Every application of an antibiotic drug triggers strong natural selection favoring the bacteria that are most resistant. And bacteria have very short generations—more on the order of 25 minutes than our 25 years. As a result of their rapid reproduction, a few bacterial strains have already evolved resistance to almost all known antibiotics, in not much more than a single human lifetime! Here you see that understanding evolution has practical applications, like why it's important to use antibiotics in a restrained and thoughtful way—because every time we use them we promote the evolution of more virulent (dangerous) bacteria.

RAPID EVOLUTION IN EUROPEAN LIZARDS

I suspect that most of my readers have never seen a bacterium and, at least in healthier moments, don't think much about them. In this chapter I'll give two examples of relatively rapid evolution—evolution that we can easily observe and measure—in species that are large enough for you to see. You know that selection pressures originate with the environment. One of the fundamental ways that animals contact their environments is through their feeding ecology—what they eat and how they get it. Feeding success is one prerequisite for reproductive success. (When we get around to exploring human evolution, you will see the importance of feeding ecology in shaping our own adaptations.) The first example I'll discuss concerns an evolutionary experiment. How would you do an evolutionary experiment? You'd make an important change in the environment and observe whether the target species' adaptations changed in response to that environmental change.

The first study I'll describe was done by Anthony Herrel and his collaborators, and it involves a lizard transplantation experiment. To anticipate their findings, they showed how a shift to a new food source caused evolutionary change in the animal's feeding-related adaptations. Their basic question was this: How quickly can natural selection create new adaptations? To begin the experiment, 5 male and 5 female lizards, all belonging to a single species, were removed from one island where they occurred naturally and then released on a small nearby island where they previously did not occur. In other words, one island was "seeded" with a lizard species from elsewhere to see what would happen. At the time the report was published, the experiment had been running for about 30 lizard generations. Was that enough time to see any adaptive changes in the transplanted population? As you will soon see, the answer is yes. But first, let's meet the cast of characters.

The scientific name of the study species is *Podarcis sicula*. Because this species is not found in English-speaking countries, its English common name is not yet stable; it is variously called "Italian wall lizard" or "Istanbul lizard." The great virtue of scientific names is that they are the same in every language. Regardless of whether you speak Mandarin or Malay, you will know what animal I am talking about when I say "*Podarcis sicula.*" Similar to your name, scientific names have two parts. The first part is the genus name. It is the more inclusive part of the name in the sense that there may be more than one species in a genus—just as there may be more than one Bach in the Bach family. The second part is the species name. By convention, the genus name is always capitalized and the species name never is, even when it is based on a person's name, such as *Rhea darwinii*, a large flightless South American bird. Both parts of a scientific name should be italicized as they are here (or underlined if you cannot italicize). Just as a genus may include several species, higher levels can include several genera (the plural of

```
┌─────────────────────────────────────────────────┐
│          Squamata (scaled reptiles)              │
│  ┌──────────────────┐  ┌─────────────────────┐   │
│  │                  │  │  Lacertilia (lizards)│   │
│  │                  │  │ ┌─────────────────┐  │   │
│  │                  │  │ │     Iguania     │  │   │
│  │   Serpentes      │  │ │ Agamidae (dragon lizards)│   │
│  │   (snakes)       │  │ │ Iguanidae (iguanas)│  │   │
│  │                  │  │ └─────────────────┘  │   │
│  │                  │  │ ┌─────────────────┐  │   │
│  │                  │  │ │  Scleroglossa   │  │   │
│  │                  │  │ │ Gekkota (geckos)│  │   │
│  │                  │  │ │ Lacertidae (wall lizards)│   │
│  │                  │  │ └─────────────────┘  │   │
│  └──────────────────┘  └─────────────────────┘   │
└─────────────────────────────────────────────────┘
```

Figure 2-1. Squamata (scaled reptiles): An abbreviated picture of relationships among the species referenced in Herrel's article. The study species, Podarcis sicula, is in the family Lacertidae (wall lizards). Wall lizards and geckos are included along with several other kinds of lizards (not shown) in Scleroglossa. Likewise, all Scleroglossa lizards are grouped together with all Iguania lizards (and several others not shown) to form the most inclusive group of lizards, Lacertilia. This, in turn, is grouped with Serpentes to form the Squamata, scaled reptiles. (What other reptiles are there besides the scaled ones? After you master Chapter 10, you will be ready to understand that there are also feathered reptiles, commonly called birds.)

genus). The next level up from genus is family. The genus *Podarcis* is in the family Lacertidae, which includes all the species of wall lizards. An abbreviated picture of the array of reptiles mentioned in Herrel's original article is shown in Figure 2-1. The lizards in this experiment were taken from Pod Kopište, the "original island," and they were released on Pod Mrčaru, the "colony island." Are you wondering what Herrel and his team found?

Observations showed that the lizards were eating very different diets on the two islands. On each island the diets do change somewhat with the season, but that is not the most dramatic difference. On the original island, Pod Kopište, where the lizards have presumably lived for many generations, they eat mainly arthropods (insects, spiders, etc.). But on Pod Mrčaru, the colony island, they eat a lot of plant material, especially in the summer. Let's talk numbers. On Pod Kopište, plant material makes up between 4% and 7% of the diet. But on Pod Mrčaru, the colony population eats between 36% and 61% plant material,

roughly ten times as much as on the original island! This is a big change in diet; presumably the lizards had to make this change because there are fewer insects on the colony island. The point of the article, however, is not why they changed their diet, but what happened when they did. Did selection design different adaptations to match the different diets of these two populations?

What are the key differences between an insect-based and a plant-based diet? Plant foods contain a lot of cellulose, a tough material that makes up the cell walls of plants. The leafy parts of plants—which the transplanted colony population was depending on— are especially high in cellulose. Eating cellulose is problematic in two ways. First, it is tough and fibrous. This toughness makes it difficult to bite off and chew mouthfuls of plant leaves. Second, cellulose is indigestible by all vertebrates (you and lizards are both vertebrates). No lizard can break it down and release the food energy packaged within those cellulose walls. The only way for a vertebrate to get food energy out of cellulose is to recruit the help of commensal invertebrates to live in their guts and do the digestion for them. Usually, as has happened in cattle and so-called leaf monkeys, the digestive system of the plant eaters evolves to form multiple sub-compartments. These modifications do two things: they slow the passage of food through the gut and create special environments, giving the invertebrate helpers both extra time and special places to do their digestive work.

Let's review the data. The colonists came from a population--their immediate ancestors—where leaf material was a minor part of the diet. But recently—within the last 30 generations—the colonists began eating a lot of cellulose-laden leaf material. This leaf material is hard to bite and can be digested only with commensal assistance. Knowing these facts, we can make some predictions about the kinds of adaptive changes we should expect in our colony population:

1. There will be changes in the head anatomy that increase bite strength.
2. There will be changes in the gut anatomy that give time and space for cellulose digestion.

Note that specifying the environmental challenges in this precise way allows us to predict specific outcomes of evolution. And these predicted adaptive changes are precisely what Herrel and his team found. Let's start with the digestive changes. The cecum is part of the digestive system. When comparing many species, it is clear that the cecum is large and complex in species that eat a lot of plant material, but small and simple in species that eat mainly animals. When the cecum is complex, it is segmented by a series of cecal valves that break it up into smaller chambers that slow the passage of food and that harbor commensal organisms that break down cellulose. Both of those changes were observed (only) in the colonist population: the cecum was large, segmented by a series of valves, and it contained cellulose-digesting nematodes (small worms). Importantly, the lizards that remained on the home island and that continued to eat very little plant material have no cecal valves or chambers and no nematodes.

In parallel with these digestive changes Herrel found that the anatomy of the head and jaws was different in the ancestral and colony populations. In particular the colonists had larger heads and jaws that allowed them to generate significantly more bite strength, a trait that we predicted given their dependence on tough, cellulose-rich leaf material. Thus, both the harvesting (biting) and processing (digestive) components of the colonists' feeding anatomy changed in a way that match their dietary shift.

This study by Herrel and his colleagues also illustrates ways of thinking that will be useful to you. First and foremost is the idea of *planned comparisons*. The most obvious comparison is the one between the original population and the colonists. This comparison lets us ask whether a change in diet produced adaptive changes in the lizards' feeding and digestive anatomy. Because we know the colonists are very recent descendants of the original population, this comparison is a direct way of assessing how much evolution has occurred.

The second comparison is one between the study species and other species of lizards (and snakes). Here is the logic the authors used. We know that the colonists' closest relatives—the original population of *Podarcis sicula*—lack cecal valves. But just how great an innovation is it for the colony population to evolve this feature of the gut? A good way to explore this question is to see how many of *Podarcis sicula*'s more distant relatives have cecal valves. For example, the authors noted that another species of *Podarcis* (*Podarcis melisellensis*) lacks cecal valves. They also stress that less than one percent of all scaled reptile species have cecal valves. And the few that do have them—in their own family, Lacertidae, and in the more distantly related families Igaunidae and Agamidae—are all plant eaters. In other words, the pattern of evolution among lizards seems to suggest that cecal valves are adaptive only for plant eaters. This kind of comparative evidence for adaptation is one of the evolutionist's most powerful and versatile tools: It will be demonstrated more explicitly in Chapter 8.

I have placed this study close to the front of your textbook because it introduces so many important issues (e.g., adaptation, classification, comparative methods). One more topic that is at least hinted at in Herrel's research is the question of how new species arise. We can see that the selective pressures of different diets have moved these two populations of lizards apart in terms of their feeding adaptations. But the authors suggest they have not moved far enough apart to be considered different species. Actually they didn't do the definitive test that would allow them to be sure about that, which would

have been a cross-breeding test. I'd be curious about the results of that test but it's just idle curiosity on my part. The key issue that we will explore in more detail later is *how* new species arise. The majority of modern evolutionists think that the lizard experiment sets up precisely the kinds of conditions necessary for the emergence of new species: different selection pressures operating on populations that don't have much opportunity to interbreed. In other words, when new species do arise, it's caused by ordinary natural selection. It would almost always take longer than the 30 or so generations of the lizard experiment, but if different selection pressures operated on relatively isolated populations for long enough, they would eventually become so different anatomically and genetically that they could no longer interbreed (see Chapter 7).

In conclusion, Herrel's research shows that adaptive evolutionary change can occur in a relatively small number of generations. In this study we have a very good estimate of how long these changes took because we know exactly when the lizards were introduced to the new island and when their diet changed. This dietary shift to plant eating changed particular head features and gut features that were advantageous in the transplanted population. The lizards that had any genetic tendency to develop these advantageous traits were more likely to survive and reproduce on Pod Mrčaru. Consequently, their advantageous traits spread through the population in a mere 36 years.

Figure 2-2. A native American lizard, *Anolis carolinensis.*

WAS THIS REALLY EVOLUTION?

I want to describe a second study to highlight a subtle but important issue that Herrel's study did not address. I have purposely chosen a study that is rather similar but more recent and more complete in the sense that it considers multiple different hypotheses. It is by Y. E. Stuart and colleagues and focuses on American lizards in the genus *Anolis* (Figure 2-2). The only species in this genus that is native to the United States is *Anolis carolinensis*, but some of its geographic range in Florida has recently been invaded by a closely related Cuban species, *Anolis sagrei*. Both species are sit-and-wait predators that dash out and capture insects and other arthropods from perches in the forest understory. *Anolis sagrei* seems to be dominant to *Anolis carolinensis* because, where the two species occur together, *Anolis carolinensis* is forced to use higher (and hence smaller) perches than where it occurs without *Anolis sagrei*. Like Herrel, Stuart studied islands (which make nice natural laboratories), but Stuart studied multiple islands, including some where *Anolis sagrei* invaded on its own and some where it was intentionally introduced, as well as some where *Anolis sagrei* was absent. Again the evolutionary time frame was short; Stuart could document that a maximum of 20 generations of lizard reproduction had occurred since the first invasions of *Anolis sagrei*.

In the case of these American lizards there was no change in diet for either species; they both continued to eat insects. But, in the presence of *Anolis sagrei*, *Anolis carolinensis* had to hunt in finer branches. Stuart hypothesized that this ecological shift would induce natural selection for better gripping ability that could

be measured as an increase in toepad area (the size of the gripping surface) and an increase in the number of lamellae (adhesive scales) on the toes (Figure 2-3). These increases should, of course, be limited to the populations of *Anolis carolinensis* that have been forced onto finer branches by *Anolis sagrei*. These predictions turned out to be correct: On the islands where *Anolis sagrei* shifted it to higher perches, *Anolis carolinensis* had lager toepads with more lamellae than it did where *Anolis sagrei* was absent.

What Herrel's study and Stuart's study have in common is that they were able to identify a particular environmental change, and predict which traits of the organism should be modified by natural selection to meet the new environmental challenge. And actual observations showed those predictions to be correct. That's impressive. But can we be confident that we're seeing evolutionary change? Taking the American example, were these changes the result of genetic recipes for larger toepads (and more lamellae) making it into more offspring? Maybe, but perhaps these changes were not evolutionary; perhaps they were merely developmental. In other words, perhaps they were like calluses, just the result of a certain kind of stimulation during the maturation process. Now, I don't mean to suggest that a developmental finding would be uninteresting; but it would no longer be an example of rapid natural selection for different traits in different environments. In fact, I will have a fair bit to say about callus-like traits soon (in Chapter 5). But to clarify the interpretation of the lizard studies, we'd like to be able to examine this alternative developmental hypothesis.

Figure 2-3. Toe pad lamellae on a lizard's foot.

Herrel's team didn't address this issue but Stuart's team did. Can you guess how? They harvested eggs from *Anolis carolinensis* females living on both invaded and un-invaded islands. Of course, because of the influence of *Anolis sagrei*, females on the invaded islands had larger toepads and more lamellae. But what would happen when all these *Anolis carolinensis* eggs were hatched and reared to adulthood in a single common environment where no *Anolis sagrei* were present? Would their feet reflect their shared rearing environment and all be similar? Or would their feet reflect genetic differences between their mothers and therefore differ based on whether the eggs had come from invaded or un-invaded islands? In fact, the toepad and lamella differences persisted, with the offspring resembling their mothers, despite their identical rearing conditions. With this approach Stuart was able to rule out a developmental effect, and hence did convincingly show rapid evolution of foot anatomy in these American lizards.

CHAPTER SUMMARY

Evolution by natural selection is a ubiquitous process, happening everywhere and always. Changes in the environment will generally cause selection to favor somewhat different traits. Depending on the strength of natural selection—how many more offspring successful individuals produce compared to unsuccessful individuals—and on how quickly one generation follows another, natural selection can produce new adaptations fairly rapidly. Examples from two kinds of lizards show that they evolved rapidly enough for humans to see and measure the consequences over just a few decades.

CITED REFERENCES

Anthony Herrel, Katleen Huyghe, Bieke Vanhooydonck, Thierry Backeljau, Karin Breugelmans, Irena Grbac, Raoul Van Damme & Duncan J. Irschick (2008). "Rapid large-scale evolutionary divergence in morphology and performance associated with exploitation of a different dietary resource. *Proceedings of the National Academy of Sciences, USA. 105*: 4792-4795.

Y. E. Stuart, T. S. Campbell, P. A. Hohenlohe, R. G. Reynolds, L. J. Revell & J. B. Losos (2014). "Rapid evolution of a native species following invasion by a congener." Science 346: 463-466.

FIGURE CREDITS

CHAPTER 3

MENDELIAN GENETICS: THE ACCOUNTING SYSTEM OF EVOLUTION

It is impossible to teach—or learn—about evolution without paying attention to how inheritance works. In fact, by the time Darwin died in 1882, his theory of evolution by natural selection was under serious attack precisely because it would not work—at least not very well—under the prevailing model of inheritance.

THE PROBLEM OF BLENDING INHERITANCE

In the 19th century, the prevailing model of heredity was *blending inheritance*—the complete merging of hereditary material from the two parents to form the offspring. I call it a model rather than a theory because no one formally described or advocated it; it was a folk idea that shaped the way most people—scientists included—thought about heredity. To get yourself into their frame of mind, imagine that the "stuff of heredity" is a liquid—that offspring resemble their parents because of some fluid substance their parents pass to them. As you know, if you mix two (similar-viscosity) liquids together, they will dilute each other. Suppose I have a bottle of orange juice and a bottle of water and I pour half of each into a third container. The result will be neither

OJ nor water, but something in between. Tasting it, you'd call it watery juice or juicy water. If blending inheritance were true, the two parents' attributes would mix and merge in the same way. As a result—just like the juicy water—any offspring would be intermediate between its parents, on every inherited trait.

So I don't leave you with an erroneous idea (even briefly), let me stress that the blending model of inheritance is wrong. But in Darwin's day, no one (except Gregor Mendel) knew that. Science is constantly rejecting bad models in favor of better ones, and the rejection of blending inheritance is just an ordinary example of scientific progress. As usual, the model was rejected because people began to notice that it didn't fit their observations. Darwin himself questioned blending inheritance. In 1866, he wrote in a brief letter to his co-author Alfred Russel Wallace: "I crossed the Painted Lady and Purple sweet peas, which are very differently coloured varieties, and got, even out of the same pod, both varieties perfect but not intermediate." (If you like historical things, you can see the actual letter at: http://www.bl.uk/learning/timeline/item106279.html). This quote is multiply ironic. First, it was written the year *after* Mendel published his ideas. Second, it concerned hybrid crosses among various strains of pea plants, precisely the sort of experiments Mendel had performed. And third, it pointed to the very same kinds of evidence that Mendel emphasized: the preservation of the original types and the lack of intermediates.

As mentioned above, in a world governed by blending inheritance offspring would always be intermediate between their parents. A tall parent mated to a short parent would produce a child who, when grown, would be shorter than its tall parent but taller than its short parent.

The same thing would, of course, happen in all families, and in every generation. As a result the range of variation in the population would inevitably shrink over time. By now, after hundreds of thousands of years of human mating, we should have all converged on a single average value. Obviously, that has not happened; there is still a lot of variation in human height and in many other traits. This is another way of seeing the problems with the blending model.

When I said "problems" in the last sentence I was referring to the various observations that make us question the blending model. But there is another sense in which the blending model is problematic: If blending inheritance were true it would seriously compromise the power of natural selection. Here's why.

As you know, selection results from the struggle for existence. Those individuals that are better suited to the prevailing environment produce more offspring. Darwin and Wallace assumed that these successful parents would transmit the same traits that allowed their success to their offspring. But, naturally, *what parents transmit depends on how heredity works.* Any new trait is likely to be rare when it first arises. This suggestion doesn't depend on the nature of the hereditary system. Whether parents pass particles (as in a Mendelian system) or fluids (in a blending system) it's unlikely that a large segment of the population would be born with the very same new trait. (If, for some reason, that kind of event were common, it would be a major evolutionary force in its own right; think about it.) Remember, what we want to explain is adaptation (the core problem of biology) and how it gets built. We have the theory of natural selection that seems to do that explanatory work; but wait. What happens to a favorable new trait in a blending system? Because it's rare, only one member of the mating pair will probably have it. As a result, their offspring will have the helpful trait, but diluted by half (because either its mom or its dad *didn't* have it). And *its* offspring would have the trait diluted by half again, etc. In other words, in a blending system any useful trait that did arise would be rapidly "washed out" of the population by the act of reproduction itself, before selection would ever be able to spread it very far. It was this exact criticism, leveled by an engineer named Fleeming Jenkin that cast serious doubt on Darwin and Wallace's theory in their later years.

Though Gregor Mendel published in 1865, neither Darwin, nor Wallace, nor Jenkin had read his work. Had they done so they would have understood that the blending model is wrong. As Darwin's own sweet pea experiments showed, the offspring are not intermediate between their parents and the two parental varieties were both present—in undiluted form—among the offspring. Let's see what Mendel did and how his research solved the puzzle of heredity that stumped Darwin and Wallace.

MENDEL'S MODEL OF HEREDITY

Sometimes scientists make fortuitous (lucky) discoveries; in the course of pursuing one research question they happen to make an observation that answers a very different one. That was not the case with the Austrian monk, Gregor Mendel. He set out quite intentionally to figure out how heredity works. He assumed that the mechanism of heredity was the same in all organisms, a hunch that turned out to be correct (and that in itself provides rich evidence

for evolution). So, reasoning that it didn't matter what species he studied, he choose the readily available pea plants in the monastery garden. Remember that Mendel could not see the hereditary material itself. He could only observe the traits of the parents and the traits of their offspring so, from those observations, he had to infer how the hereditary mechanisms worked.

Before launching his famous experiments, Mendel began by creating what he called "pure" strains of pea plants. To Mendel "pure" simply meant that it always bred true: If the parent had a particular trait, the offspring always had it. Any time he found a discrepancy, where the offspring and parent did not match, they were eliminated (probably by being tossed in the soup pot). This was an important preliminary step that you'll understand better after you've seen his experimental results. At the end of this purification phase he had several contrasting strains that differed on particular, easy-to-observe traits. For example Mendel had purified two strains that differed in the color of the pea pods, one bearing green pods and the other yellow. He had a strain were the peas were wrinkled and angular and another where they were smooth and round. He had a strain where the plants were tall and slender and another where they were short and bushy. By the end of the purification stage, each of these six strains bred true, and he was ready to begin his experiments, which are summarized in Figure 3-1 and explained in the next few paragraphs.

In what we call the "F1 hybrid cross" Mendel took a contrasting pair of strains, for example the tall strain and the short strain, and he intention-ally interbred them. He took pollen from tall plants and put it on the flowers of the short plants, and likewise transferred pollen from the short plants to the flowers of tall plants. When these fertilized flowers produced pea pods, Mendel harvested the peas, planted them and waited to see what kind of plants developed. Do you know what he found? Before you answer, let me ask a different question: What *should* have happened if the blending model was true? That's easy: The plants should have been intermediate in height between their tall and short parents. But that's not what Mendel found. He found that they were all tall—just as tall as the tall parents. There had been no blending at all!

What happened to the hereditary material of the short parent? Where did it go? Was it present but somehow hidden? To figure this out Mendel took his F1 offspring—the tall plants that had one tall parent and one short parent—and interbred them to produce the so-called F2 generation. When he did this something even more amazing happened: ¾ of the resulting offspring were tall but ¼ were short, just as short as their short grandparent. This is one of the most famous experimental results in all of science, and Mendel deserves his place among the great biologists just for conceiving it, but that was not his most brilliant contribution. His scientific legacy rests on his *explanation* of the F1 and F2 results. Let me dissect it for you. There are four elements of Mendel's model:

1. The stuff of heredity is particulate. It comes in discrete units that don't blend. Don't think in terms of fluids; instead imagine marbles.
2. Adults carry this heredity material in pairs, one member of each pair coming from the mother and the other coming from the father. The technical name for this paired state is *diploidy*.
3. In reproducing, each parent gives one and only one member of its paired hereditary units to each of its offspring. The technical name for the simple, unpaired state is *halpoidy*. Diploid parents produce haploid sex cells that fuse with the haploid sex cells of other parents to produce new diploid individuals.
4. Some particles are *dominant* to others such that, when the two occur together, only the effects of the dominant particle are observable.

Both Mendel's experimental results and his model of the hereditary mechanism that could produce these results are summarized in Figure 3-1. The hereditary particles are represented by letters ("*T*" for a tall particle and "*t*" for a short particle—trust me, that's how it's done). Each parent has two particles because each is a diploid adult. When a parent passes hereditary material to the next generation it passes only one of its two particles, via haploid sex cells. In the offspring the haploid sex cells come together producing a new diploid individual.

In the F1 hybrid cross (at the top of Figure 3-1) the parents have matching particles (*TT* or *tt*) because each is pure—pure tall or pure short. That was the effect of Mendel's purification phase: getting rid of any individual whose particles did not match. When the tall parent gives one of its particles that particle will have to be a T (that's the only kind it has) and, for the same reason, the short parent will have to give a t. That means that each of their resulting offspring will receive one *T* from its tall parent and one *t* from its short parent and therefore have a diploid makeup of *Tt*, *different* from either of its parents. Why were all of these F1 hybrid offspring tall? Because of the fourth

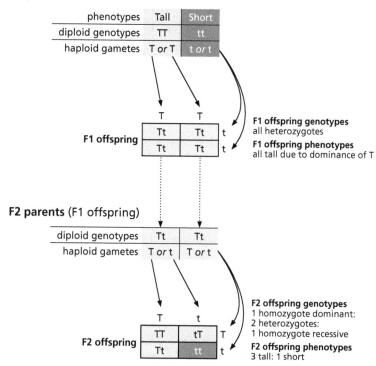

F1 parents

phenotypes	Tall	Short
diploid genotypes	TT	tt
haploid gametes	T *or* T	t *or* t

	T	T
F1 offspring	Tt	Tt
	Tt	Tt

t

t

F1 offspring genotypes
all heterozygotes
F1 offspring phenotypes
all tall due to dominance of T

F2 parents (F1 offspring)

diploid genotypes	Tt	Tt
haploid gametes	T *or* t	T *or* t

	T	t
F2 offspring	TT	tT
	Tt	tt

T

t

F2 offspring genotypes
1 homozygote dominant:
2 heterozygotes:
1 homozygote recessive
F2 offspring phenotypes
3 tall: 1 short

Figure 3-1. Results of a two-generation breeding experiment.

element in Mendel's model: dominance. *T* particles are dominant to *t* particles so, when they occur together, only the T particle is expressed thus making the offspring tall. Let's continue on to the next generation and then we'll circle back and introduce some useful terminology.

The parents of the F2 generation are the very same *Tt* individuals that were the offspring in the F1 generation. Each of these parents can give either a *T* or a *t* to its offspring and these two outcomes are equally likely; half the time it will give a *T* and the other half it will give a *t*. Since this is true of both parents we can compute the chance that an offspring will end up with two *T* particles: Half of the time it gets a *T* from its "mom" and

on half of those occasions it will also get a *T* from its "dad". Half of a half is ¼, so ¼ of the F2 offspring will be *TT*. By exactly the same logic ¼ of the F2 offspring will be *tt*. The remaining ½ of the F2 offspring will be *Tt*, having received a *T* from one parent and a *t* from the other. In the Figure the boxes let you visualize these various outcomes. The *TT* offspring are of course tall and, because of dominance, so are the *Tt* offspring. Only the tt offspring are short. Thus in the F2 generation, ¾ of the offspring are tall and ¼ are short.

Remember that Mendel had other pure strains: strains producing wrinkled seeds and strains producing round seeds, strains producing green pods and strains producing yellow pods. He carefully performed the very same F1 and F2 experiments with each pair of strains. The especially exciting result was that, in each case, one type (green pods, wrinkled seeds) was, like short plants, completely absent among the F1 offspring, but reappeared in ¼ of the F2 offspring.

Mendel's model—of particulate hereditary material, present in pairs in (diploid) adults, but passed to offspring singly via (haploid) sex cells, some of which may be silent in the presence of a more dominant particle—is perfectly consistent with the observed outcomes in both the F1 and F2 generations. I suggest that you could test your understanding of Mendel's model by trying to predict the outcome of a different breeding experiment. In this new experiment let's mate an F1 offspring (*Tt*) with a pure short individual (*tt*). What kind of offspring will this cross produce? As we've seen before, the *Tt* parent will give *T* half of the time and *t* of half the time. But the short parent will always give a *t*. Thus, half of the offspring will be *Tt* and hence tall, and half will be *tt* and therefore short. Note that if you don't know what hereditary particles the parents contain and can only see whether they are tall or short, this looks like Mendel's F1 cross, right? In the F1 cross shown in Figure 3-1, a tall parent is mated to a short parent, and in the cross we just discussed the same is true. But the outcomes are different: The F1 hybrid cross produced nothing but tall offspring, whereas our new experiment will produce tall and short offspring in a 50:50 ratio. You should be sure you understand why these two experiments produce different results. In both crosses one of the two parents was pure short (tt). And both included one tall parent, but the hereditary makeup of this tall parent differed: In the original F1 cross the tall parent was pure tall (*TT*), whereas it was *Tt* in the new experiment. That explains why the outcomes were different.

GENE AND ALLELES

Let's update our terminology so we can talk about hereditary materials in a less clumsy, more modern way. Though he did not use the term, Mendel's particles have been called *genes* since the early 1900's. An individual's genetic makeup is called its *genotype*. In Figure 3-1 there are three possible genotypes (*TT* or *Tt* or *tt*). The outward manifestation of these genotypes—the actual traits of the organisms—is called the *phenotype*. How many phenotypes are there in Figure 3-1? Just two; because of dominance the *TT* and *Tt* genotypes produce the same tall phenotype.

When an individual's diploid pair of genes is the same (*TT* or *tt*) that individual is *homozygous*. When the genes differ (*Tt*) the individual is *heterozygous*. Now we can define dominant and its opposite, *recessive*, more precisely. Recessive genes are expressed in the phenotype only when homozygous; dominant alleles are expressed in the phenotype even when heterozygous.

T and t are genes that both affect the height of the plant. As you know, Mendel studied other genes, for example genes affecting pea shape (round versus wrinkled) and pod color (green versus yellow). In these examples, each trait (height, pea shape, pod color) comes in two versions. The genes that code for different versions of the *same* trait are *alleles* of each other. This is sometimes a source of confusion, so let's take a little time with it.

We can often use the words gene and allele interchangeably. The distinction matters in only a few contexts (but there it is important). I could say "a gene for green pods" or "an allele for green pods" and no professional geneticist would be bothered by either phrase. An allele is a gene, a version of a gene, so either way of saying it is fine. Here is the key issue: For genes to be *alleles of each other*, they must be *versions of the same gene*. In the example we were just discussing, "green" and "yellow" are alleles (versions) of a pod-color gene. Shifting to a different trait—a critical shift—"round" and "wrinkled" are useful names for alleles of a pea-shape gene. Here's the critical point: "green" and "round" are *not alleles of each other*. One is a pod-color allele and the other is a pea-shape allele. There can't be a "round" (or "wrinkled") version of the pod-color gene. And there can't be a "green" (or "yellow") version of the pea-shape gene.

Let me suggest a food analogy? Vanilla and pistachio are versions ("alleles") of what you might put in a waffle cone. Scrambled and fried are versions of egg preparation. But vanilla and scrambled…yeah; they have nothing to do with each other. They are both foods ("genes") but, beyond that, there is no sense in which they are alternative versions of the same thing.

Because I know it's tricky to use these words correctly, here's one more analogy. If I say "Sean is a guy" or if I say "Sean is my brother" in either case you will know that Sean is a male human. But one class of people, guys, is much larger than the other, guys who are my brother. "Brother" is a relational term that identifies two or more entities as belonging to the same family. And likewise, allele is a relational word that identifies two or more genes as possible substitutes for (or alternatives of) each other. "Green" can substitute for "yellow" but it can't substitute for "round" or "wrinkled."

There is nothing magic about the number two. The three genes discussed so far have only two alleles each. The pod-color gene has green and yellow alleles, the pea-shape gene has wrinkled and round alleles, and the height gene has tall and short alleles. But genes can have any imaginable number of alleles. You may already know that the human blood-type gene has three alleles, *A*, *B*, and *O*. Some human genes involved in building our immune systems have hundreds of alleles. And many human genes have only a single allele, for which every living human is necessarily homozygous. Do you see how that might have come about? Taking the first step towards joining our Darwinian ideas about natural selection with our Mendelian ideas about heredity, consider this perspective: By promoting higher rates of reproduction, alleles that build better adaptations spread at the expense of alleles that build inferior ones.

CHROMOSOMES AND LOCI

From Mendel's pioneering work we learned that organisms have many different genes. We also learned that these genes (and their various alleles) can shape a wide array of phenotypic traits. Mendel did not know what these genes are made of, how they shape phenotypes (important themes of Chapter 4), nor even where they are. Today we know vastly more about genes than he could have imagined. Building on the basically correct foundation that Mendel laid, let's begin to outline a 21st-century picture of genetics.

Each species of organism has a characteristic number of genes; for contemporary humans that number is about 19,500. These genes don't just float around chaotically inside our cells. They are linearly arranged into very long strands called *chromosomes*. However, it would not be correct to imagine genes on chromosomes "like beads on s string" for the simple reason that there is no "string." A chromosome just is a series of connected genes.

When I say that genes are "linearly arranged" on chromosomes I don't mean that you would see any logic to that arrangement. For example, the genes affecting nose width are not adjacent to the genes for nose length. It's nothing like that. By arrangement I simply mean that the *sequence of genes is the same in all (normal) members of any particular species*. Just as a surgeon would know where to cut to find your pancreas (because everyone's pancreas is in the same place) your growth hormone gene is at a particular place on a particular chromosome (and when we get around to tinkering with such things—as we undoubtedly will—a "genetic surgeon" will know where to find it).

As we precede let me remind you that we humans are, like peas, diploid. This means that we have two (possibly different or possibly identical) versions of each gene. The way that works is simple: We have two copies of each chromosome, one copy that came from our mom and one that came from our dad. All normal humans have 22 of these maternal/paternal chromosome pairs, plus a matched (in the case of genetic females) or unmatched (for genetic males) set of sex chromosomes. Figure 3-2 is a diagram of the human chromosomes, showing the 22 diploid pairs, plus the matched (female) and unmatched (male) 23rd set. Scientists have agreed to the convention of numbering the chromosomes with 1 as the longest and 22 as the shortest. That's not especially interesting but this is: In the absence of rare genetic mistakes, the linear arrangement of genes will be identical on the paternal and maternal copies of each chromosome pair. In other words, the gene layout on the Chromosome 1 that came from you mother will *precisely* match the layout on the Chromosome 1 that came from your father. Likewise, your maternal Chromosome 2 will have the same "map" as your paternal Chromosome 2, and so on.

Let's stick with that map analogy. Because chromosomes are linear, like streets, the location of a particular gene can be given an address, just as we do for a particular building. That much is straight-forward, but unfortunately, there are several different addressing systems in use. According to the briefer

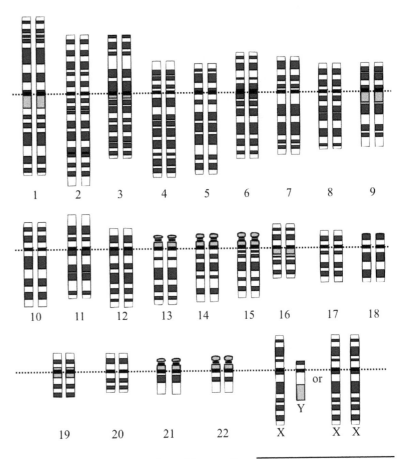

Figure 3-2. Diagram of human karyotype showing 22 pairs of autosomes and sex chromosomes.

but more opaque one, the address of the growth hormone gene is 17q23.3, and according to the longer but more transparent one it's 17:61,994,559-61,996,205. Notice that the first two numbers of these addresses are the same—17. That first number indicates that the gene is on the 17th chromosome (counting chromosomes from longest to shortest). Sticking with our geographic analogy we could say that the gene is on 17th Street. But where on 17th Street? That's what the rest of the number tells us, in two different numbering systems. When you learn about the small units that genes are made of (in Chapter 4), the second numbering system will be clear because it simply counts those units. Thus the growth hormone gene is 1646 units long, beginning at unit 61,994,559 and ending at unit 61,996,205 on Chromosome 17. It's a lot of counting but, conceptually, the approach is simple enough.

No matter which addressing system we use, the place—the address—where a particular gene is found is called its *locus*. Just to keep life interesting, the plural of this Latin-derived word is *loci*. One locus, two loci. The "c" in locus is hard (like "k") but the "c" in loci is soft (like s). Using the shorter addressing system (see above), the human growth hormone gene is found at locus 17q23.3. Now, we can use our understanding of locus as the gene's position (address) along chromosomes to revisit and clarify the subtle distinction between the words "gene" and "allele."

Previously we said alleles are different versions of a gene. For example we might talk about "red" and "blonde" alleles of the hair color gene. We can now make our definition of "allele" more precise. Alleles are versions of a gene *that can occur at the same locus*. Let me show you why this is more precise. It turns out that human hair color is *not* controlled by genes at a single locus; instead, several loci are involved. For example, the OCA2 gene has several alleles that affect hair color at locus 15q12-q13, as does the MC1R gene at locus 16q24.3, the TYR gene at locus11q14.3; and even this list is not complete. So the various versions of the OCA2 gene at locus 15q12-q13 are alleles of each other. But even though they all affect hair color, they are not alleles of the various versions of the MC1R gene or of the TYR gene, because those genes occur at *different* loci. The bottom line: The various alleles of any given gene occur at the same locus.

"OVERLEARNING" MENDEL'S MODEL

In my experience some of the most challenging parts of teaching and learning involve uncovering and correcting mistaken ideas. Your predecessors in this course have been especially helpful in this respect, since their questions bring these misunderstandings to the surface. Here I want to lay out two ideas that many students "learn" from Mendel that are *not* part of his model. These are incorrect conclusions—I call them overgeneralizations—from Mendel's model.

The first overgeneralization I'd like to address is the "one-gene/one-trait" model. Mendel probably cast around for a while, in his preliminary purification phase, to find traits that were largely governed by the alleles at a single locus; and finding such traits was essential to the success of his famous F1 and F2 experiments. So, yes, there are some traits where the one-gene/one-trait model is true: where the genes at a single locus perfectly predict the phenotype. But the more we study the avenues by which genes shape phenotypes, the more we realize that such traits are in the minority—perhaps quite a small minority--of traits. For most traits the state of the phenotype depends on the additive influences of alleles scattered across several to many chromosomes and loci. Traits affected in this way are said to be *polygenic*, a good name since they are affected by multiple genes. Height in pea plants is largely shaped by the tall and short alleles at one locus, but height in humans is affected by the summed effects of alleles at quite a few loci. We'll explore polygenic traits in a bit more depth in Chapter 11.

There's another reason the one-gene/one-trait idea should not be overgeneralized. Not only are some traits influenced by genes at several loci, sometimes the genes at a single locus affect multiple phenotypic traits. Still sticking with the height example, a gene that makes the leg bones grow longer can be expected to have similar effects on the arm bones and even the finger bones. A gene like this, that has multiple effects on the phenotype, is said to be *pleiotropic*.

The second overgeneralization concerns the role of the environment. Mendel's results seem to suggest that, if we know what the genotype is, we know what the phenotype will be. Once again, in his limited experiments, this was true. And once again, that was because he intentionally chose traits where it was true. If the traits he was studying had been affected by the environment as well as by genes he could not have tracked the passage of genes across the generations of his experiments. Remember, he couldn't see the genes; he could only see the phenotypes. If the phenotypes had not been a simple reflection of the genes, if they had been affected by environmental factors as well, he could never have unraveled how heredity works. So, as for overgeneralization one, it is true that there are some traits where the influence of the environment is minimal. Your blood type is an example. But there are many traits where the phenotype depends on interactions between the genes an individual has and the environments she experiences. A key goal of Chapter 5 is explain how those gene-environment interactions work.

THE MECHANICS OF GENE TRANSMISSION: MEIOSIS, RECOMBINATION, AND LINKAGE

Sex is fancy, really fancy. Of course sex is not the only way that genes get passed to the next generation, but it's the way we (and peas, and many other types of organisms) pass on our genes, so we need a basic understanding of how it works. Don't get too excited. Here I'm only concerned with the gene-copying and gene-transfer aspects of sex. Later, in Chapters 20 through 22, we'll explore other (for example, behavioral) aspects of sex, which will then be more comprehensible in light of the ideas discussed here. To build the needed foundation we're going to link together much of the knowledge from the preceding parts of this chapter, about genes, diploidy, haploidy, chromosomes, and loci. So, not only will we learn about the machinery of sex, we'll also consolidate our knowledge about basic genetics.

In most of the species you think about regularly, adults are diploid and make haploid sex cells containing just half of their genes. Because you'll need to know this later, the process of reduction from a diploid cell to a haploid cell is called *meiosis*. When the (meiotically produced) haploid sex cells of a male and female unite, a diploid cell is produced (1/2 +1/2 makes a whole), and if conditions are right, that diploid cell may begin to divide and grow into a new diploid individual. If successful, such diploids will eventually produce haploid sex cells that unite with other haploid sex cells to produce new diploids…in a series that may endure for many millions of years. (You are the contemporary apex of such a series; congratulations.)

As you might be able to deduce from the preceding section on "Chromosomes and Loci", in the production of haploid sex cells each parent gives *one* Chromosome 1, one Chromosome 2 and so on. When *both* parents do this, every offspring necessarily ends up with *two* copies of each chromosome, the normal diploid state. One of the most intricate aspects of sex—one of the fancy parts I alluded to above—is the *way* parents produce the chromosomes that they put in their sex cells. Hang on; we're going to a dance, a dance of chromosomes.

Remember that one copy of your Chromosome 1 is from your dad and the other copy is from your mom. Likewise, if you look at say, *your* mom, one copy of *her* Chromosome 1 came from *her mom* and one copy came from *her dad*. Now, here's the big question: Which Chromosome 1 did she give you? The one from her dad or the one from her mom? The answer is neither. Instead, she gave you a *mix* of genes from her dad's Chromosome 1 and from her mom's

Chromosome 1. Of course, everything I just said about your mom is also true for you dad.

At this point you might feel a growing panic and I feel a corresponding need to quickly soothe any anxiety I might have caused. Here's the problem that I imagine could cause you to panic. If your mom were to form a new Chromosome 1 by simply "mixing" the Chromosome 1 material from her mom with the Chromosome 1 material from her dad, you would almost certainly end up with too many copies of some genes and no copies of others. And that would, in most cases, be fatal. You're alive; I'm alive; billions upon billions of organisms are alive because that's *not* how sex works. How does meiosis (remember, it's the process that makes haploid sex cells) insure that nothing is passed on in too many or too few copies?

The key lies in something I stressed above: The map of all normal copies of Chromosome 1 is the same. All the loci are laid out in the exact same sequence. During meiosis, and *before* they mix any material, the paternal and maternal copies of Chromosome 1 lie next to each other, precisely assigned, so that each locus is adjacent to its corresponding locus on the matching chromosome. Then and only then do they exchange material, insuring that any such exchange will be perfectly reciprocal and that no material will be doubled or left out. There's nothing special about Chromosome 1. Chromosomes 2, 3, 4, and so on all do likewise, lining up their matching loci and only then exchanging genetic

Figure 3-3. Recombination is an exchange of genes between maternal and paternal chromosomes that occurs during meiosis.

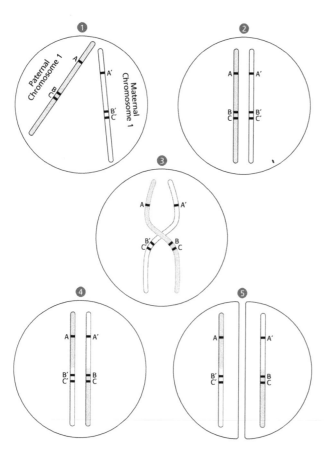

material. This exchange of genetic material during meiosis is, quite sensibly, called *recombination*. In females the two X-chromosomes engage in recombination. In males relatively small sections of the Y-chromosome recombine with the X-chromosome.

This process of recombination has a simple physical basis which is laid out sequentially in Figure 3-3. For simplicity, only one diploid chromosome pair is shown but all of the chromosome pairs behave the same way. Beginning with a resting phase where there is no alignment (1), the paternal and maternal copies of each chromosome then line up so that each locus is physically next to the corresponding locus on the matching chromosome (2). Three example loci are shown for reference (A B C) and I'll mark them slightly differently (A' B' C') on the maternal member of the chromosome pair just to remind you that the matching loci could be carrying different alleles. Next, maintaining their precise locus-by-locus alignment, the paired chromosomes physically overlap (3); the loci where they overlap are called cross-over points. At these cross-over points, each chromosome breaks and attaches to the corresponding segment of its paired chromosome (4). The result is two new versions of the chromosome which then separate to be packaged in different haploid cells (5).

Recombination has many important consequences. For example, recombination all but guarantees that each new individual—who is a result of recombination in her mother and recombination in her father—will have a genotype that never existed before. (The only "exception" to this is identical twins, and they are not really an exception because they are the result of just one fertilization event.) For now I'll emphasize only one more consequence,

called *linkage*, which also has a clear physical basis. Linkage is a sensible term for this phenomenon because it describes the observation that alleles at nearby loci tend to travel across the generations together; they tend to be *linked*. Let's look again at Figure 3.3. The farther apart two loci are, the more likely they are to have a cross-over point fall between them. Loci A and B are more likely to have a cross-over point fall between them than B and C are. And that's what happened in this example. The alleles at B and C stayed together (made it into the same haploid sex cell at step 5), but the alleles at A and B were separated into different haploid sex cells. Linkage has implications for how natural selection *can* operate, but it also provides us with a powerful tool for understanding how it *has* operated—what traits it has favored—in the recent past (see Chapter 18).

CHAPTER SUMMARY

Evolution by natural selection must rest on a system of heredity. Beneficial traits will accumulate in the population only if successful parents pass on the traits that permitted their success. Blending inheritance, the mistaken model of inheritance that was uncritically accepted during Darwin's lifetime, is wrong. Instead, inheritance is based on particulate genes, which never blend with each other. This is important because, if blending inheritance were true, favorable new variations would be diluted down to uselessness before selection could spread them through the population. These particulate genes may come in different versions (alleles) and are inherited in highly predictable ways that were first described by Gregor Mendel. Within each species, genes are arranged in a consistent way across the chromosomes, with each gene reliably occurring at its own unique locus. This consistency is critical to sexual reproduction because it allows every individual to mix genetic material from her father and her mother during the formation of her haploid sex cells. In most instances the state of the phenotype will depend on genes at multiple loci as well as on gene-environment interactions.

In Chapter 1 we noted that it's individuals who succeed or fail—having many, or few, or no offspring. But, no matter how successful they are, all individuals eventually die. With the knowledge of genetics gained in this chapter we can begin to see that alleles are important players in the evolutionary drama. The alleles that build reproductively successful individuals will get passed on to future generations and consequently endure—potentially for eons. Here's a simple summary: Alleles audition for the future by building individuals, and the

alleles that produce better-adapted individuals will be passed on more often.

CITED REFERENCES

G. Mendel (1865). "Versuche über Pflanzen-hybriden". *Verhandlungen des Naturforschenden Vereins in Brünn, 4*. An English translation ["Experiments in plant hybridization"] was published by Harvard University Press on the Centennial in 1965.

FIGURE CREDIT

3-1: Image created by Judith Geiger.

3-2: National Human Genome Research Institute, https://commons.wikimedia.org/wiki/File:Karyotype.png. Copyright in the Public Domain.

3-3: Image created by Judith Geiger.

CHAPTER 4

MOLECULAR GENETICS: WHAT GENES ARE AND WHAT THEY DO

Just from the few examples discussed in the previous chapter it's clear that genes can shape many different aspects of the phenotype. And they can transmit the instructions for shaping phenotypes from parents to offspring, generation after generation. Those are two pretty impressive capabilities. But what precisely are genes? What are they made of, and how do they influence the development of phenotypes? The answers to these questions are among the greatest achievements of 20th-century science.

In contemporary terminology, genes are nano-technology. I'm sure you know that nano-tech and nano-engineering are hot new research areas. But you may not know that the structure of genes—first described by James Watson and Francis Crick in 1953—represents a kind of nano-technology that had been hacked together by natural selection *billions* of years earlier. In Chapter 1 I suggested that we can usefully think of genes as recipes. Now it's time to take a look at how the genetic nano-technology both spells out recipes and transmits those same recipes to offspring.

GENE STRUCTURE: DNA

The key insight here is that *everything* genes do is a result of their detailed *chemical structure*. Genes are extremely long, stringy molecules that are made up of a very limited set of smaller molecular components. The long stringy molecule—the hereditary material—is called *DNA*, and its components are:

1. A specific kind of sugar (deoxyribose),
2. A certain phosphate, and
3. Four kinds of chemical bases: adenine, thymine, guanine and cytosine.

The arrangement of these components of DNA is not at all random; quite the opposite, it's highly regular. Two "backbones" are identically built out of alternating phosphate and sugar molecules (phosphate, sugar, phosphate sugar, etc.). Instead of merely lying parallel to each other the backbones are twisted into a double spiral or helix. It might help you to think of DNA as a spiral staircase. On that analogy, the phosphate-sugar backbones form the supporting structure, and the four bases work in pairs to form the rungs or treads of the staircase—the part you would step on—and they always connect to the backbone at the sugar molecules. Before we continue let's take a minute to convert to the base-labeling system that biologists conventionally use and that we will use in the rest of the book, because it's simpler! Adenine is A, thymine is T, guanine is G and cytosine is C: easy enough.

I said "the four bases work in pairs to form the rungs" because it always takes two bases to make each one of the rungs; but only certain pairs will work. A will only build a solid, stable rung with T and, likewise, G will only build a solid, stable rung with C. That's because of the detailed atomic bonds that each of these kinds of bases can form. These atomic constraints amount to what are called DNA's *base-pairing rules*. Neither G nor C will ever bond with A or with T.

In my experience students find it helpful to periodically circle back and connect new knowledge with previously learned material. Let's do that. Remember that genes are linearly arranged along chromosomes (Chapter 3). Now we have learned that genes are DNA molecules; in that case, what are chromosomes? The answer is that they are just *much longer* DNA molecules. If you were looking at a chromosome you would not see any boundaries between the genes. A chromosome is just a very long strand of DNA that includes many genes along its length. "How long?" you might ask. Remember that the 22 human chromosomes (plus the sex chromosomes) differ substantially in length, so it's slightly artificial to talk about the "average" chromosome; but with that caveat in mind we can do a simple calculation. A haploid human genotype contains about 3.3 billion base pairs; dividing by 23 chromosomes tells us that the average human chromosome would be a bit under 145 million base pairs long. Yes, as I said; chromosomes are *very* long strands of DNA. I can now tie up one more loose end for you. Do you remember when we talked about how locus addresses are specified? I said that one of the addressing systems simply counted "units" and I gave the example of the human growth hormone at 17:61,994,559-61,996,205. I imagine that you have now guessed that those "units" are bases. So the gene for this particular hormone begins 61,994,559 bases from the end of the 17th chromosome and is 1,646 bases long.

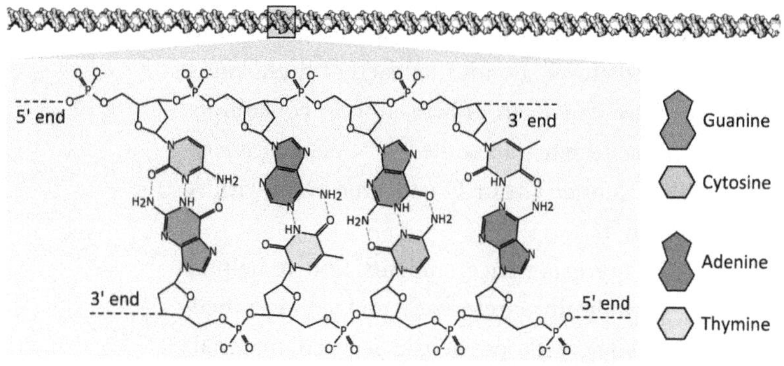

Figure 4-1. The structure of DNA. See text for a full description.

Now that we have a general picture of what DNA is, let's take a few minutes to look at Figure 4-1. Running along the top of the diagram is a stretch of DNA in its normal double-spiral configuration. Below that, shown at a much higher level of magnification, we see just four "rungs" of the DNA ladder. As mentioned above, each rung is composed of two bases, either guanine and cytosine (G and C) or adenine and thymine (A and T). At this fine scale it's apparent why some base pairings are impossible. Because of their structure, G and C are stable only when they form triple bonds. Conversely A and T need to form double bonds. Running above and below the base pairs we also see the structure of the two backbones; phosphates and sugars alternate, with the bases always attached to the sugar molecules. The backbones have an upstream and downstream direction, designated 3' and 5', which determine the direction the DNA is read. (You can only make sense out of the words on an English page if you read from left to right, and DNA has a very similar restriction.) In terms of building blocks, DNA is assembled from *nucleotides which each include one base, one sugar, and one phosphate*. For example, in the upper left of the Figure, next to the words "5' end" there is first a phosphate, bonded to a sugar, bonded to a cytosine. That group of three molecules is one nucleotide. Nucleotides are attached end-to-end to make one side of the spiral staircase and mated with the complementary nucleotides that form the other side. Let's move towards a picture of how that assembly happens.

Please do a brief thought experiment with me. Suppose I had a special molecular tool that would let me take the spiral staircase of DNA and cut it right down the middle. If I did that, on each side of my cut I'd have one phosphate-sugar backbone plus a sequence of detached bases, missing their "rung partners." Now, let me ask you the key question. Imagine that on the left side of the cut I saw a G. What would be directly opposite on the right side of the cut? Of course, it would be a C; only C can pair with G. In fact, no matter what sequence of unmatched bases I had on one side, I could specify with absolute certainty what the complementary sequence would be on the other side: The base-pairing rules determine it.

Why is that interesting? Because any hereditary material must be able to copy itself. A parent still has its genes after reproducing because it passes *copies* of its genes to the offspring. It's DNA's base-pairing rules that allow it to copy itself. You see, the thought experiment you did is much more than an experiment: It's exactly how DNA copies itself! The DNA spiral staircase "unzips" along its midline and *both halves* of the molecule recruit the missing phosphate-sugar-base components they're missing. When that process is complete there will be two identical copies of the original DNA molecule. Figure 4-2 shows this process in some detail. The key elements are just what we have outlined. The DNA opens up and each half of the molecule captures the nucleotides needed to complete itself. By this process one molecule becomes two that are exactly the same. Every time a cell divides (whether that division is for growth of the individual or for the production of sex cell that will form the next generation), this is precisely how DNA copies itself.

Now we see how DNA accomplishes one of the fundamental things that any kind of hereditary material would have to do: making copies of itself that can be passed to offspring. If there were life on other planets (and I strongly suspect that evolution has created it many places), that life would need some kind of hereditary molecule that could, like DNA, copy itself. I don't expect that, for example Martian "genes", would be made out of DNA, but they would need to have some physical machinery that allowed the kind of accurate copying that DNA is capable of.

Besides making very precise copies of itself DNA, has a second equally important task. It's not a mere trinket passed from one generation to the next. It carries information, the information necessary to build phenotypes. So the hereditary system has to be a code, a kind of language, for phenotype construction.

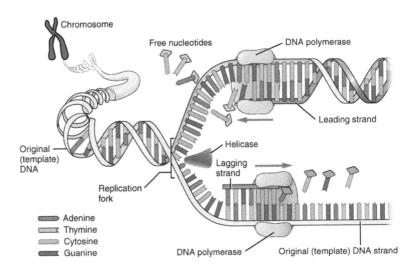

Figure 4-2. The mechanism of DNA copying. Each unzipped base recruits its complementary nucleotide.

If you ever invented a secret code (for sending messages to your friends?) you realize that any information-carrying system needs some variable elements that can be put together in different configurations to encode meaning. There don't necessarily have to be lots of variable elements. For example, Morse Code has just two: dots and dashes. Each letter was assigned a unique combination of dots and dashes (for example, A is dot, dash; B is dash, dot, dot, dot). This code was extensively used to transmit information before voice transmission was invented and is in fact still in use in various situations today.

An analogy with Morse Code suggests that the sugars and phosphates could be the information-carrying parts of the DNA molecule. How does that possibility sit with what you're learned about the structure of DNA? I hope you'll say "not very well." What we know is that the two DNA backbones consistently alternate phosphate, sugar, phosphate, sugar… with no variation across the entire length of a DNA molecule, and you now know how long that is! To carry information the way the dots and dashes of Morse Code do, the phosphates and sugars would have to occur in different combinations: PSPPPSSPSSSPPSPSS. Since they don't, they can't carry information. What we have left as the possible information carriers are the bases, A, C, T, and G, and they do occur in every imaginable combination. An A, for example, can be followed by a T, C, G, or by another A (right; it has to be mated to a T, but it can be followed by any of the four letters). All such sequences are easily found. So that mystery can be solved on simple structural evidence: only the bases vary in the way that information carriers would. More than half a century ago researchers used this same logic to reach the same conclusion—and won the Nobel Prize for doing so. But what kind of information do the bases carry, and how is that information read?

GENETICS AS A LANGUAGE: RNA, RIBOSOMES, AMINO ACIDS, AND PROTEINS.

I'm going to start with the punch line so you can see where we're heading. Earlier I used the analogy of genes as recipes. Actually that description was more like reality than analogy, because genes *are* recipes, recipes for the assembly of proteins. The reading of those recipes is more complicated than the process of DNA copying (above) but it does depend, all along the line, on the same kinds of base-pairing rules that permit DNA copying. Let's continue to take a top-down approach; we'll get around to the detailed mechanics after you understand the overall gene → protein road map.

You can think of the four possible bases (A, C, T, and G) as the "letters" of the very brief "genetic alphabet." Now, most single letters don't mean anything in your language, and they don't mean anything in the genetic language either. In language we use sequences of letters to make words that do have specific meanings. Likewise, in genetics the four possible bases are used to spell "genetic words" (called *codons*). While English words vary in length, codons always have exactly three letters (for example, GTT, or CGA). To continue the analogy with language, each three-letter codon has a meaning: It specifies a particular amino acid. In language we string words together to make sentences. In genetics, amino acids are strung together to make proteins. We started out by saying that genes are recipes for proteins and now we have mapped out how that works: Genes are strings of three-base codons that specify amino acid sequences which form proteins (see Figure 4-3).

Proteins are the building blocks of all life. As just mentioned, they are sequences (linear chains, as first assembled, but folding into complex 3-dimensional structures) of their component amino acids. Although there are only 20 kinds

Figure 4-3. Both language and genetics are systems of progressively larger units that can be combined only according to specific rules.

letters ⟶ words ⟶ meanings ⟶ sentences

bases ⟶ codons ⟶ amino acids ⟶ proteins

of amino acids, many different proteins can be assembled from this limited set by ordering them differently and by building amino acid chains of different lengths. The shortest known proteins are less than two dozen amino acids long, but such brevity is very unusual; the longest proteins in your body are tens of thousands of amino acids long! Yes, that's right; to specify a 30,000 amino-acid protein, it takes 90,000 bases. But remember, that's still a tiny fraction of your 3.3 billion bases.

You might have noticed an apparent mismatch. Four letters can make 64 different three-letter words, but there are only 20 amino acids. How does that work out? The answer is simple: Just like your language, the genetic language has synonyms. I can say "bright," "clever," "intelligent," "quick-witted," etc. and they will all be taken to have more-or-less the same meaning. Likewise, for most of the 20 different amino acids there are multiple codon-words that specify it. Consider Figure 4-4. There you can see that there are six different codons that specify the amino acid arginine. There are four that call for proline, and there are two that specify lysine. You might notice that most, but not all, of this synonymousness concerns the third base-letter of the codons.

Not only does the genetic language have letters, words, sentences, and meanings, it also has punctuation. "Stop" codons, of which there are three (TAA, TAG and TGA), are the equivalent of a period. And the equivalent of capitalization at the beginning of sentence is the unique "start" codon, ATG.

Now that you understand the basic gene → protein road map let's dig a bit more deeply into the mechanisms that "read" DNA's message. The structure of DNA that we've already described might usefully be called DNA's "resting mode." In that mode all of the A=T bonds and all of the C=G bonds are zipped up tight. The protein recipes are there, coded in the A, T, C, and G bases, but they can't be read, just as the words in a book are there but can't be read until you open it up.

So naturally, the first step in reading any DNA sequence—any protein recipe—is to open it up: The DNA needs to unzip along its midline to expose its bases. What happens then is very similar to what happens when DNA copies itself because it depends on base-pairing rules, but there are a couple of critical

Figure 4-4. The 64 possible DNA codons and their amino acid "meaning." Note that some amino acids can be specified by more than one codon.

Amino Acid	Codons					
Tryptophan	TGG					
Tyrosine	TAC	TAT				
Cysteine	TGC	TGT				
Glutamic Acid	GAA	GAG				
Lysine	AAA	AAG				
Glutamine	CAA	CAG				
Serine	AGC	AGT	TCA	TCC	TCG	TCT
Leucine	TTA	TTG	CTA	CTC	CTG	CTT
Arginine	AGA	AGG	CGA	CGC	CGG	CGT
Glycine	GGA	GGC	GGG	GGT		
Phenylalanine	TTC	TTT				
Aspartic Acid	GAC	GAT				
Histidine	CAC	CAT				
Asparagine	AAC	AAT				
Start codon — Methionine	ATG					
Alanine	GCA	GCC	GCG	GCT		
Proline	CCA	CCC	CCG	CCT		
Threonine	ACA	ACC	ACG	ACT		
Valine	GTA	GTC	GTG	GTT		
Isoleucine	ATA	ATC	ATT			
Stop codon — ———	TAA	TAG	TGA			

differences. In DNA copying (Figure 4-2), both sides of the opened-up DNA chain actively recruit their complementary bases, and that happens along the entire length of the chromosome. But in this first step of the gene → protein process the DNA unzips *only for the length of a single gene, and only one side of the unzipped DNA is active.*

Very much as it does in DNA copying, the active side recruits complementary bases, but it doesn't form a matching half-strand of DNA—since it already has one that it can zip back onto. Instead, the complementary bases it recruits form a new single-stranded molecule called *messenger RNA*, or mRNA for short. It's called messenger RNA because its role is to carry the message contained in the gene to the part of the cell where the protein will be made; more on that shortly. Being single-stranded, mRNA has only one phosphate-sugar backbone and it uses a different sugar than DNA does. The base pairing-rules that determine the mRNA sequence are also slightly different from DNA's base-pairing rules. In building the mRNA molecule, G on the exposed DNA recruits a C, and C on the exposed DNA recruits a G. T on the exposed DNA recruits an A; but here's the difference. A on the exposed DNA recruits a U on the mRNA (U stands for a different base called uracil). So if the exposed DNA reads TTCGCCACA it would specify an mRNA molecule that reads AAGCGGUGU.

Of course any real tRNA strand will be longer than these brief examples. You know that they must have three times as many bases as there are amino acids in the corresponding protein. After it is formed, this mRNA molecule might be further edited (having some bits clipped out), but when it is "mature" it leaves the cell nucleus where the DNA resides and enters the cytoplasm of the cell. I like to think of the cell nucleus as the rare-book room where the irreplaceable materials are kept. As you know, you can't check those materials out. You can go in there and read the rare books (the DNA) and you can take pictures (the mRNA) of parts of them with your cell phone; and you can take those pictures with you. On this analogy, the cytoplasm of the cell is the work space, for example your desk at home with various tools: laptops, e-readers, pens, pencils, paper, etc. There you can review your pictures and interpret their message.

Back to reality. In the cytoplasm there is a big, complicated piece of cellular machinery called a ribosome whose only job is to interpret the message of the mRNA. Ribosomes actually have two unequal parts—a large subunit and a small subunit—that clamp down on the mRNA. This message-interpretation phase is the first context in which we would notice that the genetic information is read as three-letter "words" (the codons discussed above). The ribosome reads the mRNA by moving along it, three bases (one codon) at a time. This reading process again involves base-pair rules (see how important they are?). For each codon on the mRNA, say UCG, the ribosome finds a molecule of *transfer RNA* (tRNA) that has a complementary triplet of exposed bases; in this case that would be AGC. Let me explain "exposed bases." Molecules of tRNA are, like any kind of RNA, single-stranded molecules with a phosphate-sugar backbone and sequences composed of A, C, G, and U bases. But these tRNA strands don't lie flat. They ball up on themselves because the base sequence of particular regions happens to be complementary to the base sequence of other regions elsewhere along its length. This balling-up process leaves three adjacent bases that are not bonded to any other region on the tRNA molecule and are hence "exposed," and therefore free to bond with a codon on the mRNA. There are, of course, 64 kinds of tRNA, one for each of the possible three-base combination of A, C, G, and U. In addition to having three exposed bases, every tRNA molecule carries at its tip (can you guess?) an amino acid. The "reading" actually occurs when the ribosome "mates" the three exposed tRNA bases with an mRNA codon. At that instant the tRNA molecule releases its amino acid. The just-used tRNA molecule is then discarded (recycled actually to recruit another molecule of its specific amino acid), and the ribosome moves on to read the next codon. As the ribosome moves along the mRNA strand, reading codon after codon, the amino acids that are being released bond to each other to form an amino acid sequence which, when complete, will be a protein.

Figure 4-5 visually reviews this process. I haven't bothered with the step of making the mRNA since that's so similar to DNA copying. Here we see the already formed mRNA (which is of course single-stranded). As each three-letter codon comes into position between the large and small units, the ribosome finds the right type of tRNA (one that has the complementary codon exposed), and forms a very brief bond between the mRNA codon and the tRNA. This bonding ejects the amino acid that the tRNA had been carrying at its opposite end, and this just-released amino acid is then tacked onto the amino acid released by the previous tRNA molecule. So, as the ribosome runs along the mRNA "tape," it spins out a growing amino acid chain. It's at this stage of the process where we can see codon-amino acid correspondences laid out earlier in Figure 4-4. (Those are DNA correspondences; you can tell because there are no U's. You should now be able to produce a similar table with mRNA correspondences and tRNA correspondences.)

So now we see that the gene → protein process has a few intermediary steps and players. Genes unzip long enough to have their base sequences transcribed into mRNA. The mRNA transcripts leave the nucleus and are glommed onto by ribosomes in the cytoplasm. These ribosomes facilitate very brief bonds between three-base codons on the mRNA and exposed three-base anticodons on molecules of tRNA. During those brief bonds the tRNA releases the amino acid it has been carrying. And each successively

Figure 4-5. Through the intermediary of mRNA, DNA specifies the amino acid sequences of proteins.

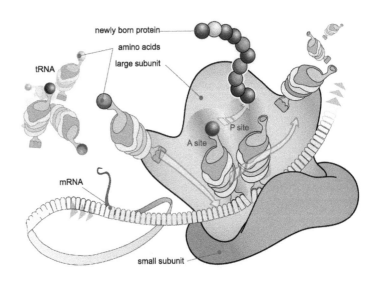

released amino acid bonds to the one before it to, eventually, form a protein.

It's true that proteins are not phenotypes. But they are components of phenotypes, and interact in various more and less complex way to build phenotypes. For example, the different pod colors of peas in Mendel's experiments were due to alternative alleles that code for different pigment proteins. In Chapter 1 we met the human hemoglobin molecule, responsible for carrying oxygen throughout the body. With your new knowledge I can now explain that human hemoglobin is actually a complex formed by the union of two proteins, one coded by a locus on Chromosome 11 and one coded by a locus on Chromosome 16. Human growth hormone is a protein that affects the activity of other proteins, coded other genes. Also, proteins coded by genes at one locus can affect whether or not—or how much—genes at other loci send their mRNA messages, and therefore how much of their protein is produced. It's these interwoven cascades of protein effects and interactions that build phenotypes.

CHAPTER SUMMARY

Two processes fundamental to all life on Earth are discussed in this chapter: how genes copy themselves and how they influence the development of phenotypes. When we look under the hood of Mendel's genes we see a marvelous realm of precisely tuned nano-technology: physical interactions among tiny components that are limited by the kinds of chemical bonds that are and aren't possible. The chemical base A can bond with T (or U) but not C or G. These base-pairing rules allow genes to make extremely precise copies of themselves. And, through the intermediaries of mRNA, ribosomes, and tRNA, they allow genes to specify the recipes for proteins that then interact in myriad ways to assemble phenotypes like yours and mine.

FIGURE CREDITS

CHAPTER 5

ADAPTIVE EVOLUTION IN HUMANS: THE CASE OF SKIN PIGMENTATION

Natural selection builds adaptations by filtering the flow of alleles from each generation to the next. Of course that process happens in every species, including our own. A useful way to deduce what selection is favoring, and why, is to compare different populations confronting different environmental challenges. We'll formalize the *comparative method* later; here we'll get acquainted with it on a more informal basis. Because environments are complex and genomes are huge it's not very effective to ask questions like "where is evolution taking us?" To make progress we need to focus on one, or a very limited set of traits, at a time.

For example, in Chapter 2 we learned about a "field experiment" where Mediterranean lizards were intentionally moved to a new environment. There, they confronted new food sources, and natural selection reshaped both the "front end" and the "back end" of their food-processing systems, allowing them to survive and reproduce better in that new environment. And we saw that American lizards also evolved different grasping adaptations depending on whether or not a competitor species was forcing them to use hard-to-grasp perches. Both examples illustrate selection's ability to redesign particular traits in response to particular environmental shifts.

Our human ancestors have colonized a larger proportion of the planet than almost any other species, and thus experienced some dramatically different selective regimes. Those various selective regimes can be viewed as natural experiments performed by natural selection. As we saw in the lizards, we should expect that specific human traits would be favored where they were useful and deleted or reduced elsewhere. In this chapter we'll use this kind of comparative approach to consider the adaptive significance of a single human trait—skin color—and try to understand how selection has acted on it as humans have moved around the planet.

HUMAN SKIN PIGMENTATION

Let's start with a basic question: What makes skin dark or light? The main molecule of interest is called melanin, and it is a dark-colored pigment. All humans who are not albinos have genes that allow them to make melanin—they have a protein recipe for it. Individuals can differ in the particular melanin alleles they have and, partly because of those genetic differences, they differ in how much and exactly what kind of melanin they produce. Because melanin is a dark pigment, those whose genes synthesize more of it have darker-looking skin. Those whose genes make less of it are more lightly pigmented. In other words, more darkly pigmented people tend to have different melanin alleles than more lightly pigmented people.

In the lizard experiment we discovered that lizards experiencing different selection pressures (as a result of having different diets) evolved different feeding and digestive adaptations. If we saw only their feeding and digestive adaptations, we would probably hypothesize (guess) that they had different diets—a hypothesis we could test with field observations of their feeding behavior. We find ourselves in a similar situation when we try to understand skin color. Evolution has already done the "experiment," producing different skin colors in different parts of the world. Our task is to work backwards to figure out what the relevant selection pressures were. Why did natural selection favor alleles that produce light skin in some areas and alleles that produce dark skin in other areas?

To take this problem apart, as scientists like to do, we can start with the source of the difference—the melanin molecule itself. Superficially we can see that more or less melanin makes people darker- or lighter-skinned. But there must be a reason this particular protein recipe exists; what does the melanin molecule do besides making skin darker? Or, put another way, what is the advantage of darker skin? One clue comes from where melanin is produced. The genes that code for the melanin protein are present in almost all of your cells—muscle cells, liver cells, bone cell, brain cells and so on. So, because they have the recipe, any of these cells could make melanin; but most don't. Most of the melanin in a person's body is produced by cells in the surface layers of her skin. Why there? Research has revealed that melanin has a unique property, a photochemical property. It absorbs sunlight in a narrow band of wavelengths called ultraviolet-b (UVb). This is a critical observation because it turns out that UVb is the precise wavelength of light that poses the *greatest risk of skin cancer*, especially the often-fatal kinds of skin cancers known as melanomas.

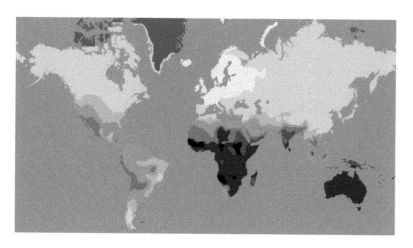

Figure 5-1. The indigenous distribution of human skin color. Darker shading indicates darker sknin colors.

Now we're making progress. Melanin is a UVb blocker. The genes that make melanin stash this special molecule in the top layers of the skin. There, at the body's outer boundary, it prevents the cancer-causing kinds of sunlight from penetrating to deeper layers where it would do damage. Given the precise photochemical activity of the melanin molecule—blocking a very narrow and very dangerous wavelength of light—and the observation that it is concentrated in the surface layers of the skin, a biologist would be inclined to conclude that melanin had been shaped by natural selection for this very purpose. In other words, we can hypothesize that the melanin protein is an *adaptation* for protecting against the risk of skin cancer.

Let's be clear what it means to claim that melanin is an adaptation for protecting against skin cancer. It means that, in ancestral populations, individuals who produced sufficient melanin were less likely to die of skin cancer and consequently more likely to survive long enough to reproduce. As a consequence, alleles that produced the right amount of melanin accumulated in the population. Yes, saying melanin is an anti-cancer adaptation entails all of that. So, how could we test this adaptive hypothesis about melanin? We can look for evidence of natural selection's influence on skin color. Let me suggest two possible categories of evidence: 1) the natural distribution of skin color around the globe, and 2) the rates of skin cancer in people with different skin colors living in the same environment. What does that evidence suggest?

If melanin protects against skin cancer then selection should have favored higher levels of melanin production where skin-cancer risks are greatest. Figure 5-1 shows the indigenous distribution of skin color across the planet. By "indigenous" I simply mean the skin colors of the resident populations before ships, airplanes, and the large-scale migrations of people that have occurred in just the last few centuries. This skin color distribution is not random; there is a clear pattern. Darker-pigmented skin is found near the equator, especially in areas with less cloud cover and less forest (both clouds and trees block some UVb). The earth's atmosphere also blocks UVb, so the more atmosphere the sun's rays have to pass through, the less UVb reaches the ground. That's important because the sun's rays are more perpendicular to the earth, and therefore pass through less atmosphere, at the equator. At progressively higher latitudes (moving towards the poles in either direction from the equator), the sun's rays strike the earth at a more shallow angle and therefore transit more atmosphere before reaching the ground. These three factors (angle of solar incidence, cloud cover, and forest cover) do a good job of explaining the pattern of skin color in Figure 5-1. Populations that experience more solar radiation (because they live near the equator and get little shade from clouds or trees) have the darkest skin colors.

But another aspect of this pattern may have caught your attention. The equator-to-poles gradient I just described is much stronger in the Old World (Africa, Europe, and Asia) than it is in the New World (the Americas). In both of these world areas people are lighter-skinned towards the poles and darker-skinned towards the equator, but the differences between polar people and equatorial people are noticeably larger in the Old World. Why should that be? This answer also makes evolutionary sense. As you'll learn later in the course, our species (*Homo sapiens*) has been in the Old World about ten times as long as it's been in the New World. Thus, there has been more time for selection to build the equator-to-pole gradient in the Old World. We'll explore this more in the second half of the course when we unearth (literally) the details of where our species arose and how it came to occupy so much of the planet. So, when we consider the natural distribution of human skin color, dark pigmentation (more melanin production) seems to be restricted to areas of high UVb exposure. That pattern is evidence in favor of our hypothesis that melanin evolved to protect against the cancer-causing effects of UVb.

Let me now turn to the second category of evidence: observations about what happens when people lack the protection of melanin. The idea is simply that, if melanin evolved to protect against skin cancer, those without such protection will show higher rates of this cancer. Of course this kind of evidence would be most relevant if it came from areas of the world with high UVb exposure. Mel Greaves (2014), a British cancer researcher, has collected this kind of evidence. If you're following the evolutionary argument you might expect that skin cancer rates would be the same everywhere, because each population would produce enough melanin to deal with its particular level of UVb exposure. That's nice adaptive thinking on your part, and it's broadly correct. It's the perspective we used to explain the world-wide distribution of skin color (Figure 5-1). But don't forget about entropy. Things tend to fall

Figure 5-2. The level of exposure to solar radiation varies with the seasons.

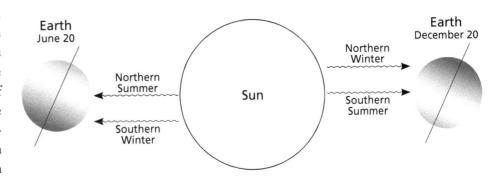

apart; mistakes happen. We need a very brief digression here to explain that even genes occasionally fall apart.

I'm going to introduce a very important idea, one with many implications for our understanding of evolution: *mutation*. In Chapter 4, I stressed how accurately genes copy themselves (because of their base-pairing rules), and that is overwhelming correct; I have no intention of retracting that claim. But very, very rarely gene-copying errors do occur. That's what a mutation is: a mistake in gene copying. We will revisit the notion of mutation many times in this book. For now we are interested only in one specific mutation—the one that causes *albinism*. Because of this gene-copying error people with albinism—albinos—cannot make melanin. It's quite possible that you have never met an albino, but they do occur at very low frequency (approximately 1 in 17,000) in most human populations. If melanin is an anti-cancer adaptation, what do you predict about the skin cancer rates of albinos?

That's the question Mel Greaves asked and he chose to focus on Africa and other low latitude areas. UVb exposure is greatest there and the majority of people in such regions have protective, darkly pigmented skin. Comparisons between albinos and non-albinos should be most revealing in such areas. The sad answer is that albinos suffer greatly from skin cancer. In low-latitude areas of Africa they have skin cancer rates up to 1000 times higher than the skin cancer rates of non-albinos. By age 20 roughly half of African albinos have skin cancer, decades earlier than non-albinos, whose skin cancers are mostly confined to their post-reproductive years.

This is stark evidence; it contrasts people who have high melanin production with people who have *no* melanin production in an area where UVb exposure is high. And, as predicted, it shows the strong action of natural selection, removing the mutant alleles that derail melanin production, via the early deaths of albinos. Australia provides similar evidence. Much of this country lies at low latitude and most of it is extremely arid, having little cloud cover and not much shade-providing vegetation. As you might expect, the native peoples of Australia generally have quite high levels of melanin production. Beginning less than 250 years ago, people from a cloudy, high-latitude area (Britain) began immigrating to Australia in substantial numbers. Predictably, Australians of British ancestry have one of the highest rates of skin cancer in the world, a rate many times higher than the native Australians do (Condon et al., 2003). As useful points of comparison, British people who live in Britain don't have high rates of skin cancer; and those who moved to Australia don't have higher rates of non-skin cancers than native Australians. The elevated risks suffered by the British colonists seem to be restricted to their lack of protection from high levels of UVb.

IS UVB ALWAYS BAD?

Why do people living farther from the equator produce less melanin? "Economy" could be the answer. In other words, there's no free lunch: Everything has to be paid for. Matter (amino acids) and energy (calories) are both required to make melanin. So, if you don't need much melanin (because you don't need to block much UVb), then don't spend a lot of resources making it. You'll see this idea more fully developed in the Chapter 7; but since it's not the primary reason that people from higher latitudes make less melanin, I'll save the economic perspective for later. Until now we've looked at only the harmful effects of UVb, but it turns out that UVb is also essential to humans! That's because UVb catalyzes (makes chemically possible) the synthesis of vitamin D. *We can make this vitamin only in the presence of UVb.*

Let's take a minute to think about vitamins from an evolutionary perspective. Substances are called vitamins when they are metabolically essential for life. We need to get certain vitamins from food, but others we can make, if we have the necessary precursors ("ingredients"). To exemplify the contrast, vitamin C and vitamin D are both essential for humans; eventually you'll die if you lack either of them. We can make vitamin D (with the help of UVb), but we can't make vitamin C under any circumstances. The better way to say this is that our lineage has lost the ability to make vitamin C, since other species (e.g., most members of the order *Carnivora* such as your dog) can. This loss could have happened only if our ancestors habitually ate a diet that included sufficient amounts of vitamin C. The opposite must be true for vitamin D. It must have been scarce or absent in our ancestors' diets and they therefore needed the ability to make it.

OK, back to our analysis of skin pigmentation. We can make vitamin D if we get enough UVb. But, melanin blocks UVb and that blocking effect could become a problem because UVb has two effects, one harmful and one helpful—in fact essential. UVb blocking protects against skin cancer but it *inhibits vitamin D synthesis.* Across the planet, the relative risks of vitamin D deficiency and skin cancer vary inversely. Skin cancer is a big risk on the equator but vitamin D deficiency is not. In cloudy northern areas the opposite pattern prevails: a low risk of skin cancer and a high risk of vitamin D deficiency. So let's combine these ideas to formulate a prediction. In different areas of the globe, selection should favor different melanin-producing alleles, blocking more or less UVb depending on which risk (skin cancer or vitamin D-deficiency) is greater. That's a fuller explanation for the indigenous distribution of skin color (Figure 5-1).

Skin color makes very good evolutionary sense. It's not an arbitrary, superficial trait at all. It reflects important biological functions and a well-designed trade-off between two potent selection pressures. The meta-lesson (the bigger lesson sitting on top of the stated one) is that much can be learned by beginning with the assumption that traits are designed (by selection) and asking what they are designed for. Patterns of human variation across the planet are the essential data for answering these kinds of questions.

FACULTATIVE ADAPTATIONS

There is one more educational pearl lurking in this particular oyster—one that we will invoke many times as we deepen our understanding of human biology. You already know that UVb levels vary with latitude and cloud cover. Here's an inescapable Terran twist: Because the earth's axis of rotation is tipped relative to the plane of its orbit, UVb also varies seasonally. Regardless of whether you live in the northern or the southern hemisphere, you get more UVb in your summer, when your part of the world is tipped toward the sun, than you do in your winter, when it's tipped away. This seasonal variation means that the optimal (ideal) amount of melanin isn't constant anywhere on the planet; it changes seasonally with shifts in UVb exposure. Is there any way selection can solve this problem? Yes there is; in fact such solutions are common, and they are called facultative adaptations.

Selection builds facultative adaptations when key environmental challenges vary within the lifetimes of individuals. In the skin-color case, the relative risks of skin cancer and vitamin D deficiency shift with the seasons. What do you call the particular facultative adaptation that lets you respond to these changing risk patterns? Sun tanning. Not only do your genes set your baseline level of melanin synthesis, but they also encode a rule about how to change that level (within certain limits) in response to your *current* dose of UVb. Note how well designed this mechanism is: your sun-tanning response is not uniform over your whole body, but instead tracks how much solar radiation each area of skin receives. If you regularly wear a watch on your wrist, for example, much less melanin is produced by the skin under the watch.

The existence of this facultative adaptation is one more piece of biological evidence that our explanation about skin color is correct. UVb has both positive and negative effects. Melanin evolved as a UVb blocker. The amount of blocking that's needed varies both geographically and seasonally because UVb exposure varies geographically and seasonally. Both the geographic and the seasonal patterns of human melanin production match the patterns of UVb exposure. Natural selection nicely explains human skin color.

I don't want to distract you from the important messages in this chapter, but as I've mentioned before, I think it's also important to connect ideas across chapters. In Chapter 2, we noted that Stuart et al. (2014) was keen to demonstrate that the changes in the grasping adaptations of *Anolis carolinensis* were not "mere" developmental effects. This was accomplished by taking eggs from females living on islands with and without the invader species and showing that the resulting offspring manifested their own mothers' grasping traits, even when reared in a single common environment. In terms that you are now better prepared to understand, the point of this common-rearing experiment was to show that these particular *grasping changes were not facultative.* That is interesting, and I understand why it was important to Stuart (who wanted to show rapid evolutionary change) to rule out other possible explanations. Well done!

On the other hand, I also want to stress an even more sweeping idea: Facultative adaptations are, first and foremost, adaptations. What I mean is that *the ability to track and respond to the environment in particular ways must itself have been designed by selection* in the lineage under study. Patterns of so-called *developmental plasticity* are products of natural selection. To help you wrap your mind around this idea, I expect a human infant to be able to productively adjust its development to its elevation above sea level (oxygen availability), the language its parents are speaking, and the supply of available calories, among other things. Why? Because these environmental factors would plausibly have varied over human history, and because taking a local "reading" could usefully cue the infant about what developmental pathway might be best in that environment. On the other hand, I do not expect a human infant to make productive accommodations to the amount of carbon monoxide in the atmosphere its breathing, or the number of starfish in the sea. Why, not? Carbon monoxide, though fatal in even moderate doses, was not part of our species evolutionary history (since it is a product of fossil-fuel combustion), so our ancestors would not have experienced natural selection to accommodate it. And, although starfish numbers may have varied, their abundance was probably not an important determinant of human reproductive success—so why "pay attention" to it during development?

Students have taught me that examples work well because they stick in the mind. But I can recap the last paragraph for those who like their ideas distilled. If a feature of the environment has varied significantly over the lifetimes of individuals, and if the optimal adaptation is different in those different environments, we should expect selection to have designed a facultative adaptation—one that takes a reading of the environment and adjusts certain features of the organism appropriately.

CHAPTER SUMMARY

Like all other species, humans are constantly subject to the force of natural selection. Human pigmentation (skin color) provides a useful case study. The molecules affecting skin color block UVb radiation from the sun. Since this radiation causes skin cancer but also facilitates our synthesis of vitamin D, melanin production is under the influence of two opposing selection pressures. The demand to minimize skin cancer is greatest in high UVb zones and the demand to maximize vitamin D production is greatest in low-UVb

zones. Thus the world-wide distribution of skin pigmentation is expected to—and did, before mechanized travel—match the trade-off between these two priorities. Comparisons among individuals or populations that differ in their melanin production but are exposed to similar levels of UVb amount to natural experiments. The results of these natural experiments clearly demonstrate the adaptive benefits provided by UVb.

Facultative adaptations are among the most complex of selection's designs. They track regularly varying and evolutionarily relevant features of the environment and orchestrate productive adjustments across the organism's lifetime. Sun tanning is a good example.

CITED REFERENCES

Mel Greaves (2014) "Was skin cancer a selective force for black pigmentation in early hominin evolution?" *Proceedings of the Royal Society, B, Biological Sciences. 281*: 20132955.
http://dx.doi.org/10.1098/rspb.2013.2955

J. R. Condon, B. K. Armstrong, A. Barnes and J. Cunningham (2003) Cancer in Indigenous Australians: A Review. Cancer Causes & Control 14: 109-121.

FIGURE CREDIT

CHAPTER 6

NATURAL SELECTION IN A MENDELIAN WORLD

Though Gregor Mendel lived at the same time as Darwin and Wallace neither read his work. Had they done so they would have understood that the blending model of inheritance is wrong (Chapter 3). As Darwin's own sweet pea experiments showed, the offspring are not intermediate between their parents and the two parental varieties were both present—in undiluted form—among the offspring. So when Mendel's work was eventually "rediscovered" in 1900 it laid the foundation for a resurgence in evolutionary thinking, and significant efforts to join Mendelian and a Darwinian ideas. Those efforts resulted in what is called *modern synthetic theory of evolution*—because it is a synthesis of two bodies of theory—and it is the subject of this chapter.

Since Mendelian genes are "particles" rather than "fluids," they pass intact and undiluted from parents to offspring. Thus a new particle could eventually end up, unchanged, in millions of descendants of its original carrier. Whether it will, of course, should depend on its adaptive value—on its contributions to survival and reproduction (see Chapter 1). But it's their "undilutability"—their fidelity—that makes Mendelian genes stable enough to be targets of selection over long periods of evolutionary time. Let's see why.

UNITING MENDELIAN AND DARWINIAN IDEAS

My goal is to help you understand natural selection in the most powerful and general way possible. The benefit of that kind of understanding is simply that it's more useful: It can be applied in a wider array of contexts. General framings are almost always more abstract than more narrow and specific ones, so I'm going to take your picture of natural selection to that more abstract realm. I'll support your transition with a simple diagram.

In Figure 6-1 we have two reproducing entities, type A and type B. In this example it's apparent that type A individuals reproduce at a higher rate—leave more offspring—than type B individuals. As time goes by, the natural result of this reproductive difference (as shown in the top panel of the Figure) is that type A individuals will become progressively more common relative to type B individuals. This is not surprising; it may be the way that you have already pictured natural selection—which is fine. But there is a hidden assumption here, one that goes unnoticed because it matches our every-day expectations about the world. The hidden assumption is that when A reproduces, its offspring are also A. What if they weren't? What if every time A and B reproduce, each is equally likely to produce an A or B offspring, just like a coin toss. This thought experiment is shown in the bottom panel of the same Figure. Very shortly we can address whether this situation is at all realistic. But just please acknowledge that, in a world like this, a

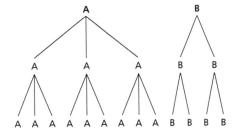

High-fidelity inheritance

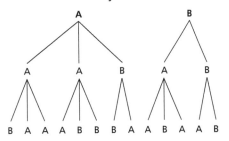

Low-fidelity inheritance

Figure 6-1. Unless reproduction is sufficiently faithful the advantaged type will not spread.

reproductive advantage would *not* cause the advantaged type to become more common. That's because, in the bottom panel, *copying errors* are swamping A's reproductive advantage. The type that is reproducing at a higher rate is not spreading because it is not systematically producing offspring of its own type.

I know it can be mentally uncomfortable to entertain ideas that seem obviously wrong, as the lower panel of Figure 6-1 probably does. But I'll never take you for a ride without a reason, so here's my reason. The two panels in Figure 6-1 are simply intended to be the two ends of a logical continuum. The top panel assumes that inheritance is perfectly reliable: A always produces A, and B always produces B. The bottom panel assumes that inheritance is perfectly *un*reliable: A produces either A or B randomly, and B does the same. In the real world of life on earth, inheritance is not perfect but it's clearly not random. Here's the point: Natural selection only causes favored types to spread if the hereditary system is reliable. OK, but how reliable? We need a *quantitative* answer to the question, "how reliable does inheritance have to be for natural selection to operate?" Or, put the other way around, "how many copying errors will it take to prevent the favored type from spreading? The copying errors must not swamp the reproductive advantage; if they do, the favored type will not spread (Williams 1966).

Thus, to unite Mendelian and Darwinian ideas we need to begin by first paying attention to the reliability of the Mendelian, gene-based hereditary system. Based on the principle we just worked out, do genes copy themselves reliably enough to support natural selection—to allow favored types to spread? In a word, yes. Genes copy themselves with very high accuracy; they are *not* perfectly reliable but their error rates are very low. We'll return to more detailed calculations later but for now we just need the right order of magnitude. Genes copy themselves incorrectly roughly 1 time out of 10,000. Think about what that means for natural selection: Even very tiny reproductive advantages will still cause the favored gene to spread. For example, if those who carry allele M average 1.001 offspring compared to 1.000 offspring on average for carriers of allele N, and the gene copying error rate is, as we said, 1/10,000, then the reproductive advantage is still 10 times larger than the error rate and allele M will spread.

Simply put, this is why genes loom so large in the modern theory of evolution: They copy themselves very accurately. Thus selection will cause the spread of genes that improve the fit between the organism and the environment, *even if the improvement is quite small*. With gene-based inheritance even small improvements will not be cancelled out by errors, since genetic errors are so rare. This analysis has an important "flip side" that might not be obvious. Unless they provide very large reproductive advantages, most non-genetic hereditary units (e.g., "culture") do *not* replicate faithfully enough to support the spread of adaptive traits by natural selection. That's why there's no discussion of culture in this book.

EVOLUTION'S RAW MATERIAL

The various alternative genetic recipes—the alternative alleles—in any population are natural selection's raw material; they are the stuff selection can choose among in designing adaptations. How different are these recipes?

In Chapter 2 we learned that a normal human *genome* (what we can think of as a complete set of self-assembly recipes) consists of about 19,500 genes. You know that these genes are made up of smaller elements, the four bases of the genetic alphabet (A, T, C, and G), and that it takes roughly 3.3 billion (3,300 million) of these bases to spell out your whole recipe set. Let's do an experiment. Let's list out all 3.3 billion of your bases, in sequence (something we can now actually do!), and line all of them up next to the 3.3 billion bases of some other randomly chosen human. On average how far would you need to scan down the sequence before you'd find a difference between the two of you? Well, of course you're unique, right? So maybe by the 20th or 30th base there would be a difference; surely you could find one by the time you'd scanned 100 bases down the sequence. These intuitions are just wrong. Even when you choose one person from Nigeria and one from China, or one from England and one from the Amazonian jungles, they differ on average on only 1 in 1,000 bases! The 1-in-1000 variable locations (where we humans are not all exactly the same) are called *single-nucleotide polymorphisms* (SNPs) and they are interesting for many reasons. On the practical side, forensic scientists use them to identify individuals, because each of us has our own unique set of these 1-in-1000 base differences.

Is 1 in 1000 a lot or a little bit of variation? Importantly, it's both. Obviously, if I say only 1 in 1000 students is going to get an A in my class, you'll think that's a pretty small fraction—just one tenth of one percent (0.1%). (Don't worry; that's not the grading curve!) But remember that, in the case of the human genome, we're starting with a large denominator, 3.3 billion bases. So 0.1% of 3.3 billion is still 3.3 million bases. That means that natural selection currently has several million alternatives—different SNPs—to choose from as it shapes human adaptations; that's quite a bit of raw material.

Without questioning or undermining that conclusion at all, there is another way to look at the same numbers. If 0.1% of our genetic bases differ, then 99.9% are the same! Why would we all be so similar? Again I want to suggest an analogy (based on what biologists call a null model, but don't worry about the name for now). Let's take two extremely large decks of cards, which as you know have four suits: hearts, clubs, diamonds, and spades (I want the decks to be large because the human genome is large.) The four suits are my stand-ins for the four bases of the genetic alphabet, and the two decks represent my two different people. Let's shuffle each of the decks and then start turning over pairs of cards, one card from each deck. How likely is the first pair to be a match (say, both clubs or both diamonds)? On average they will match 1 in 4 times (25%), and the same is true for each successive pair. That means that the first two pairs should both match (25% X 25%=) 6.25% of the time. The first three would match 1.56% of the time. The first ten pairs would be expected to match 0.00009% of the time. For the first fifty pairs, our calculation gives a result with 29 zeros to the right of the decimal point. And that's just fifty matches; I invite math-minded students to estimate how likely it is that the first 999 pairs would match (the answer is 0.25^{999}). Remember, that's the level of matching we find when we compare the A's, T's, C's, and G's of two people: 999 out of every 1000 of their genetic bases are going to be the same.

Is this a math "trick"? Why is the result so different with card suits than it is with human genetic elements? OK; what process affects whether two cards match? It's just chance, naked probability; that's why I said my analogy was based on a null model. That's a fair thing to do because it gives a picture of what would happen if only chance forces were at work. But, what process affects whether two human's genetic bases match? Is it just chance? No! It's billions of years of natural selection throwing away what doesn't work. Natural selection is actually the furthest thing from chance we can imagine. The opposite of chance or random is "skewed" or "biased." Natural selection introduces bias because certain genetic recipes (ones that build adaptive traits) are much more likely to be passed down the generations than others. The sequence of A's, T's, C's, and G's is so similar in different people because natural selection has already gotten rid of all but the best (most adaptive) base at 99.9% of positions. Why else would our recipes be so overwhelmingly similar? What other process could produce such a highly non-random (anti-entropic) result?

To summarize, genomes are very big, very complicated sets of recipes for building organisms. In any particular ecological niche, certain traits are more suitable than others. By its normal process of throwing away what doesn't work and holding onto what does, natural selection has already "found" most of the genetic recipes that build those adaptive traits. However, despite selection's incessant editing, there is usually some remaining variation in the population—about 1 out of every 1,000 bases in contemporary human populations. This variation is raw material that selection can choose among in building even more precise adaptations.

WHY ARE INDIVIDUALS DIFFERENT?

Why is there *any* remaining variation? Why hasn't natural selection found the best base at *every* position in the genome? Moreover, in order to find the best base at 99.9% of positions, selection had to sort through a lot of variation in the past: Where did all *that* variation come from? Because Darwin and Wallace didn't know what caused heredity, they couldn't have known what caused variation—differences in what is inherited. Today we know that genes cause heredity and that *mutations—gene copying errors*—produce heritable variation. OK, but what causes mutations? Ultimately, the answer to this question is our old friend, entropy. Let's dig into that.

When entropy has its way and the sandcastle or the skyscraper tumbles down, it's always a result of physical forces—tides, wind, rain, rust, gravity, and earthquakes, to name a few. The same is true of mutations: They have physical causes such as cosmic radiation, environmental toxins, and the like. But it's critical to understand that, while *mutations are caused, they are caused randomly* and are therefore undirected. In other words, mutations are *not* aimed in any sense at improving the organism. This is precisely the same sense in which an ocean wave is *not* aimed at improving the sandcastle. A mutation is just an error caused by some physical force of nature. The simplest kind of mutation, called a point mutation, is just the swap of one base for another in a DNA sequence. (It's also possible for larger mutation to occur, such as the deletion of several bases.)

Mistakes—and mutations are mistakes—don't generally improve things. Take your Apple watch and throw it against the wall (OK, let's make this just a thought experiment rather than a real one). Do you think the impact would make your watch work better? No, probably not. And when, for example, ultraviolet radiation strikes a genetic base and changes it from a T to a C, is that going to make the genetic recipe work better? Again probably not, and for the same reason. A watch and a genetic recipe are both finely tuned mechanisms—one tuned by human engineers and the other tuned by natural selection—to accomplish particular functions. If you change it, it will probably work less well. That's a prediction. Let's take a look at whether this prediction is supported by evidence.

Rafael Sanjuán and his associates at the University of Valencia in Spain tested the prediction that mutations are generally bad, using a virus as their experimental organism. They randomly changed single bases in the virus' genetic code and measured the effects of these changes on the viability and reproduction of the virus (Figure 6-2). They created 48 different clones, each with a different single-base mutation. About 40% of those single-base changes were lethal. Another 30% were harmful; they reduced the virus' ability to reproduce. About 27% were neutral, meaning that they had no effects on survival or reproduction. (See Figure 4-4 to remind yourself why some base changes have no effect). And just over 4% actually increased the virus' reproduction. This is what we would expect if the virus' genetic code had already been fairly thoroughly edited by natural selection: Most mutational changes were bad, about one quarter had no effect, and a small proportion was helpful. And these are the results for the smallest possible mutations—changes of just a single base. Larger-scale mutations are expected to be even more disruptive.

The key idea here is that genes copy themselves quite accurately, but mistakes—mutations—sometimes occur. These mutations are not aimed in any sense at improving adaptation; they are just random. But any mutation, by definition, creates a new allele. Even a point mutation—a change of a single base letter such as C to T—creates a new allele, in the form of a new SNP.

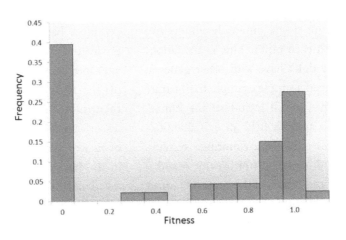

Figure 6-2. Fitness: 0=lethal; <1=harmful; 1=neutral; >1=beneficial.

And selection can then evaluate whether that new allele has better or worse effects on the fit between the organism and its environment than alternative alleles at that same locus. Of course selection "evaluates" these alleles in terms of the reproductive success of the individuals who carry them. Let's explore how selection works at the level of alternative alleles.

ALLELES AS EVOLUTIONARY COMPETITORS

As you know, a gene is a protein recipe that affects one or more traits of an organism. As discussed above and elsewhere, many genes have multiple alleles (versions). The various alleles of a given gene affect the same trait(s) but each can produce different phenotypic results, results that might make a difference to the fitness of the individual carrying that allele. As we will develop in the remainder of this chapter, the alleles of any given gene—the different versions of a gene that might occur at the same locus—stand in a special, intensely competitive relationship to each other. This is a relationship that they don't have with other genes at other loci. I need a simple example to illustrate this perspective, so I'll introduce the human CLOCK gene, at locus 4q12 (or 4:56,294,067-56,413,075 in the base-counting system). "Morning" and "evening" (for brevity, m and e) are names for two alleles of this gene that affect so-called diurnal preference (when a person prefers to be active; Katzenberg et al. 1998). Remember, loci are like addresses, places where something (or somebody) sits. Here's the key insight in analogy form: If Hanna is renting the house at 2716 Pueblo Avenue, then you can't because it's already occupied; it's unavailable.

The same displacement idea applies to genetic loci. True, you have a pair of CLOCK genes (the one you got on the Chromosome 4 that came from your mom and the one you got on the Chromosome 4 that came from your dad). And every other member of the population also has two 4q12 loci, because we're all *diploid* (see Chapter 3). So how many 4q12 loci are there? Simple: two times the number of people in the population. But, no matter how big a number that is, displacement rules: Every one of those 4q12 loci that is occupied by the m allele is currently unavailable to the e allele. If m occupies 60% of the 4q12 loci in the population, only 40% are available for e to occupy. That is precisely how evolutionary geneticists describe populations: in terms of *allele frequency*. In this case the frequency of m = 0.6 and the frequency of e = 0.4.

The last sentence would be a snapshot at one moment in time, but natural selection can and does change things. Just suppose, for example, that the filtering action of natural selection is biased in favor of m, because it produces better adaptation in the prevailing environment. That will mean that (on average) individuals who have (one or two copies of) the m allele will produce more offspring than individuals who have (one or two copies of) the e allele. As a result the frequency of m will increase (will be greater than 0.6) in the next generation, and the frequency of e will decrease proportionately. This is what evolutionary change looks like down in the trenches. And if this selective regime continues (if the adaptations that m builds continue to fit better with the environment than the ones that e builds), the eventual frequencies of m and e will be 1 and 0, respectively. Do you see that? At that point we could say that m had crowded e right off the 4q12 locus. An evolutionary geneticist would say that m had *gone to fixation*, an admittedly arcane phrase. However we say it, it's clear that any "wins" for allele m will always be "losses" for its alternative allele at the same locus: If m increases in frequency, e *must* decrease. Of course m's wins would have no similar automatic effect on the evolutionary fate of alleles at *other* loci. This is why I said that the different alleles of a single gene are locked in competition in a way that genes at different loci are not.

Now that we are linking Darwinian and Mendelian perspectives we can define evolution in a fully modern way: *Evolution is change in allele frequency*. Note that individuals cannot evolve: They have the same genes throughout their lives. (Instead, individuals *develop*, as their genes are expressed.) What can evolve is a population—a collection of individuals. It's at the level of the population that we can measure allele frequencies, and determine if they change from one generation to the next.

MENDELIAN GENES PROVIDE A LEVEL PLAYING FIELD FOR NATURAL SELECTION

The picture of natural selection that we have developed so far suggests that it causes organisms to fit well with their environments because it spreads alleles that build good adaptations. In order for that to work, there can't be any inherent bias or skew in the genetic system itself. Selection is biased; absolutely. That's why some alleles become more common and others are eliminated—or so our theory claims. But if the genetic system itself were biased that would call into question whether selection is responsible for evolutionary change.

So the very first job of the modern synthesists (the folks who first joined Mendelian and Darwinian theory) was to ask this question: Is the genetic system a "fair dealer" or is the game rigged? Does the process of passing genes from parent to offspring change gene frequency all by itself (without any selection)? To anticipate the answer, it doesn't. The particular solution I'm going to share with you is called the *Hardy-Weinberg Equilibrium* and is named for the mathematician and physician who independently worked it out. It's actually very simple and was far below the pay-grade of Hardy, at least.

To avoid needless complication let's stick with our CLOCK example. Remember there are two alleles, *m* and *e* with initial frequencies of 0.6 and 0.4 respectively. To facilitate the math, I want these frequencies to be variables so let's call the frequency of the *m* allele p, and call the frequency of the *e* allele q. Let's assume these frequencies are the same in males and females (the potential moms and dads), and that there is *no selection*. No selection means that the *m* allele and the

e allele have equal chances of getting into an offspring. If you're wondering why a selection maven like me is assuming no selection, it's because the purpose of this exercise, remember, is to see what the genetic system does all by itself.

Figure 6-3 is designed to help you picture the math. This Figure is similar to Figure 3-1 except that you will notice that this one is asymmetrical; some boxes are bigger than others. That's because I want to show *allele frequency*. I'm letting the horizontal line at the top of the Figure 6-3 represent the maternal *gene pool*—the collection of CLOCK genes added up across all the women in this population. Since we know that 60% of women's CLOCK genes are the *m* allele and 40% of them are the *e* allele, I've divided the line unequally with 60% of it on one side of the dividing point and 40% of it on the other. We agreed in the preceding paragraph that these allele frequencies are the same in men and women, so I can divide the vertical line on the left of the Figure in the same 60/40 way to model the paternal gene pool. What each line is intended to represent is your chance of getting an *m* or an *e* allele if you randomly grabbed a CLOCK allele from the maternal or paternal gene pools. I think you can see that your chance of getting either is simply its frequency; you'll get an *m* allele p proportion of the time, and an *e* allele q proportion of the time. Of course, since *m* and *e* are the only possibilities (there are only two alleles in this example), p + q = 1.

Offspring are formed, of course, by contributions from both the maternal and paternal gene pools. So what is the chance that *both* the mom and the dad will give an *m* allele? Since moms will give it 0.6 proportion of the time and dads will do the same, the chance that both parents will give an *m* allele is $p^2 = 0.6 \times 0.6 = 0.36$. Put another way, 36% of the offspring produced by these moms and dads are expected to be *homozygous m* (both of their CLOCK alleles are *m*). By the same logic, the chance that both parents will give an *e* allele is $q^2 = 0.4 \times 0.4 = 0.16$. So 16% of the offspring should be homozygous *e*. Finally, the chance of mom giving *m* and dad giving *e* is $pq = 0.6 \times 0.4 = 0.24$. But, don't forget, there is a second way that a *heterozygous* offspring (one with two different alleles) could be produced: dad could give the *m* and mom could give the *e*, and that should happen another 24% of the time, so the proportion of heterozygous offspring is actually $2pq = 2\ (0.6 \times 0.4) = 0.48$. As I mentioned, Figure 6-3 is intended to convey all of this visually in a way that makes the math transparent, but those who prefer their math unadorned have probably noticed that the Hardy-Weinberg Equilibrium is an example of the binomial-squared rule: $(p + q)^2 = p^2 + 2pq + q^2$ (hence my earlier comment about its simplicity).

The first thing to notice is that we haven't lost anybody: 0.36 + 0.48 + 0.16 = 1.00. But what has happened to the allele frequencies? Are they the same in the offspring generation as they were in the parental generation? If they aren't, the genetic system isn't a level playing field. We'd better find out!

This is even simpler than what we've already done. We just need to count up the alleles. I'm going to use p' and q' to denote the allele frequencies in the offspring generation to distinguish them from the allele frequencies in the parental generation (p and q), and to allow for the possibility that they might be different. Let's count the *m*'s first. The *mm* homozygotes are "pure" *m*, and the *me* heterozygotes are "half" *m*. So that gives us:

$$p' = p^2 + ½(2pq) = 0.36 + 0.24 = 0.6.$$

Have we seen that number before? Yes; it's p, the frequency of *m* in the parental generation. In other words $p' = p$. We could quit here because we know that $1 - p' = q' = 0.4$, but let's finish up properly and actually count the *e* alleles. In parallel to our previous calculation, the *ee* homozygotes are "pure" *e* and the *me* heterozygotes are "half" *e*. Thus:

$$q' = q^2 + ½(2pq) = 0.16 + 0.24 = 0.4.$$

dads \ moms	*m* p = 0.6	*e* q = 0.4
m p = 0.6	*mm* $p^2 = 0.36$	*me* pq = 0.24
e q = 0.4	*me* pq = 0.24	*ee* $q^2 = 0.16$

Figure 6-3. This figure shows expected genotype frequencies in the offspring generation given known allele frequencies in the parental generation.

Once again, there is no change from the parental to the offspring generation. That's the outcome that we were hoping for. It shows that there is no inherent bias in the genetic system.

Let me summarize what we did in this section of the chapter. We started with a parental generation where we knew the allele frequencies. We used that to determine the proportion of each genotype among the offspring of those parents. Then we counted the alleles in those offspring genotypes to calculate the allele frequencies in the offspring generation. When we did that we found that the allele frequencies were unchanged. That shows that the hereditary system, by itself, doesn't produce any evolutionary change. Now you can see why it's called the Hardy-Weinberg Equilibrium. An equilibrium is a balance point where things don't change.

SELECTION ACTING ON MENDELIAN GENES

Evolution is change in allele frequency. Because, by itself, it can't change allele frequency genetics can't be the cause of evolution. You might think of an analogy with the physics concept of inertia. According to that idea, an object at rest tends to stay at rest unless acted on by some external force. Likewise, gene frequencies tend to stay stable unless acted on by an outside force. What might that outside force be? While there are others, the one that will consistently change allele frequencies in an adaptive direction is (all together now!) natural selection. Selection would be at work if individuals with certain genotypes contributed fewer genes to the next generation. It only takes one simple step to build selection into our equations. All we need is a number (something less than 1) that measures how much less they reproduce.

For reference, here are the offspring genotypes with *no* selection (what we've already shown):

$$1 = p^2 + 2pq + q^2$$

Now let's start to build selection into our model. Here is an example of *moderate selection against a recessive allele* (by convention the frequency of the dominant allele is defined as p, and the frequency of the recessive allele—if there is one—is defined as q):

$$p^2 + 2pq + 0.8(q^2)$$

The decimal 0.8 is just an example. What it says is that homozygous recessive individuals (*ee* in our example) reproduce only 80% as much as the other two genotypes. The *selection pressure* against *ee* is defined as $(1 - 0.80 = 0.20)$. In this case, *with selection acting*, will the gene frequencies change after one generation? They'd better. Let's find out. The first thing we need to notice is that population size is going to change. The equation above is *not* going to add up to 1, because 20% of the ee individuals are being eliminated by selection. Continuing to use p = 0.6 and q = 0.4 we see that:

$$p^2 + 2pq + 0.8(q^2)$$
$$= 0.36 + 0.48 + 0.128 = 0.968$$

Thus we need to use 0.968 as our denominator when we calculate the relative frequencies of the two alleles after selection. So:

$$p' = [p^2 + \tfrac{1}{2}(2pq)] / 0.968$$
$$= (0.36 + 0.24) / 0.968$$

$$= 0.61983$$

And to calculate q´ we need to incorporate both the new denominator and the relative fitness (0.8) of the ee homozygotes. Thus:

$$q´ = [0.8(q^2) + \tfrac{1}{2}(2pq)] / 0.968$$
$$= (0.1283 + 0.24) / 0.968$$
$$= 0.38017$$

Everything checks because p' + q' = 1 (0.61983 + 0.38017 = 1). In words, what did we learn from this example? While the genetic system holds gene frequencies stable in the absence of selection, gene frequencies do change when selection operating. In a case where selection was disfavoring the homozygote recessive genotype by 20%, the frequency of the dominant allele increased from 0.60 to approximately 0.62 in a single generation; and the frequency of the recessive allele decreased from 0.40 to approximately 0.38 in the same time frame. Note that the changes are in the expected direction.

Of course, selection does not always disfavor the recessive allele and we can use similar techniques to model other modes of selection. Selection *against a dominant allele* would look like this:

$$0.75(p^2 + 2pq) + q^2$$

Again the decimal is arbitrary, but here both homozygous dominant and heterozygous individuals experience reduced reproduction because the harmful allele is dominant (and therefore expressed in both homozygotes and heterozygotes). You might try to solve for p' and q' using 0.6 and 0.4 for p and q (as we have

been, or using any other starting frequencies you choose.

Finally, for completeness, here is an example of *selection in favor of heterozygotes*:

$$0.7(p^2) + 2pq + 0.9(q^2)$$

I chose two different selection pressures (0.3 and 0.1) to illustrate that the two homozygotes won't always be equally disfavored. Again, you have the tools to solve this equation.

These kinds of calculations amount to mathematical proofs of natural selection. A mathematical proof is not a scientific proof since, as I argued in Chapter 1, in is impossible to prove evolution or any other scientific hypothesis. But a mathematical proof demonstrates that a process can operate if its assumptions are satisfied. The assumptions of the modern theory of evolution by natural selection are that genes are relatively faithfully transmitted from parents to offspring (with few spontaneous copying errors; Figure 6-1), and that the rates at which they are transmitted will depend on their effects on the survival and reproduction of potential parents.

NATURAL SELECTION'S LIMITATIONS

The theory of evolution by natural selection nicely solves the central problem of biology: It can explain how inanimate forces shape adaptation out of mutation, by automatically weeding out what doesn't work. In fact, organisms seem to be balanced on an adaptive peak in the sense that even very small perturbations—changing one base in millions or billions—will often be fatal. Biologists are greatly impressed with the power of natural selection to sculpt intricate adaptations out of the raw "junk" of mutations. (Echolocation, which evolved independently in bats and dolphins, is one of my favorite adaptations.) And yet we also know that selection has its limits. There are some things it cannot do, and we need to appreciate these limitations as well.

Suppose that an organism's environment is changing. As a consequence, the particular suite of traits that had been most adaptive is no longer meeting all the challenges of the new environment. This organism is not necessarily doomed. Depending on how fast its environment is changing and just how far off the new mark its old adaptations are, it may be able to survive and produce some offspring as natural selection works to cobble together some adaptive adjustments. But, and this is selection's first important limitation, *selection cannot produce the particular new mutations that would address the new environmental challenges*. Of course it would be handy if natural selection could create mutations that would meet current needs, but the process has no such capability.

Think about what selection is. It's merely the preferential retention of certain *existing* variants. Right; it's just a filter that lets some alleles pass and weeds others out. Filters don't create anything; they just determine what gets through. To pass the filter, an allele has to already exist. All new alleles come into existence by the *random* process of mutation. So it will sometimes happen that populations go extinct because the mutation(s) that would have saved them just didn't happen. Biology is not paradise. It's not mystical. It operates by certain principles, natural selection being the most important. But selection cannot create

particular mutations; it can only evaluate those that arise by chance.

There is another important limitation of natural selection and there are big payoffs from understanding this limitation. Every individual is a developmental result of the very large bundle of genes that constitute its full genome. If the organism is alive, most of those genes are pretty good. But that doesn't mean that all of its genes are equally good: Some are probably better than others. Why does this matter? Remember that natural selection keeps or weeds out genes based on how well the carriers of those genes meet the tests of their environment. But *the filtering process of natural selection evaluates whole individuals*. It can't preferentially retain some of the adaptations of a successful individual. Whole individuals survive to breed or die young. Whole individuals have offspring or don't. And when an individual does reproduce, every gene it carries—whether it's a great, good, merely acceptable, or somewhat harmful gene—has an *equal* chance of making it into the offspring.

Again I'll use an analogy, this one borrowed from Richard Dawkins. Think of the individual as an athletic team; its various genes are the team members. When actual athletic teams compete, the whole team wins (or loses) the championship. If the team does win, every player gets a trophy regardless of how many or few points she scored. She was a member of the winning team so she wins. It's the same for individuals competing in the evolutionary process. If an individual wins (has offspring), then each of that individual's genes has an equal chance of getting passed on. I trust the conclusion is obvious: Some genes that are just average or even somewhat harmful can ride on the coat-tails of other genes that are especially good—they can hitch-hike. This means that natural selection won't always be able to weed out low-quality adaptations. When low-quality adaptations happen to be carried by an individual who also has many high-quality adaptations, both will be passed on at the same rate. Thus, this is a second limitation of natural selection: *It cannot assess genes one-by-one*, but must evaluate them as members of the large "teams" of genes that comprise individuals. This makes natural selection a somewhat dull knife, but let me show you why it's still sharp enough to prune away maladaptive traits and thereby sculpt adaptation.

I pointed out that a gene for a low-quality adaptation can hitch-hike into the next generation when it happens to be in a body that carries many genes for high-quality adaptations. But will this low-quality adaptation *always* be so lucky; will it always have such good company? No, there's no reason to expect that it would. The "law of averages" says that half of the time a low-quality gene will have better-than-average company (which will help it get passed on); and half of the time it will have worse-than-average company (which will hurt its chances of getting passed along). And these two situations should cancel out. In other words, on average, any gene should have average company and thus, on average, get neither help nor hindrance from his fellow-travelers. If that's true, then what does predict a gene's chances of getting passed on? *Its effects on survival and reproduction, averaged over all the individuals who carry it.* As long as it has no special trick for always insinuating its way into individuals with especially good adaptations, it's going to have to make it into the future on its own merits. The bottom

line: If it builds low-quality adaptations it will eventually be weeded out.

That fate is relatively certain, as long as the law of averages applies—as long as the disadvantageous gene occurs equally often with better and worse genetic companions. But we need to consider one class of exceptions: rare genes, ones carried by a small number of individuals. Please allow me one more analogy. If I have a fair coin and I flip it many times, you'd expect the result to be very close to 50:50 heads and tails. That's our law of averages again. But suppose I flip it just a few times; let's say four. Many four-flip series will *not* come out 50:50. In fact, more than 12% of the time they will come out all heads or all tails. (You can flip some coins or try to model the process if you like.) What is the point of this comparison? Something I suspect you already know: The law of averages only applies when the set of cases is large.

Do you see the point of this analogy? If a gene occurs in many individuals (equivalent to many coin flips), it will have a 50:50 chance of having good or bad genetic company; the law of averages will apply, and the gene's own virtues (or lack of them) will determine its evolutionary fate. But if it occurs in just a few individuals (equivalent to a small number of coin flips) it could have mostly good luck or mostly bad luck in the kind of genetic company it gets. In other words, a rare gene will be retained or eliminated not because it helps or hurts adaptation, but because it happens to fall in with good or bad company. Selection can't get an accurate read on the quality of a rare gene because it hasn't seen that gene play on enough different "teams." As a result, natural selection won't automatically spread a rare beneficial gene to lots of offspring, and it won't automatically filter out a rare harmful gene. Their frequency (how many copies of the gene there are) will just drift up or down, blown by the winds of chance. In fact, this phenomenon is called *genetic drift*. The fate of rare gene is driven more by (random) genetic drift than it is by (biased) natural selection.

As you know, *all genes first arise by mutation*. Mutations don't happen very often and there are billions of specific sites that could mutate. If we put these observations together we can predict that it would be fairly unlikely for many people to experience the very same mutation. In other words, most mutations will be rare when they first appear. Because rarity is the starting point for most genes, we can see why selection's handling of rare genes is important. If we work through the possible fates of rare new genetic recipes, we'll finally have a serviceable model of evolution.

Taking the ugly part first, sometimes an adaptive (helpful) new gene will encounter a run of bad luck and be fairly quickly eliminated by the vagaries of genetic drift. Many favorable recipes probably perish early in this way. On the other hand, the law of averages tells us that, while some genes will drift down in frequency (perhaps all the way to zero), others will drift up, becoming more common. Since drift is random some of the ones that drift up will be adaptive and others will be maladaptive. But as they drift up, natural selection begins to exert its influence. Do you remember why? Drift is important when there are too few copies of a gene for its effects on survival and reproduction to be clear—when the company it happens to keep is determining its fate. But as a gene occurs in more and more individuals, its company should average out to being neither helpful nor harmful in the aggregate.

Thus, as a gene becomes more common, it will occur in a wider range of genetic company, and selection will get a more and more accurate "read" on its contributions to survival and reproduction—on its *adaptive value*. At that point selection will start filtering out any bad genes that have drifted up into its sights, and it will start to spread the good genes (via the additional offspring they generate).

Genes naturally differ in their adaptive value. Some increase survival and reproduction a lot, some give only a small increase, some may be neutral (have no effect—like the 27% of mutations in Figure 6-2), and some cause a small or large decrease. You can picture these effects arrayed along a number line from plus infinity (for very adaptive traits), through zero in the middle (for neutral ones), to minus infinity (for very maladaptive ones). Their adaptive value matters, obviously, to whether selection is likely to retain them. But it also determines selection's effectiveness. In terms of the interplay between drift and selection discussed above, *the farther the adaptive value is from zero, the smaller the number of copies it will take for selection to "see" its true effect*. The converse is also true. The closer its adaptive value is to zero, the larger the number copies required before selection begins to spread or eliminate it. For a trait sitting right on the zero point, selection has no effect; regardless of how many copies there are, drift will be the only force affecting its frequency.

To summarize the limits of natural selection:

1. Selection cannot create entirely new alleles; mutation does that, and selection can only "prefer" certain mutation-created recipes over others;

2. Selection is constrained to assess the adaptive value of alleles as bundles because they never "perform solo"; they only collaborate in creating individuals;

3. Consequently, when an allele exists in only a few individuals, selection will not be able to get an accurate assessment of its adaptive value;

4. When an allele has neither positive nor negative effect on adaptive value, it will increase or decrease in frequency only by drift. (Sometimes this is interesting; stay tuned.)

CHAPTER SUMMARY

Natural selection operates only on entities that replicate faithfully. The smaller the reproductive advantage they provide, the more faithfully they must replicate for natural selection to operate on them. Since genes replicate extremely faithfully even genes that provide small advantages can be expected to spread, and genes are consequently the primary basis of evolution by natural selection on planet earth.

Contemporary humans are very similar to each other at the genetic level, differing on average on only 0.1% of their DNA base pairs, but this still provides millions of alternatives for selection to choose among. The mutations that produce these allelic differences between individuals are entirely random and usually harmful, because they disrupt what are already quite good designs for reproduction.

Alternative alleles are evolutionary competitors in the sense that one allele can only increase in frequency in the population to the extent that another allele decreases. There is nothing in the mechanics of Mendelian inheritance that will tend to change allele frequency. Instead, genetics provides an unbiased playing field on which selection can alter allele frequencies.

In addition to mutation there are other random components to the evolutionary process. Genetic drift refers to chance (random) fluctuations in allele frequencies. It is most important for alleles at low frequency or with neutral or near-neutral effects on fitness. Unlike natural selection, drift is not expected to produce adaptation.

CITED REFERENCES

D. Katzenberg, T. Young, L. Finn, L. Lin, D. P. King, J. S. Takahashi & E. Mignot (1998) "A CLOCK polymorphism associated with human diurnal preference." *Sleep* 21:569-576.

Williams, G. C. (1966) Adaptation and Natural Selection. Princeton, NJ: Princeton University Press.

FIGURE CREDIT

CHAPTER 7

TWO LESSONS OF GRADUALISM

Academics, and everyone interested in ideas, will have many "-isms" in their vocabularies. An "-ism" is simply a way of thinking. No doubt you're familiar with a range of political and religious "-isms" but there are also philosophical and scientific "isms." This chapter is about a key evolutionary "ism"—gradualism—but I'm going to begin with another "-ism" one that has even broader implications, being a cornerstone of all scientific thought.

UNIFORMITARIANISM

Uniformitarianism is a way of thinking about causal processes. It is easy to state but sweeping in its implications. *Uniformitarianism is the idea that the causal processes operating in the universe are constant.* Wherever we look we should see the same causal processes, driven by the same forces, operating in the same ways. Be careful. Uniformitarianism doesn't claim that these processes always operate with equal intensity or equal speed, or that their outcomes will always be the same. It simply claims that these processes are driven by a consistent set of forces that operate by consistent rules.

I know; that's pretty abstract. Let's get some examples on the table. In classical physics, *gravity* describes the attraction between two objects. In Newton's formulation, gravity increases with the product of the masses of the two objects, and decreases with the square of the distance between them. By these rules, the pull of gravity won't be the same for different pairs of objects. Nor does uniformitarianism claim that it should be. It's not the *outcome* that should be uniform; it's the *forces*. A uniformitarian says, "See; gravity is always the result of the product of the masses and the square of the distance; it works the same way always and everywhere." Objects with very little mass (subatomic particles) or at great distances (stars that are light-years apart) exhibit negligible gravitational attraction. That's as it should be, because it's the forces (mass and distance, either of which could be large are small) that determine the outcome. So uniformitarianism doesn't predict the same outcome everywhere; but it does insist that the forces producing that outcome are the same, and that those forces interact in the same ways.

Here's an example you can see: erosion. Erosion is caused by fluids (wind and water), picking up particles of soil or rock in one location and moving them to another. A uniformitarian view says that it's always these same forces but, because of that, erosion would happen at a faster pace where there is more rainfall or more wind, or flakier rock. Use your uniformitarian imagination to compare the rate at which equal-sized mountains would be worn down on earth and on our planet's moon, which has no atmosphere and hence no wind or rain. Right; the outcome is not the same but the causal processes are.

What is important about uniformitarianism's prescribed way of thinking? It is, quite simply, the *bedrock principle of all science*. Uniformitarianism is an assumption that

scientists have agreed to make about the nature of the universe: The universe is not fickle and capricious; I doesn't operate by one set of rules today and a different set tomorrow. That's important because, if it operates by an invariant set of rules, then hard and careful work can discover them. An experiment performed to certain specifications in Lab A should produce the same outcome if performed the same way in Lab B, because the same forces will be at work. If that weren't true there could be no science, of any type. Only if processes are uniform can we make discoveries that have any predictive value beyond the instant of discovery. Fortunately, the universe does not seem to be capricious. It seems to conform to the expectations of uniformitarianism. Scientists don't need to give up and go home!

Because Uniformitarianism is the bedrock of science, it plays a critical role in the way we *do* science. You've already had a glimpse of this in the section of Chapter 1 called "Only a Theory." Theories are (nothing more and nothing less than) claims about causal processes. Here's the key point: If uniformitarianism is correct (that causal processes are constant), then a theory's causal processes should be operating everywhere and always—anytime we look! A scientist can't say, "Oh, my process only operates when nobody's watching." (Or if he did, he wouldn't actually be a scientist!) This uniformitarian approach is a very handy as a way of debunking bad theories. If I have a theory, I need to be able to show my theory's causal process(es) at work, now. If I have a wind-and-rain theory of erosion I need to show that the amount of erosion taking place in any given time period is directly proportional to the amount of wind and rain in that same time period. If there is sometimes erosion without wind or rain, or there is wind and rain but no erosion, guess what; my theory is wrong. If I have a theory that natural selection causes evolution, I need to show (at a minimum) that some types are leaving more offspring and that those types are increasing in frequency in the population. It can be useful to view science as a project to find peep holes into causal processes: At what point can we cut into the process and see it operating? This is the way we test our theories.

As indicated in the title, we are going to tackle two evolutionary questions in this chapter. The first of those problems is: *Where do new species come from?* The reason I introduced uniformitarianism is that I wanted to be sure we agreed on the basic ground rules. Whatever explanation I offer for the origin of species, that theory needs to be uniformitarian; that means it needs to invoke processes that can be observed. It can't be something that happens only when everybody's sleeping. What process(es) *can we observe* that could cause a species to change? Based on what we've seen in Chapters 1-6, we can nominate natural selection. Acting generation after generation, selection favors individuals who fit better with their environments and thus changes gene frequencies (causing some alleles to become more common and others to become less common or even disappear from the population). And we've shown the corresponding changes in head, gut, and foot anatomy, melanin production, etc., that are the apparent results of such changes in gene frequency. Is this enough to support the suggestion that natural selection can not only change foot anatomy, but can also change one species into another? Logically speaking, these kinds of naturally selected changes in gene frequencies and traits

are unbounded in time. They could go on for decades, centuries, millennia, millions or even billions of years. What might happen if natural selection, sculpting organisms to meet their (always changing) environments, operated over very long periods of time? Might it change one kind of creature into a new one, one species into another?

I'll return to that question shortly, but a brief retracing of our erosion theory can provide a useful analogy. Geologists believe that, as suggested above, erosion is caused by the action of wind and water. Indeed, we can observe that process in the little rivulets of mud that flow down even a gentle slope in the rain. That's important for the erosion theory: Its hypothesized process is observable. Now, do you think that very same process could have carved the Grand Canyon of the American Southwest? It would certainly take more water and more time! In fact we could calculate how much time it would take by measuring the erosive effects of water on the actual rocks that comprise the Grand Canyon. Having done that, geologists think it would have taken about 6,000,000 years for the process of erosion—the same process we can see and measure all around us today—to carve the Canyon. In fact, the very roots of modern geology spring from exactly these debates about whether the earth is old enough for measureable processes like erosion to have such dramatic cumulative effects. For the record, our planet is about 4.5 billion years old. That's 750 times longer than the time required to carve the Grand Canyon. In other words, erosional processes that we can observe, operating in the same way they operate today, could have easily made the Canyon in the time available. That doesn't mean that these processes did, but if they didn't make the Canyon, what did? And can we observe *that* process? Because if we can't, then this "alternative" is not a uniformitarian theory and therefore not a scientific theory.

Do you see why I wanted to present this example from geology? Geology and biology have several things in common. (By the way, Charles Darwin greatly admired some of the early geologists, such as Charles Lyell, corresponded with them, and read their work avidly.) For example, both geology and biology invoke forces which often act slowly, but whose cumulative effects over long periods of time can be quite dramatic.

In returning to our "origin of species" question I will begin by recreating the same kind of argument I used for the erosional origin of the Grand Canyon. Just as we know the Grand Canyon exists, we know that the collection of species on earth has changed over time—as testified by the fossil record. Just as we can measure the erosional force of any given amount of water, we can measure the amount of change natural selection can produce in one generation, and we can estimate how many generations it would take to produce proportionately larger changes (e.g., 30 generations to produce cecal valves). Natural selection has billions of years to act (just as erosion does). Thus selection's changes would accumulate essentially without limit—producing enough change to create (many) new species.

No one has to accept this Grand-Canyon-style argument. That's the great strength of science. Everyone is always free to offer an alternative theory of speciation, or of anything. But, if we are to stay in the realm of science, those alternative theories need to be uniformitarian: They need to be testable in the sense of identifying and demonstrating their hypothesized

causal process(es). So far no theory other than natural selection has been able to do that.

Still, a diehard skeptic might say, "Alright, I know natural selection is real. I know it can change the traits of a species, but I can't see any examples where it has created an entirely new species. So, even though I don't have a better theory about where new species come from, I'm going to reject yours unless you have better evidence." Scientists love skeptics; they make us do our best. I'm going to present two quite different examples, but first we need to address a question that we've ignored for the last four pages (although I did briefly mention it in Chapter 2): How do we decide whether two populations are "different species" or not? The problem is messy for asexual species, but I'm betting you don't care much about them anyway. For sexual species, it's easy in principle. If typical members of two different populations can mate and produce viable, fertile offspring, they are the same species. If they cannot, they are members of different species. That's the definition. I realize this approach leaves a few problem cases like "ligers," but let's not worry about them now; gradualism will take care of them. To put it briefly and precisely, different species are defined by reproductive isolation.

OK, now we know what we're looking for. The first of my two examples is anything but exotic; you may have a dog in your own backyard. Let me say at the outset that dogs are not products of natural selection alone. Intentional breeding by humans ("artificial selection") has also been important in shaping canine traits. But I don't think that rules out this example. I believe the question at hand is this: Could "mere" differential reproduction—some individuals leaving more offspring than others—cause a population to change so much that it would be deemed a different species. If that is the question, then it shouldn't matter whether it's nature (as in natural selection), or people (as in artificial selection), or some mix of the two, that's causing the differential reproduction. The question is, "Is any amount of differential reproduction sufficient to create a new species?" Or is some other kind of process needed to produce that magnitude of change?

Dogs were domesticated from wolves, and some domesticated dogs can and do breed with wolves and produce fertile offspring. So why did I bring up this example? It seems like the kind of evidence my skeptic would offer: no evidence of speciation. But wait, could a wolf breed with a Chihuahua? Certainly not; in fact the wolf is very likely to treat this diminutive dog as potential prey, not as a potential mate. What if we forget about wolves and limit our analysis to dog breeds? Then, wouldn't it be equally fair to say that Chihuahuas (5 pounds) are reproductively isolated from Irish Wolfhounds, or from Mastiffs (150 pounds or more)? If a future paleontologist dug them up as fossils, he or she would almost certainly conclude, from their 30-fold size difference, that they were different species. So, I suggest that selection—"mere" differential reproduction—has created some

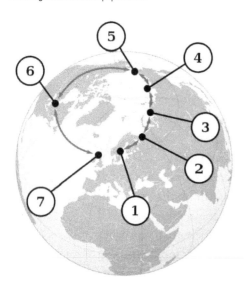

Figure 7-1. Numbers label adjacent populations and arrows indicate interbreeding between those populations.

reproductively isolated "populations" of dogs. What this example shows is that the simple process of *some individuals having more offspring than others* can move two populations so far apart that they are no longer possible mates for each other, and hence different species (different gene pools). But I have a better example.

Remember; what we are trying to show is that the process that creates new species is just the accumulated result of the process that produces smaller-scale adaptive changes within species. In other words, we're arguing for a uniformitarian theory of speciation. I'm going to offer one more class of evidence, evidence that also forms a clear bridge to the concept of gradualism. The evidence concerns what are called *ring species*, and I say that it's a class of evidence because there are several known ring species, though we only need to discuss one for you to understand their relevance to the speciation problem. I'm going to share the Herring Gull/Lesser Black-backed Gull case. Why two names? That's the point: from one perspective these birds represent two species, and from another they have to be seen as one. The evidence hinges, precisely, on this apparent paradox.

Even if you're not a birdwatcher (you're not?!) you could easily tell these two kinds of gull apart. A typical (American) Herring Gull (*Larus argentatus*; "6" in Figure 7-1) has *pink* legs and *pale gray* wings and back, with sharply contrasting black wingtips. A typical (European) Lesser Black-backed Gull (*Larus fuscus*; "1" in Figure 7-1) has *yellow* legs and *very dark* wings and back, with much less contrast between the wing and the wingtip. Note the different scientific names, signaling that these gulls are thought to be different species. Actually, these gulls form a set of adjacent populations in a doughnut-shaped band between 35° and 70° latitude in the northern hemisphere (Figure 7-1). The hole in doughnut is the polar region where these birds can't survive, and the hole is important because it forces the populations into a linear arrangement.

Members of adjacent populations show smaller differences than the Herring and Lesser Black-backed Gulls do. For example, the eastern Siberian birds ("5" in Figure 7-1) have somewhat darker gray wings and backs than the American birds, but the two types fairly regularly interbred. Likewise "4" birds are yet darker than "5" birds but members of these two populations also interbreed with each other. And that's true all the way around the globe—populations getting darker as we move westward from America, but still able to interbreed with their neighbors—with one exception: When Herring Gulls make it to Europe ("7"), they *cannot breed* with the dark-backed gulls ("1") they find there. Let's see why not.

Though lay people call them all "seagulls," most can't drink salt water, so gulls are more coastal birds than sea birds. This is important because if you look at the map you will see that there is a nearly complete land connection at these latitudes. For example, there is very little ocean gap between Alaska and Siberia (so the "6" and "5" birds get together fairly often). The largest gap is the North Atlantic Ocean, between eastern Canada and the British Isles. Birds from opposite sides of that gap don't see each other very often. And it turns out that,

when they do, they can't produce viable offspring together. *That means that they are different species.* Let that sink in. Lesser Black-backed Gulls in England can breed with similar, dark-backed birds in Sweden. And those birds can breed with similar birds farther east, and those with birds still farther east…all the way to eastern North America! Even though a Herring Gull and a Lesser Black-baled Gull can't make offspring together, a gene from a British Lesser Black-backed Gull could get into an American Herring Gull if it leap-frogged, one generation at a time, through the several intervening populations.

This is a delicious paradox and wonderful evidence for a uniformitarian theory of speciation. As just demonstrated, these gulls are all united in a single gene pool. Through adjacent populations, they can pass genes around the entire ring. So they must be one species. But if we look at the two ends of the ring, we see two species, because they are reproductively isolated—they can't directly breed with each other. The point of this example is not to make you dizzy. No; the point is to show that speciation—*the emergence of new species—is just the accumulated result of the process that produces smaller changes within species.* And that is precisely what any ring species shows. A ring species lays out the cumulative effect of many small changes across a geographic landscape and shows that, at the ends of the ring, they add up to a species-level difference. Evolutionists claim that precisely the same process explains how new species emerge over time. Members of one generation could certainly interbreed with members of the following generation, and those with the next. So, just as for geographically adjacent populations of gulls, temporally adjacent generations will be members of the same species. But, across a sufficient amount of time—a sufficient number of generations—the many small changes that separate each generation could add up to reproductive isolation, just as it does across a sufficient geographic distance for the gulls.

Lest my imaginary critic grasp at straws and say that one bizarre example can't support a theory, let me emphasize that there are other well-studied ring species. For example, there is ring species of *Phylloscopus* leaf-warblers in central Asia where the doughnut hole is the Himalayas. There is a ring species of moisture-loving *Ensatina* salamanders, where the doughnut hole is the hot dry central valley of California. There is a ring species of *Euphorbia* shrubs in Central America and the Antilles where the doughnut hole is the Caribbean Sea. Other cases are known and more will certainly be discovered, if we don't completely crush our planet's biodiversity.

Before we leave ring species, they have one more important lesson for us. Note that we cannot draw a "species boundary" line on the gull map. There is no boundary; the changes that produce reproductive isolation *accumulate gradually* all around the ring. The same would be true in the temporal dimension. If we could look at a long enough series of successive generations, the oldest and the most recent may be different species but, again, we couldn't say that the transition from one to another occurred there, say, at generation 421. (A mother never gave birth to an offspring that was a different species from her!) In such a series, there could be no "speciation event," a careless phrase that ignores the important observation that the species transition is not a *point* (in space or time), but a cumulative, incremental *process*. Which brings us to our second "-ism," *gradualism*.

GRADUALISM

Gradualism has slightly different meanings in the various sciences. But let's be clear from the outset; its meaning in biology is *not* that evolution is always slow. In fact, from Chapter 2 you already know that evolution can be fairly rapid. Gradual doesn't mean slow; it means "by small increments." *Gradualism is the idea that natural selection is much more likely to favor small changes than big changes.*

Why should selection work that way? The answer is quite parallel to our explanation of why mutations are generally harmful. In the previous Chapter we argued that, if something already works pretty well, a change is probably going to make it worse (and we gave evidence on that point in Figure 6-2). Here we suggest a corollary of that argument: *The bigger the change, the worse the outcome*. Thus, the smallest changes have the best chance of being helpful and are therefore most likely to be preserved by natural selection. This idea stretches all the way back to one of the architects of the modern synthesis, R. A. Fisher, who (much to my satisfaction) explained it with an analogy—what is still called "Fisher's microscope analogy." Allow me.

If you've used a microscope you know that, to focus it, you turn a knob that moves the viewing tube closer to or farther away from the "stage," where your subject of study sits. Imagine that you have been turning the knob and now have it almost in focus when, oops, your lab-mate bumps it. Here's the question: Will that bump improve the focus? Fisher's answer was: That depends on how big the bump is. Since the viewing tube was almost in focus, it was either slightly too close to the stage or slightly too far away. Of course the bump could move it in the right or the wrong direction (with equal probability). But (and here's Fisher's point) if it's a big bump then it doesn't matter whether it's in the right or the wrong direction; because, even if it's in the right direction, a big bump will overshoot and go past the focal point. The smaller the bump, the more likely it is that the (50% of those) small bumps that happen to be in the right direction won't overshoot. Here is a diagram that shows what Fisher had in mind with respect to mutations and selection (Figure 7-2).

I'll explain, with parenthetical references to the microscope analogy. The horizontal axis in Figure 7-2 represents the range of possible sizes of some hypothetical trait, say, beak length, with small values toward the left and large values toward the right. The current (average) value of the trait in the population is indicated by the dotted line, and the best possible value is indicated by a dashed line. In this example, the best value is slightly larger than the current value. The best is only slightly different from the current value because we assume that selection has been continually shaping this trait, constantly improving it, so it's already pretty close. (This is equivalent to your microscope being almost in focus). Now, just as your microscope might get bumped in the right or the wrong direction, a mutation could either make the trait a little smaller, moving it away from the optimum, or a little bigger, moving it towards the optimum. But (again Fisher's point) a large mutation is not going to

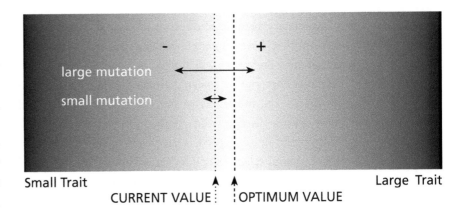

Figure 7-2. The effects of small and large mutations on the likelihood of improvement. Large mutations are always harmful, but roughly half of the very smallest mutations will be helpful.

help in any case; even if it's in the right direction, it will overshoot (like a big bump of the microscope). The very smallest mutations have the best chance of being helpful because the 50% of those that are in the right direction may not overshoot.

Yes, that's right: Fisher was arguing in favor of gradualism. It's not that big mutations can't occur. Of course they can; that's just entropy (things falling apart). It's that *big mutations won't tend to make it into the next generation* because they mess things up so badly. To make sure you take away the right message let me explain that a big mutation is one that has a big effect on what the allele builds. A small mutation is one that only slightly changes what the allele builds. The notions of big and small mutations depicted in Figure 7-2 should *not* be measured, for example, in terms of how many bases in the DNA code are changed. That is irrelevant (though, on average, more base changes could be expected to have greater effect). For Fisher's argument to be valid, changes have to be defined as "big" or "small" up at the level of the trait—at the level where natural selection acts.

In summary, because of the eons of natural selection that have already occurred, most traits of most organisms will already be nearly as good as they can be—near their optimum. For this reason, mutations of big effect will almost always disrupt good adaptations and will therefore be disfavored. That means that most of natural selection will be gate-keeping; it will be *negative selection* that rejects harmful mutations. But some mutations of quite small effect will be helpful, and these are the new alleles that selection will spread through the population. These insights mean that evolution will generally proceed by small, incremental steps, not by large, dramatic leaps. Evolution will be gradual.

GRADUALISM AND SPECIATION: THE ALLOPATRIC MODEL

At this point we have laid so much of the groundwork that you can probably anticipate what comes next, but for completeness, I'm going to lay out the standard *allopatric model of speciation*. As you may have noticed, it takes some "separation" to get speciation. The gulls at the two ends of the chain interact rarely enough that their gene pools have diverged to the point that they are no longer reproductively compatible. In contrast, gulls of adjacent, regularly interacting populations exchange genes more often, and this has kept their gene pools similar enough that they can continue to interbreed. Likewise for our temporal series. Members of adjacent generations naturally share most of their genetic material, but if we look at more distant generations we could see that here again, genetic difference would accumulate with the number of generations of

separation. So how do populations become different species? Yes, separation is a key element. Speciation is unlikely where populations regularly interbreed.

The allopatric model (*allo*, meaning other; *patric*, referring to country; hence the "other-country" model) assumes that sometimes the populations of a single species become separated. There are many reasons this could happen; tectonic (geological) forces can build mountains or cleave continents. New river valleys can be carved. Climatic changes may create uninhabitable zones. As a result, populations that previously had frequent contact and exchanged genes thorough interbreeding, would no longer do so, or would do so much less often. Figure 7-3, shows a hypothetical species that inhabits a continental peninsula north of a large mountain range.

In panel 1 the individuals of this species can freely mix and interbreed with each other throughout the peninsula. In panel 2 a climatic change substantially widens the river, pushing its headwaters well into the mountains, and since these creatures can't swim, their population is cut in two. Any environmental differences between the areas west and east of the river can favor different adaptations in the two areas. Maybe there are different predators or parasites in the two areas; or different foods may be available. And here's another factor: Perhaps certain beneficial mutations arise in one population and different beneficial mutations arise in the other. Because mutations are rare, the occurrence of a particular mutation in one population is nothing like a guarantee that it will occur in the other. Any new alleles contributing to each population's new adaptations will be confined on their own side of the river (panel 3). The longer this situation continued and the more different the selection pressures in the two areas, the more genetically different the two populations would become. The allopatric model assumes that such conditions could *gradually* cause enough genetic difference that, even if reunited (panel 4) the member of the two populations would not be able to interbreed.

To review the core elements of this model, the barrier is initially necessary to prevent the distinctive adaptations evolving in population A from being passed to population B, and vice versa. But after the gene pools of the two populations become sufficiently different (due to different mutations and different selection pressures), they would be unable to interbreed. The reasons for that inability don't really matter. They may be too different in size; they may breed at different times or the year; they may not recognize each other as potential mates; eggs from one population might be incompatible with sperm from the other; there are many possibilities. Regardless of the reason, the two populations will have *gradually become different species*.

ALLOPATRIC SPECIATION IN OUR BACKYARD

Pardon me for playing to my hometown audience, but I'm going to choose an example from California. The California Scrub-Jay (*Aphelocoma californica*) is common at low elevations in the mainland US west of the Sierra Nevada Mountains. You could find them easily in San Diego, Los Angeles, San Francisco, or Sacramento. The species has a wide distribution, including my yard in Santa Barbara. But just 25 to 30 miles south of

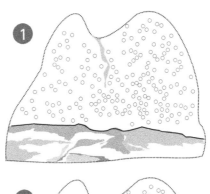
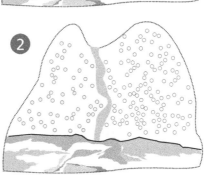
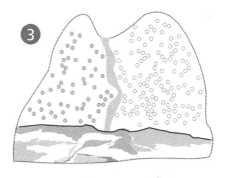
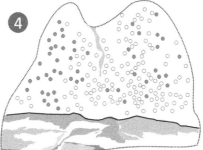

Figure 7-3. The allopatric model of speciation assumes an initial physical barrier to interbreeding.

Santa Barbara there is a group of islands where, despite the species' wide geographic range and proximity, there are no California Scrub-Jays at all. However, the largest (about 250 km²) of those islands, Santa Cruz, is home to a similar species, the Island Scrub-Jay (*Aphelocoma insularis*). I trust I need to say nothing more. This is a clear example of allopatric speciation. California Scrub-Jays occupy roughly 100,000 square miles on the mainland. But a relatively narrow ocean channel was a sufficient barrier to allow a few colonists from the mainland to evolve into a distinct species on a nearby island.

I have chosen this example out of thousands because of recently published research by Kathryn Langin and her colleagues. She focused on the island species and noticed that the scrub-jays on Santa Cruz occur in two different habitats, oak forests and pine forests, where they eat different foods: acorns and pine seeds. Like Herrel's lizards, these birds might be expected to differ in their feeding adaptations. Specifically, Langin hypothesized that longer, more slender bills would be better for extracting seeds from pine cones, but that shorter stouter bills would be better for pounding and prying open acorns. There are several interesting aspects of her study. The first is that there are three separate pine forests on the island and that, in each of those pine forests, the local scrub-jays do have longer and shallower bills than the scrub-jays in the surrounding oak forests. She found that the change in bill shape was smooth across the habitat: Bill length declined gradually with increasing distance from the pine forest. There was no sharp boundary. Her conclusion is that, while there are interesting adaptive specializations on Santa Cruz (related to divergent feeding habits), these Island Scrub-Jays are unlikely to split into two distinct species. Why not? There is no barrier equivalent to the ocean channel. Thus, the distinct adaptations within each group are constantly eroding due to interbreeding with birds from the other habitat.

This pair of examples suggests that different selection pressures are generally not enough to produce speciation. Some initial barrier is needed to "protect" independently evolved adaptations from spreading to adjacent populations.

WHAT ABOUT LIGERS?

Before I leave the topic of speciation, I promised you an answer to the liger dilemma. In case you haven't heard of this creature, a liger is an offspring of a mating between a tiger and a lion. Lions and tigers are different species so why can they produce offspring together? OK, hold on; just because we see differences between them and have different names for them doesn't mean they *are* different species. That will be determined, definitionally, by their ability or inability to interbreed. Since they can interbreed, they're actually one species. But let's not play word games. There is a real and interesting issue here.

There are more (probably many more) than 5 million species on the planet. Pick two of them at random, say some squid species and some mushroom species. Are they reproductively isolated? Sure. Pick another two (an oak tree and a newt). Are they reproductively isolated? Yes again. Keep going. Now, 5 million X 5 million is a pretty big matrix but if you were to create it you would see, I guarantee, that 99.9999% of those species pairs would be reproductively isolated from each other—completely unable to interbreed. A very, very few would show some limited capacity to interbreed. Is that an embarrassment to any argument we have advanced in this chapter? Absolutely not; it is evidence in favor of our arguments. Gradualism suggests that species differentiate from each other by small increments, not by sudden jumps. If gradualism is true then, at each and every moment in evolutionary time, we should be able to look around and find some pairs of populations that are right "on the cusp" of speciation. Maybe a small percentage of individuals can interbreed; maybe they can interbreed but often produce infertile offspring. These populations, that are almost but not quite reproductively isolated, would be *evidence for gradualism*.

If such situations tie our species definition in knots that is still not a problem for our theory of evolution. Our theory of evolution is predicting exactly the pattern that we see in the world: mostly reproductively isolated populations with a very small percentage close to the threshold of speciation. The problem, if there is one, is with the definition of species. The definition assumes a static, unchanging world, having been developed before the theory of evolution. Since the living world is constantly changing—evolving—static definitions will sometimes not fit. So, ligers are not a problem. Properly understood, they are—like the rest of life—evidence for the modern theory of evolution.

GRADUALISM AND COMPLEX ADAPTATIONS: CUMULATIVE SELECTION

The title of this chapter is Two Lessons of Gradualism. So far we have only seen one: Selection will generally reject all but the smallest changes, so the emergence of new species will almost always be a matter of many small steps, layered one on another, across the generations.

The second lesson concerns what biologists call complex adaptations. There is no clear line between "simple adaptions" and "complex adaptations." But an adaptation is more complex when it has more elements that must fit together in a specific way to accomplish some useful function. The classic example of a complex adaptation is the vertebrate eye. A diagram of an eye ("f" in Figure 7-4), illustrates its complexity and integration. This is a bio-engineering masterpiece; a visual sensing device made out of living cells that is more sensitive, versatile, and acute than all but the most expensive cameras. Such "organs of extreme complexity" have been a favorite point of attack since the early days of Darwinian theory—and still are. The critics' claim is that, for an eye to function properly, all of its many components must not only be present, but positioned and wired together is just the right way; otherwise the eye is useless. They immediately follow that with the second punch: No single mutation could be expected to produce all of those elements, much less integrated in the right way, and so the eye could never have been designed by natural selection.

This would be a devastating criticism if its assumptions were correct. Let's be clear. No evolutionist would challenge the second critique. A mutation that took a piece of smooth, featureless skin and turned it into a full-featured eye is utterly implausible; we don't believe such a thing could happen anymore than the critics do. But no such mutation is needed. Remember, adaptations are built *gradually*, step-by-step, out of small, incremental changes.

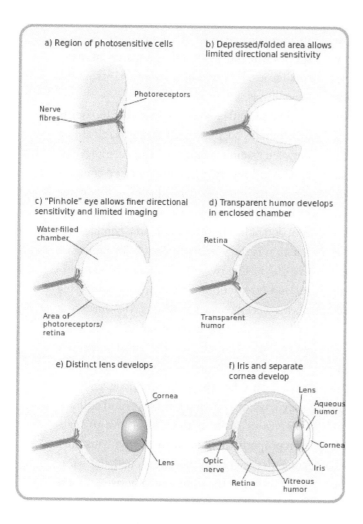

a) Region of photosensitive cells

Nerve fibres

Photoreceptors

b) Depressed/folded area allows limited directional sensitivity

c) "Pinhole" eye allows finer directional sensitivity and limited imaging

Water-filled chamber

Area of photoreceptors/retina

d) Transparent humor develops in enclosed chamber

Retina

Transparent humor

e) Distinct lens develops

Cornea

Lens

f) Iris and separate cornea develop

Lens

Aqueous humor

Cornea

Optic nerve

Iris

Retina

Vitreous humor

Figure 7-4. Kinds of actual eyes representing steps in gradual eye evolution.

There is only one constraint on building an eye step-by-step: Each element must provide an adaptive benefit on its own, when it first arises, or selection won't hold onto it. Let's be clear about that. Pardon the eye-themed pun, but *natural selection has no foresight*. For example, if there were a mutation that makes a blob of transparent tissue, selection can't retain it simply because it could be useful in the future when it might be paired up with features built by other mutations. Think about how selection works. Traits are preserved because they improve the fit between the organism and its environment; not "might improve;" not "would improve if certain other features were present". No. If a mutation doesn't have immediate adaptive value, selection won't retain it. That is why an eye could only evolve if each element were somewhat helpful when it first arose. Can we suggest an evolutionary sequence leading to a complex eye that meets this standard? Absolutely.

The first step is presumably an eyespot, just a clump of tissue that is sensitive to light. Plenty of organisms don't have even this (they're at square zero in eye evolution), but Algae and some other unicellular photosynthetic creatures (e.g., *Euglena*) do have an eyespot. Is this very basic first step useful; would selection have retained it? Yes; these organisms move in response to information from the eyespot, to position themselves in optimal lighting conditions for photosynthesis. The next step might be an increase in the size of this clump, a change which might provide increased sensitivity to light; this could be useful to creatures that live in low-light environments, or for whom small changes in light availability are important. So, in some lineages at least, this second mutation would be retained because of the improvements it made in the basic eyespot design. Now, if instead of being arrayed as a flat plate, the light sensitive material were formed into a cup, then light direction could be sensed because some parts of the cup would be in shadow and others not. If this kind of light-and-shadow information is useful—imagine the shadow cast by an approaching predator!—this further improvement would be retained by selection. A deepening of the cup would give more precise directional information (useful), and at a certain point in the preservation of mutations for deepening, the structure begins to act like a pinhole camera. You can make a pinhole camera with a cardboard box, and if you do, you'll see that it provides a crude image of what's outside the box. That sounds like really useful information and selection could be expected to retain this mutation as well.

Now I'll bring back that transparent blob of tissue that was useless by itself; once selection has established these other elements, the blob might be useful enough to be retained. To see why, take a plastic bag (a small one will work better), fill it with water and dangle in front of the hole of your pin-hole camera. You'll need to experiment with placement but you should be able to get a sharper image because the bag is acting like a lens. It's not a perfect lens but it's an improvement over no lens, so selection would retain it. Then, any subsequent mutations that improve its curvature or transparency would be favored. We can continue in this way, adding a protective cover over the lens, mechanisms to control the "aperture" and focus, and other features. As long as each mutation provides an improvement over the previous design, selection is expected to retain it. In this way, *by gradual, incremental steps* each one of which was useful when it first arose, selection could build a complex eye from the very simplest beginnings. We don't need an implausible "macromutation" that solves everything at once. We need only the continual action of natural selection holding onto whatever

works at the moment and grafting that onto what it has previously retained. One on my favorite evolutionists, Richard Dawkins, calls this *cumulative selection*. Let me be clear: Cumulative selection is not different from natural selection, but his phrase emphasizes that selection can build great complexity by layering new traits on existing ones.

As I like to do from time to time, I'm going to lead you back to ideas discussed earlier so you can see that all the parts of our modern theory of evolution fit together and form a coherent, mutually supportive framework. In this instance I want to join your new understanding about the incremental way that adaptations are built with the key point of Figure 6-1 in the previous chapter. There we saw that selection can spread a favorable trait only to the extent that the trait is reliably inherited. And we concluded that, since genes are so very reliably inherited, selection would be able to spread a gene *even it only slightly improved the fit between the organisms and its environment*. Thus genes provide a perfect foundation for the gradual improvement of phenotypes via cumulative selection.

As we "evolved an eye" over the previous two paragraphs, I suggested ways that each new modification might be useful. But is there any reason to believe those arguments? Yes, I think there is. The evidence takes the form of creatures whose actual eyes represent each of the mentioned steps. I already noted that there are creatures with eyespots; that observation suggests that eyespots are indeed useful, otherwise selection would have deleted them (I'll defend that claim in a moment). There are creatures that have sheets of light sensitive material; ones where the sheet forms a shallow cup; others where the cup is deeper; creatures with "lens-less" pinhole-hole-camera eyes; and obviously, creatures with complex eyes like yours. Again, the presumption would be that each type of "eye" is useful to the organism that has it—otherwise that "eye" wouldn't be there. In fact this entire series can be seen in a single group of invertebrate organisms: the mollusks. Cephalopod mollusks such as squid and octopi have camera-type eyes which, in at least one way, are better than our own. As explained in Dawkins' excellent book on gradualism, *Climbing Mount Improbable*, eye evolution began and progressed some distance along this sequence at least 40 separate times in the history of life on earth. There are even single-celled organisms (certain dinoflagellates) that have lens-like and retina-like structures, in essence approximating a camera-type eye (Hayakawa 2015).

If all these various eyes are useful—as I have claimed—why hasn't a scallop, which has a simple cup eye (roughly "b" in Figure 7-4), evolved the camera-type eye of a squid ("f" in the same Figure)? The answer is probably economic; it's about the balance of costs and benefits. Each trait has costs: developmental and maintenance costs in materials and energy that could have been spent on other things. And each trait may provide benefits in certain contexts. The question is, do the benefits justify the costs? If not, selection won't favor the trait. I'm going to suggest that a camera-type eye is more "expensive" to build and maintain (in the ways just mentioned) than a cup eye. Sure, the camera-type eye is sometimes worth the added cost, but is it always? Do sycamore trees have camera-type eyes? Why not? What would they do with the information? Being rooted to one spot constrains their ability to respond to visual data. I think trees *could* have eyes (some

algae do) but, given the tree's limited scope of action, the benefits don't justify the costs.

Why are the costs and benefits tallying up so differently for scallops and squid? Scallops are filter-feeders; they sit on the bottom and sieve water for microscopic plankton. They do have predators (e.g., starfish) and can move away from an approaching predator (imprecisely) by squirting water. In contrast, squid are extremely quick and agile predators; they catch fish that are, naturally, trying their best to escape. Pursuing and capturing elusive prey is aided by excellent vision. Given their particular ecologies, scallops and squid have different capacities to benefit from a high-end eye, and thus the benefit/cost balance has been struck at a different point along the eye-complexity continuum. The take-home message is that selection will not build an adaptation that is more complex than the species' environment justifies.

My best evidence for this last claim is that selection will *delete* an adaptation that was once useful if that use evaporates. The evolved function of the vertebrate eye is to form images from light reflected off objects in the environment. If that's true, what should happen—evolutionarily—when an animal with eyes colonizes an environment where there is no light to bounce off anything? Well, presumably the cost of those eyes has stayed more or less constant, but the benefits have crashed to zero. In that environment the cost of an eye is unjustified. Delete, delete, delete! Get rid of the eyes. And that is precisely what selection has done. Many different kinds of animals that ordinarily have eyes have colonized deep underground caves, where no light penetrates. And the cave-dwelling descendants of those initial colonists are typically eyeless. This deletion has happened in multiple lineages. Just as eyes have evolved many times, they have been deleted many times. There are eyeless spiders, eyeless insects, eyeless crayfish, eyeless shrimp, eyeless crabs, eyeless fish and eyeless amphibians (Figure 7-5). And the deletion can happen quickly. The Central American fish, *Astyanax mexicanus*, has surface-dwelling populations, and colonists from these surface populations have taken up residence in several different cave systems. As you should expect, the cave-dwelling populations are all eyeless, but they can still interbreed with the surface-dwellers—they are still the same species! Thus eyelessness not only evolved multiple times, it evolved relatively rapidly.

In the next chapter we'll consider vision in a bit more detail and learn about an evolutionary tradeoff between vision and the sense of smell (olfaction).

CHAPTER SUMMARY

The scientific principle of uniformitarianism requires that all theories must rest on observable processes. Because it is observable, the process of natural selection is the explanation of choice, not only for adaptive precision within species but also for the emergence of new species. Mutations with the smallest effects are the ones most likely to be beneficial, and hence evolution—both adaptation and speciation—are expected to be gradual. Ring species support this idea, as do studies of eye evolution.

(a)

(b)

Figure 7-5. a. Eyeless cave fish, *Astyanax mexicanus*. b. Eyeless cave salamander, *Proteus anguinus*.

CITED REFERENCES

Richard Dawkins (1996) *Climbing Mount Improbable*. W.W. Norton; New York.

Shiho Hayakawa, Yasuharu Takaku, Jung Shan Hwang, Takeo Horiguchi, Hiroshi Suga, Walter Gehring, Kazuho Ikeo, Takashi Gojobori (2015) "Function and Evolutionary Origin of Unicellular Camera-Type Eye Structure." PLOS One: DOI:10.1371/journal.pone.0118415

FIGURE CREDITS

CHAPTER 8

THE COMPARATIVE METHOD AND THE VISION-OLFACTION TRADEOFF

Natural selection constructs adaptations in every species, but because adaptations have costs, selection can also delete them if their benefits don't justify their costs. Thus, a significant clue to the function of adaptations is their distribution across species—where they have been built by selection, and where selection has disassembled them or never built them in the first place. As we just saw in Chapter 7, it helps us understand the function of eyes to note that selection has gotten rid of them in lightless environments. I admit that in this particular case, the structural similarities between eyes and cameras already provide pretty good evidence about the function of eyes. So you may have thought that our comparisons of cave-dwelling and surface-dwelling species were not all that necessary. But there are cases where the function of a trait is less obvious. For example, what is the function of menopause (the shutting down of reproduction in otherwise healthy and vigorous women)? It's certainly not as obvious as the function of eyes. That is why it's important to understand how we can use comparisons to help us unravel adaptive puzzles like menopause.

THE COMPARATIVE METHOD: CONVERGENCE AND DIVERGENCE

As you learned in Chapter 2, it is possible to perform actual evolutionary experiments. But, unless the species of interest has short generation times compared to the lifespans of human scientists, this approach will not be feasible. Experiments are not our only tools, however. Evolution has been going on for a long time and natural selection, acting in different environments has produced a wide array of adaptations. The *comparative method*, as used by biologists, treats the outcomes of evolution in different environments as quasi-experiments. In a normal experiment, humans manipulate the conditions, with some treatment groups exposed to one condition and other treatment groups exposed to different conditions. Of course, what we want to know is, do the outcomes differ in parallel with the treatment conditions. But, in a quasi-experiment, humans don't control the conditions. Instead they observe the outcomes under different naturally occurring conditions. For example, In Stuart's study, also discussed in Chapter 2, some of the contrasts were between islands where *Anolis sagrei* had invaded and islands where it had not. Since the lizard invaded (or didn't) on its own, this would be a quasi-experiment rather than an experiment. The outcome that Stuart observed was that certain aspects of the foot anatomy of *Anolis carolinensis* were different, depending on the presence or absence of its competitor. Stuart was applying the comparative method. Allow me to more fully unpack the logic of this method.

As evolution proceeds, changes occur: changes in gene frequencies and parallel changes in phenotypic traits. The comparative method treats these changes as the outcomes of quasi-experiments. There are two broad categories of outcomes that are of special interest to evolutionists: cases of convergence and cases of divergence. Both of these words have everyday meanings similar to their technical ones. But as I have emphasized, in science we can create difficulties if we don't distinguish between technical and everyday meanings, so let's be precise.

Sometimes species that seem quite different nevertheless resemble each other on certain traits. For example, squid have eyes much like ours. But squid are related to clams (most of which have no or very simple eyes) and we're related to monkeys who all have eyes. Why should human eyes and squid eyes be so similar when we're so different in most other respects? The likely answer is *convergence*. Selection builds adaptations (out of the raw junk of mutation) to solve whatever environmental challenge the organism faces. For this reason organisms that face similar environmental challenges often evolve quite similar traits even if they "started" from very different beginnings. Thus, *Convergence refers to any case where separate populations that are exposed to similar selection pressures evolve similar adaptations.* This is the logic of a convergence quasi-experiment: Do similar conditions lead to similar adaptations? For example, the need to move efficiently through the thick fluid medium of water caused aquatic mammals to converge on the body shape of fishes (Figure 8-1), even though the first aquatic mammals had four legs. Convergence provides general evidence of the power of natural selection, but is also a helpful tool when we want test hypotheses about the function of any given adaptation. If we think adaptation Q solves environmental challenge K, then Q should evolve

Figure 8-1. a. Shark b. Dolphins. Note similar body plans.

(a)

(b)

where challenge K exists. These tests can be qualitative: If challenge K exists, the population should have adaptation Q. Or they can be quantitative: The more K in the environment, the more pronounced trait Q will be. The same logic can be used to compare different populations within a species, as we have already done in Chapter 5. Because melanin blocks harmful UVb radiation, the more UVb there is in the environment, the more protective melanin people will synthesize. When we look for convergence, we are treating the adaptations of organisms as the outcomes of quasi-experiments (experiments done by evolution), and we ask whether or not particular adaptive outcomes systematically recur in the same environmental circumstance.

There is a second, equally important prong to the comparative approach: divergence. *Divergence refers to any case where members of one population (or two initially similar populations) that are exposed to different selection pressures evolve different adaptations.* This is the logic of a divergence quasi-experiment: Do different conditions lead to different adaptations? Quite naturally, any case of convergence will have a divergence element. For a simple physical analogy, as you walk toward the library you walk away from home; to get somewhere else you need to leave where you are. Thus, as the body shape of aquatic mammals converged on that of fishes, it was simultaneously diverging from that of its four-legged terrestrial ancestors. As the cave-dwelling fish populations lost their eyes they diverged from their surface-dwelling ancestors but they converged on the eyelessness of cave-dwelling shrimp, spiders, and amphibians.

The observation that eyelessness evolved several times independently—in different kinds of animals, and also in different geographic populations of a single fish species—is a *replicated quasi-experimental result*. In the realm of true experiments, replications increase our confidence that we are correctly identifying the cause. Likewise, quasi-experimental replications increase our confidence that the comparative method is identifying the true links between particular selection pressures and particular adaptations.

I invite you to take a short break and watch a 10-minute video that nicely demonstrates adaptive evolution of coat color in the rock pocket mouse (https://www.youtube.com/watch?v=wrTXvrKBlbc). What makes this example interesting for you now is that this species of mouse lives both on light sandy desert soils and on dark lava flows. Dark mice would be camouflaged of the lava but conspicuous in the sandy desert; light mice would be camou-flaged in the sandy desert but conspicuous on the dark lava. As you might expect, selection has favored different coat-color alleles depend-ing on which substrate the mice are living on. Mice living on the lava flows—on quite a few different lava flows—are dark; and those living in the surrounding deserts are almost all light. (Note also that selection did not modify the belly color; it's irrelevant to fitness since preda-tors don't see that side.) We can date the age of the lava flows; they are about 1,000 years old. So this change has occurred fairly rapidly. In case you're interested (though it's not central to the lesson I'm emphasizing here), the mice still belong to the same species because they can interbreed.

The more important lesson in this context is that the pocket mouse story shows us both divergence and convergence, and both are rep-licated. Before the lava flowed and there was only sandy desert, the mice were presumably all light. After the lava flowed (and cooled) and was colonized by the mice, there was strong selection for different coat colors in the two environments. Mice living on the lava flows *diverged* in coat color from those still living in the sandy desert. And that divergence was rep-licated in the sense that it happened on widely separated lava flows. In other words, the lava flows are far enough apart that we're sure the dark mice didn't simply walk from one lava flow to another; dark coloration must have evolved separately on each lava flow. At the same time, the mice on various lava flows all *converged* on the same adaptive solution of a dark coat, and that convergence happened multiple times. We know these events were independent because the mutations causing the dark coat color were different on the various lava flows. Selection was able to construct very similar adaptive solutions working with whatever gene copying errors cropped up locally. This set of observations supports the hypothesis that dark coloration provides adaptive camouflage on a dark substrate. Maybe you're not surprised by that conclusion. My goal was to demonstrate the method clearly so that you understand it well enough to apply it to more challenging adaptive questions.

A TRADEOFF BETWEEN VISION AND OLFACTION

I'm going to turn to a richer example now, one a bit closer to home since it focuses on primates (the order of mammals that includes humans), and one involving two complex traits: the sense of smell (olfaction) and the sense of vision. Most of what I'll have to say in this section is gleaned from an ambitious article by a group of scientists based at the Max Planck Institute for Evolutionary Anthropology, in Leipzig (Gilad et al. 2004). The question I'll be addressing is, has selection produced a tradeoff between these two systems? In particular, do species with more complex visual systems have less complex olfactory systems, and vice versa?

To test this hypothesis, the authors explicitly looked for convergence. The reason the authors wondered if there might be a tradeoff between vision and olfaction is—remember—*all adaptations are costly*—costly to build, to maintain, and to run. If circumstances change and a particular adaptation is no longer providing sufficient returns (in terms of reproductive success), selection will delete it. The convergent deletion of eyes in cave-dwelling fish, cave-dwelling crayfish, cave-dwelling insects, cave-dwelling salamanders, and others (Chapter 7) exemplifies a repeated cost-saving solution. Gilad and his coauthors ask if selection has simplified the olfactory system—and thus reduced its associated costs—in species with highly sophisticated visual systems.

In order to assess whether there is a tradeoff—whether one system is simplified when the other becomes more complex—the authors need a way to measure the complexity of each sensory system. Their measure of complexity for vision is a simple presence/absence measure: presence or absence of full trichromatic vision. Trichromatic vision is the more complex form. Some species of primates (the group of mammals that includes all apes, monkeys and lemurs) have full trichromatic vision, and some do not; thus some primates have more complex visual systems and some have less complex visual systems.

In everyday terms, full trichromatic vision refers to the kind of rich color vision that you have. Let me explain this exquisite adaptation. Different colors of light have different physical wavelengths; that much is physics, not biology. In the biological realm, retinas have specialized cells that are adapted to capture light—to monitor it. In species with color vision, retinal cells contain pigments that are differentially sensitive to various wavelengths. Each pigment is a protein whose amino acid sequence is encoded by a different gene (see Chapter 4 to remind yourself how genes specify protein recipes). To have "full" trichromatic vision you need three different genes: one for a pigment sensitive to short wavelengths, one for a pigment sensitive to medium wavelengths, and one for pigment sensitive to long wavelengths.

These pigment genes are not all on the same chromosome. The short-wavelength pigment gene is on an autosome. *An autosome is a non-sex chromosome*; the X-chromosome and the Y-chromosome are *not* autosomes, but all the rest are. Humans have 22 pairs (remember, we're diploid) of autosomes; in addition to these autosomes, females have two X-chromosomes, but males have one X and one Y. Where are the other two pigment genes? In the primates with full trichromatic vision, the other two pigment genes are at two different loci on the X-chromosome. The middle-wavelength pigment gene is at one X-chromosome locus, and the long-wavelength pigment gene is at another X-chromosome locus. This means that females will have two copies of the middle-wavelength gene and two copies of the long-wavelength gene, whereas males will have only one copy of each. But one copy is enough to make sufficient pigment of each, so both sexes will be able to see in all three wavelengths, that is, both sexes will see in full color—though females might have somewhat better (more acute) color vision.

What about the set of primate species which do not have full trichromatic vision? They all have the same autosomal (short-wavelength) gene. But on the X-chromosome, they have just one locus coding for a retinal pigment, not two loci. However, that single X-chromosome locus has two *different* alleles: one that codes for a middle-wavelength pigment and one that codes for a long-wavelength pigment. As a consequence, females who happen to be heterozygous at this locus *will* be able to see in full color, but females who are homozygous will not. And males will not have full color vision either; because with only one X-chromosome, they cannot possibly have both alleles. (Strictly speaking, males cannot be either homozygous or heterozygous for any X-chromosome gene; what they are is called hemizygous.)

Remember, Gilad and his coauthors categorize primates into those that have full trichromatic vision and those who do not. The situation of having three separate loci (as we humans have) provides full trichromatic vision; the authors consider this to be the more complex visual adaptation. The condition of having only two loci does not give all members of the species full trichromatic vision and is thus considered to be the less complex visual adaptation. Figure 8-2 illustrates the configuration of genes in species with and without full trichromatic vision.

Now let's turn to olfaction; we need a measure of its complexity as well, because we want to see if olfactory complexity is reduced where visual complexity is increased. Smells do not come in just short, medium, and long; there are many different kinds of smells. Because you can smell so many different odors, you would be right to suspect there are many different genes coding for olfactory receptor proteins. There are over 1,000 olfactory receptor genes in mammals.

But not all of these genes are functional in every species; some are "switched off." The "off" switch consists of one or more mutations in the gene's coding sequence that prevent the gene from sending a messenger RNA message (see Chapter 4). When a gene is switched off in this way, the protein the gene would have coded for is never assembled; it is then called a "pseudogene" because it looks like a gene but it does not specify any protein the way the real gene does. (We can still recognize that it *used to be* an olfactory receptor gene in the evolutionary past because its A, T, C, G sequence is still very similar to known olfactory receptor genes in other species.)

Each olfactory receptor gene that is switched off (converted to a pseudogene) deletes one smell component from a species' olfactory repertoire. Thus, the number of olfactory receptor genes that have been converted to pseudogenes is a measure of the simplification of a species olfactory system. More-complex

Figure 8-2. The arrangement of genes in species with (diagram on left) and without (diagram on right) full trichromatic vision. Both kinds of species have a short-wavelength gene on one of their autosomes (not shown).

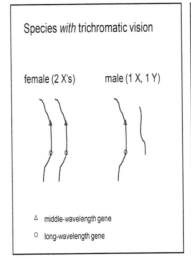

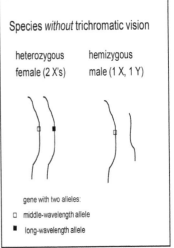

olfactory systems have fewer olfactory receptor pseudogenes (i.e., more working genes), and simpler systems have more pseudogenes (i.e., fewer working genes).

Gilad did not look at each of the 1,000 olfactory receptor genes in each species to determine which ones were real genes and which ones were pseudogenes. They might not be done yet if they had! Instead, they did what people always do when they have a lot of cases to evaluate: They took a sample. If you wanted to predict the results of an election, you would not ask every registered voter whom they were going to vote for; you would ask a sample of voters. Likewise, for each of the primate species discussed in their article the authors looked at a sample of 100 olfactory receptor genes and measured the percentage of those 100 that were turned off—the percentage that had been converted to pseudogenes.

That percentage is very different in different species. In humans, about 50% of the olfactory receptor genes are pseudogenes (about half are switched off). In other Old World anthropoid primates (African and Asian monkeys and apes), between 25% and 35% are pseudogenes. In New World primates (Central and South American monkeys), a prosimian primate (lemur), and a non-primate (mouse), generally only 15% to 18% are pseudogenes. But there is an obvious exception to this pattern. One New World monkey species, the howler monkey, has 31% pseudogenes; in this regard, howlers resemble the Old World anthropoids and are quite unlike their close relatives. This exception (marked by the lower arrow in Figure 8-3) is critical to testing the hypothesis that increasing complexity of the visual systems allows some deterioration of the olfactory system. Here is why it's critical: among the New World monkeys, only howler monkeys have trichromatic vision!

To appreciate the importance of this observation about howler monkeys we need to absorb what Figure 8-3 is telling us. This diagram is a *phylogenetic tree* of all the primates studied by Gilad.

Figure 8-3. Species with trichromatic vision are shown in gray; those without it are shown in black.

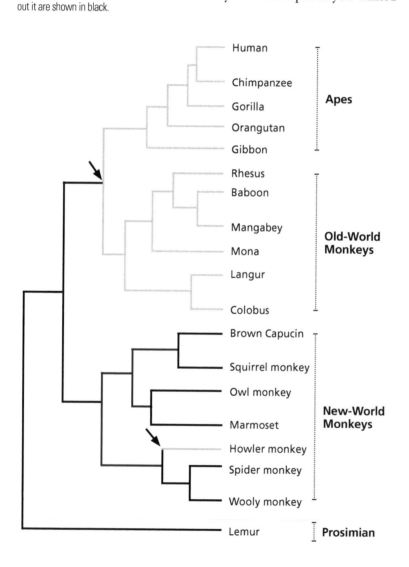

Phylogenetic trees are constructed using the *cladistic* methods you will learn about in Chapter 12. For the moment all you need to understand is that this kind of tree shows how closely related each species is to every other species. For example, our closest relative is the chimpanzee. The closest relative of the chimp-human group is the gorilla. The closest relative of the howler monkey is the spider monkey-wooly monkey group. The shorter the route between two species, tracing over the lines in the diagram, the more closely related they are; the longer the tracing route, the more distantly related.

Based on this phylogenetic tree we can now ask how many times trichromatic vision evolved in the primates. The answer seems to be two. Natural selection twice solved the problem of getting three different retinal pigments into both male and female primates: once in the common ancestor of all apes and Old World monkeys (indicated by the upper arrow in Figure 8-3), and a second time in the ancestor of howler monkeys (the lower arrow). This second solution was more recent; it probably did not occur in the ancestor of all New World monkeys because hardly any New World monkeys have it.

Now, this makes the data about the percentage of pseudogenes especially interesting. Trichromatic vision evolved twice in primates (the arrows), and *both* times it was associated with an increase in the percentage of olfactory receptor pseudogenes. Howler monkeys have *twice* as many pseudogenes as other New World Monkeys, and they are also the only New World Monkeys with trichromatic vision. Of course, this could be a coincidence, but statistical considerations that are best reserved for an upper–division course suggest it's probably not just chance. Gilad and his coauthors conclude that when the visual system becomes more sophisticated, selection allows the olfactory system to become simpler. Here is the way to picture that process.

Mutations that switch off olfactory receptor genes can occur at any time, in any species. But if they occur in a species *without* trichromatic vision, selection is more likely to disfavor them than if the same disabling mutation occurred in a species *with* trichromatic vision. Can you see why? Sensory systems like vision, hearing, and olfaction exist because they help animals to make discriminations (tell things apart), and those abilities are relevant to survival and reproduction. For example, if you can't make certain discriminations you might eat something toxic. That is why selection generally hasn't permitted many olfactory receptor genes to be switched off. But if a species has especially good vision (e.g., trichromatic), then it might be able to discriminate by sight instead of by smell. In that case selection might allow a mutation that switches off an olfactory receptor gene to spread in the population, since it would save matter and energy (by building a simpler olfactory system) but wouldn't compromise the animal's discriminatory abilities.

In terms of their high proportion of olfactory receptor pseudogenes, howler monkeys have *converged* on Old World monkeys and apes. Because this pairing of trichromatic vision and a degraded olfactory system occurred twice, our confidence is increased that there is an adaptive relationship between these two systems.

CHAPTER SUMMARY

Evolutionary convergence occurs when similar selection pressures cause similar adaptations to arise from different starting points. Divergence occurs when different selection pressures cause different adaptations arise from similar starting points. Evolutionists can use instances of convergence and divergence to test hypotheses about the functions of adaptations. Eyelessness seems to repeatedly evolve in species that live in deep caves where there is no light. Coat coloration seems to repeatedly evolve to match the prevailing substrate in pocket mice. Aquatic mammals seem to repeatedly evolve fish-like body shapes.

Comparisons among various primate species suggest that natural selection has traded-off the quality of the visual system against the quality of the olfactory system; species that have more acute visual systems tend to have less acute olfactory systems and vice versa. In general, evolutionary tradeoffs are to be expected. The matter and energy available to any organism is limited. Individuals who best allocate those resources among various demands will tend to leave more offspring and their allocation patterns should therefore spread in the population. Thus each kind of organism has evolved only the adaptations that justify their costs, given the suite of environmental demands impinging on it.

CITED REFERENCES

Yoav Gilad, Victor Wiebe, Molly Przeworski, Doron Lancet, Svante Pääbo (2004) "Loss of olfactory receptor genes coincides with the acquisition of full trichromatic vision in primates." *PLoS Biology 2*: 120-125.

FIGURE CREDITS

CHAPTER 9

THE EVOLUTION OF ALTRUISM: KIN SELECTION

An odd accident of history (and perhaps personal prejudice) is that a Nobel Prize in biology was never established. Be that as it may, another wealthy Swedish industrialist, Holger Crafoord, attempted to remedy Nobel's omission in 1980 by founding the Crafoord Prize in Biosciences. In 1993, this esteemed prize was awarded to W. D. Hamilton for his development of kin selection theory.

THE PUZZLE OF ALTRUISM

Why is kin selection such an important idea? The answer is that it was the first logically coherent solution to the puzzle of how altruism might evolve. To biologists, "altruism" does not simply mean being nice. Just as the term "selection" has a technical meaning for evolutionists, so does the term "altruism." *An altruistic trait is one that reduces the reproductive success of the individual who manifests it while increasing the reproductive success of one or more neighbors of the altruist*—the recipient(s) of the altruism. The altruist sustains an evolutionary cost and the neighbor receives an evolutionary benefit. A simple example of altruism would be giving some of your food to a hungry person, or (assuming there was a cost of doing so) warning someone of approaching danger.

When I say that altruism is a "puzzle" I don't mean it's a "problem" is the sense that we'd rather live in a world where there were no altruists. No; it's not a problem in the way that disease is a problem or tsunamis are a problem. But it *is* a problem for the theory of evolution as we have developed that theory so far. Darwin's theory of evolution by natural selection does not predict that altruism will evolve, *so it shouldn't exist*. That's why altruism is a problem. Our best theory of why organisms have the traits they do says that organisms shouldn't be altruistic, not "shouldn't be altruistic" in the moral sense, but in the sense that natural selection wouldn't have favored altruism. This is exactly the kind of problem that scientists love because it's an opportunity to make theoretical progress. So get ready, we're going to enter some new theoretical territory.

The very definition of altruism (a reproductive cost for the actor combined with a reproductive benefit for the recipient) highlights the key evolutionary puzzle: How can a trait that lowers reproductive success spread, especially when it increases the reproductive success of potential competitors? This was Hamilton's break-through contribution: He solved it by realizing that alleles have multiple possible routes to the next generation.

The obvious route is the one we have emphasized in the first eight chapters of this book: An allele could get into the next generation by doing something to improve the adaptations of the body it (the allele) is sitting in. An allele that makes its surrounding body fit better with the local environment will get passed on more often than one that doesn't. That's what I like to call the "front door" to the next generation, and that's what the architects of the modern synthesis were describing. But Hamilton (1964) found the *back door* to the next generation.

KIN SELECTION

What if, instead of conferring benefits on the surrounding body, the allele conferred benefits on *other* bodies likely to be carrying the very same allele? Conferring those benefits would require certain expenditures (costs): The surrounding body would have to *do something* to confer those benefits. From the allele's perspective it would be swapping a reproductive decrease (as a result of the cost) in one carrier for a reproductive increase in another carrier. If the decrease were smaller than the increase, the allele would be better off (more likely to end up in the next generation) than if it did not orchestrate such swaps. Think about it. If an allele could get one of its carriers to accept small costs in order to confer somewhat larger benefits on other carriers of the same allele, that *allele* would reap a net profit. In these kinds of "back-door swaps", individuals are getting costs and benefits, but it's the altruistic allele that's improving its chances of getting passed on.

I hope you see that this could work in principle, but you probably also worry that there are some bugs to be worked out. For example, how could an allele "recognize" its other carriers? Wouldn't alleles make lots of mistakes and end up helping competing alleles? The solution to this problem lies is kinship—hence the theory's name. What would cause a pair of individuals to have similar genotypes, having many alleles in common? Kinship. For example you and your siblings (brothers and sisters) have many of the same alleles because you inherited them from the same source: your parents. Let's consider the case of two full siblings (who have both the same mother and father). Now, close your eyes and randomly pick an allele in sib 1. What's the chance that the very same allele is present in sib 2? It's ½. The essential point here is that this probability is greater than zero for any pair of relatives, and less than 1 (except in the case of identical twins). For example, it's 1/8 for full cousins; it's ¼ for grandparent-grandchild. In kin selection theory this probability is called the *degree of relatedness*, and in mathematical expressions of the theory it's written as r. Now let's put the degree of relatedness together with the notion of back-door swaps.

Remember, we're taking a gene's perspective on evolution—a perspective that we mathematically explored in Chapter 6. We're doing that because the course of evolution depends *only* on which alleles get into the next generation. The theory of kin selection proposes that an allele can benefit by accepting a cost in one person who has that allele (say "carrier J,") if accepting that cost produces a large enough benefit in another person who also has a chance of having the same allele (say, "carrier K"). Let's now be precise about "large enough:" We mean large enough to make up for the fact that "carrier K" isn't always an actual carrier. The degree of relatedness, discussed above, measures how likely K is be an actual carrier. Bingo. Let's formalize this. I'm going to let c stand for the size of the reproductive cost to the altruist (J, above), and b stand for the size of the reproductive benefit received by the recipient of that altruism (K, above). And r, you already know, measures how likely J and K are

to share any given allele. Altruism is favored by kin selection whenever:

$$rb > c$$

Equations are just sentences. This one says a product has to be bigger than the cost paid by the altruist. That product is what I like to call the *devalued benefit*—the benefit downrated by the less-than-certain chance that the benefit strikes the same allele that caused the altruism (which will happen only r proportion of the time). Let's fill in some numbers. Say the cost of the altruism, c, is 1 unit of reproductive success, and the benefit, b, is 3 units of reproductive success and r=1/2 because the altruist and recipient are full siblings. In that case, is:

$$rb > c?$$
$$1/2(3) > 1?$$

Yes, it is. So, kin selection would favor an individual accepting 1 unit of reproductive cost in order to provide 3 units of reproductive benefit to a full sibling. Kin selection would favor it because any allele that induced this kind of behavior in its carriers would be helping itself, and would therefore spread in the population compared to alleles that produced no altruism.

Here is a simple way of thinking about kin selection that is very close to one of Hamilton's own summaries: Individuals should value each other in direct proportion to their degree of relatedness, and they should behave in accordance with that valuation. My sibling is, at the genetic level, half of me and I should treat her accordingly. My cousin is, in similar terms, 1/8 of me and thus not as worth making sacrifices for and my sibling is.

Kin selection takes a "gene's-eye view of evolution. In doing so it shows that altruism among individuals can evolve via genetic selfishness. In the above example, the allele in question is inflicting a cost on one individual in order to confer a larger benefit on another (potential) carrier and *thereby selfishly promoting its (the allele's) own interests*. I contend that all evolutionarily viable models of altruism will depend on turning altruism among individuals into selfishness at the level of the underlying alleles. How would an allele that regularly sacrificed its own welfare persist in the population? Any alleles like that should have been weeded out by selection long ago. In the section that follows all traits are defined in terms of their fitness effects on individuals (how they affect an individual's reproductive prospects).

THE TRAIT SPACE

We begin by noting that altruism is only one of four hypothetically possible kinds of traits. Trait X could increase (provide a benefit, b, to) or decrease (impose a cost, c, on) the fitness of individuals who have it. These effects would be shown to the right or to the left, respectively, of the origin in Figure 9-1. And the same trait, X, might simultaneously increase or decrease the fitness of the individuals' neighbors (respectively, b or c on the vertical axis). For example, if John has a mate-stealing trait, that would increase his fitness but decrease his (male)

neighbor's fitness. The conjunction of such effects, on self and on neighbors, defines the four quadrants of Figure 9-1 and therefore the four kinds of traits. John's mate-stealing trait would fall in the selfish quadrant. Selfish traits are not difficult to explain evolutionarily, because genes for these traits will get a boost from their positive effects on the reproductive success of the individuals who have them. Keep in mind, however, that altruistic traits will decrease the fitness of those who have them. That is why evolutionists have struggled to explain altruism and, consequently, why the theory of kin selection is so important.

Kin selection theory does not predict that the altruistic quadrant will be fully occupied; it predicts only limited altruism. Altruism that satisfies *Hamilton's Rule* (rb>c) is favored by kin selection; altruism that does not satisfy this rule is disfavored. We defined r, b, and c above. If you remember your analytic geometry, the distinction between altruism that is favored by kin selection (because it satisfies Hamilton's Rule) and altruism

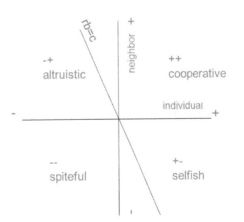

Figure 9-1. Four kinds of traits, categorized by their fitness effects on self (horizontal axis) and on neighbors (vertical axis).

that is disfavored can be seen in Figure 9-1. The diagonal line rb=c defines the boundary between altruism that is favored (above and to the right) and disfavored (below and to the left). When r is larger, as it is for more closely related kin, the rb=c line will have a shallower slope, thus bringing a larger wedge of the altruistic quadrant into the favored region. Translating back to English, kin selection theory predicts greater altruism to more closely related kin. To see if you fully understand the implications of kin selection, try to explain what it means to extend the diagonal line into the selfish quadrant.

IS KIN SECTION MORE THAN A MODEL?

So far we've been discussing a mathematical model. It's a model that imagines a particular kind of altruism-inducing gene and asks about the conditions under which such a gene might spread. Anyone can be forgiven for wondering whether this is all just math fiends gone amuck. I assure you it's not; I value your time too much to waste in on formulas that tell us nothing about the real world. But how would we—how would you—decide whether kin selection theory actually explains altruism? Well, that's why I put hypothesis testing in Chapter 1. Scientific theories are testable. Can you make some testable predictions from Hamilton's kin selection theory? Sure; it's easy. Individuals should:

Be able to assess degree of relatedness (r)
Be able to assess benefit and cost (b and c)
Respond differently depending on r, b and c
Endure larger costs for closer relatives (to whom they have a higher r).
Give small benefits to close relatives that they withhold from more distant relatives.

Discriminate among more and less closely related individuals in a wide array of social contexts.

The detailed way that these various abilities and behaviors play out could fill, not a book, but an encyclopedia. As of July 2016, Google Scholar lists nearly 14,000 citations to Hamilton's core article. The citing articles represent a wonderfully diverse collection of predictions and tests of Hamilton's ideas. They focus on a wide variety of organisms, from invertebrates to humans; they explore every imaginable kind of interaction (including interactions between mothers and their gestating fetuses); and they consider a wide range of kin-selected adaptations—anatomical, physiological, behavioral, and psychological. Why should you feel more grief when a close relative dies than when a more distant one passes? You almost certainly would. Science always asks "why?" and searches for theoretically coherent answers.

Let me finish by giving you one more glimpse of how far-reaching Hamilton's kin selection theory is. *Monogamy* refers to a mating system in which one male and one female produce all their offspring together; neither have offspring with any other individual. Looking across species, monogamy is fairly rare except in birds, where it is the most common mating system. In contrast, only about 4% of mammal species are monogamous. We'll explore the evolution of monogamy in the final chapters of this book but my concern in this chapter is not the selection pressures that could favor monogamy. Here I'm interested in how monogamy affects degrees of relatedness.

If males and females mate promiscuously, as they do in many species of mammals, then the various offspring of a female have different fathers, and the various offspring of a male have different mothers. As a consequence, these offspring are "half-siblings" to each other. They share only one parent and—here is the key point—they share only ¼ of their alleles. In contrast, if females and males mate monogamously, their offspring will be full siblings to each other and hence share ½ of their alleles—twice as many as half siblings do. I want you to get practice making predictions from theory. Does kin selection predict that full and half siblings would treat each other differently?

Absolutely. Kin selection says that, because of their higher degree of relatedness, the offspring of monogamous matings should be more altruistic towards each other than the offspring of promiscuous matings. That's easy to test. Let's pick a clearly altruistic trait that we can score as present or absent: It's called "helping at the nest" because it was first described in birds, but the same behavior occurs in other kinds of animals. In species with this kind of "helping" the helpers refrain from going off to breed on their own. Instead they remain with their parents, assisting the parents in rearing their next batch of offspring (who would be the helpers' younger siblings). The helpers go out and find food and bring it back to their siblings, monitor the home territory for potential predators, and may attack or otherwise attempt to divert any predators they do find. Because many more bird species than mammal species are monogamous, the first prediction is that more bird species will have helpers. That prediction is correct; about 1,000 species of birds regularly have helpers, but a mere handful of mammal species do (wolves are one example). But we can make that prediction more precise. Among

bird species (and among mammal species) the monogamous ones should be much more likely to have helpers. That too is correct (Cornwallis et al. 2010). And finally, the scalpel-like version of our prediction: Within any bird or mammal species, the individuals who would be rearing full siblings are more likely to be helpers. Do see how that works? Inevitably, in some breeding pairs, a mate may die and the surviving parent may take a new partner. The young of the original pair would then be only half siblings to the next batch of offspring. In those particular families the young are significantly less likely to remain as helpers (Komdeur 1994).

Kin selection is an elegant theory, and the evolutionary process it describes seems to have significantly influenced the behavior of individuals in many different species. But note that the individual decisions it shapes (e.g., helping or not helping) ramify out to structure entire social systems. In other words, groups are not random collections of individuals broadcasting indiscriminate altruism. They are kinship-weighted webs of more and less altruistic associations among highly discriminating actors. The tendrils of evolution are everywhere in the living world.

CHAPTER SUMMARY

Altruism, where individuals incur fitness costs in order to provide fitness benefits to others, is an evolutionary puzzle. The theory of kin selection provides one way of solving that puzzle, by showing that alleles for altruism could persist if they systematically aim that altruism at other carriers of the same allele. This theory highlights that idea that alleles are the enduring players in the evolutionary game, and that individuals are their disposable agents. Many detailed predictions of kin selection have been tested by comparing them to actual patterns of behavior is a wide array of animal species.

CITED REFERENCES

Cornwallis, C. K., West, S. A., Davis, K. E., and Griffin, A. S. (2010). Promiscuity and the evolutionary transitions to complex societies. *Nature, 466*: 969-974.

Dillard, J. R., and Westneat, D. F. (2016). Disentangling the correlated evolution of monogamy and cooperation. *Trends in Ecology and Evolution, 31*: 503-513.

Hamilton, W. D. (1964). The genetical evolution of social behavior. I. *Journal of Theoretical Biology, 7*: 1-16.

Komdeur, J. (1994). The Effect of Kinship on Helping in the Cooperative Breeding Seychelles Warbler (Acrocephalus sechellensis). *Proceedings of the Royal Society of London: B, Biological Sciences, 256*: 47-52.

CHAPTER 10

THE EVOLUTION OF ALTRUISM: RECIPROCITY

Here we have an interesting parallel that further empha-sizes the magnitude of the Darwinian puzzle posed by altruism. As I mentioned, in 1993, W. D. Hamilton won the Crafoord prize for his development of kin selection theory. Fifteen years later, R. L. Trivers won it for his work on "social evolution," including his formulation of the theory of reciprocal altruism. Trivers' reciprocal altruism (1971) offers a second evolutionary escape hatch from the dog-eat-dog world of perpetual competition and selfishness among individuals.

ZERO-SUM INTERACTIONS

In social species like our own, we inevitably end up associat-ing with our most serious competitors. This is true by defini-tion. The members of any species share a set of adaptations geared to their particular ecology and naturally depend on the same resource base. The food I want is the best food for you. The same goes for mates and shelter; almost anything that would enhance my fitness would similarly enhance yours. And most of these resources are "zero-sum." Zero-sum simply means that what I use is unavailable to you. If I eat a piece of fruit or meat, it's gone; you can no longer eat it. Zero-sumness is precisely what causes the evolution of competitiveness, of selfishness. In the vast majority of circumstances, individuals whose *modus operandi* was, "No, you take it, please!" had lower fitness than individuals who said, "Get your paws off it; it's mine!" My point here is not that I want to live in a mean and nasty world, but simply to remind you that you cannot take altruism for granted. Altruists seem destined to lose out in everything that matters to reproductive success—to fitness. So we need special theories to explain how altruism can win out over selfishness.

RECIPROCITY'S ESCAPE FROM THE ZERO-SUM TRAP

Reciprocity works as an escape from selfishness precisely because it can sometimes take the zero-sumness out of life. Let's imagine that we need to scratch up all our food from nature—by hunting animals and foraging for edible plants. As you will soon understand in much more detail, this is a very important thing to imagine because it was true for all humans until just a few thousand years ago. This way of making a living is challenging and it entails very big ups and downs. Sometimes you get a bonanza: You kill a big animal that yields much more meat than you can eat before it rots. But sometimes you have a string of bad foraging luck that lasts for days. How wasteful to let the bonanza rot; how painful to starve. If you just had a refrigerator you could save the leftover meat for the lean days that will inevitably come. Of course our foraging ancestors had no refrigerators. But they discovered what we might call the *social refrigerator*—reciprocity. Simply put, I give you the parts of my big kill that I do not need.

Then, next week or next month, when I come up short on calories and you have a surplus, you pay me back.

Here is another way of thinking about it. What is five ounces of meat worth in fitness terms? This is a trick question, because the answer depends on how well fed you are at the moment. If you have just eaten three pounds of meat, five more ounces will not help you much. But if you have had nothing to eat for days, the very same five ounces could keep you from dying, a huge fitness benefit. This is how reciprocity lets individuals exploit non-zero-sum situations.

A very simple mathematical model will make the gambit clear. Here is a 10-day period in the lives of two stone-age foragers, Mald and Kleg. Mostly they each eat what they find, but interesting things happen on Day 2 and Day 9. When Mald has an especially good foraging day and has more than she can eat, she gives some food to her hungry neighbor, Kleg. Later, when Kleg has been fortunate in finding food and has eaten his fill (but Mald has had bad foraging luck), Kleg repays the favor. The numbers estimate the fitness consequences, negative numbers being fitness costs and positive numbers being fitness benefits. Even though they both accept costs along the way, they both come out ahead after the exchange.

	Mald	**Kleg**
Day 2	gives food	receives food
	-1	+10
Day 9	receives food	gives food
	+10	-1
Net result	+9	+9

Note that the non-zero-sumness of the situation is what that makes reciprocity work.

In zero-sum situations, A loses whatever B gains. But here, because of their different nutritional situations, Mald pays only one fitness unit to give Kleg ten. This asymmetry guarantees that if the situations are later reversed and the roles of well-fed giver and hungry receiver are switched, both participants reap a substantial profit.

You might say that this kind of exchange is not altruism because both participants eventually end up with a net benefit. You would be right at one level; but remember, *all* evolutionary explanations of altruism must somehow convert the costs of altruism into benefits (you should be able to explain how kin selection makes this conversion); otherwise, selection will weed out altruism. Think about how this kind of reciprocity looks to an outside observer. A scientist would see that, on Day 2, Mald does indeed pay a cost to provide a benefit to her neighbor; in other words, the scientist would see an instance of altruism. The scientist would recognize that there was a net benefit to Mald only if he also happened to be around on the day of the payback. Thus, as offered by Trivers, reciprocity is a *theory* about how altruism can pay off—one that can be supported or rejected on the basis of observations of actual behavior over time.

TIT-FOR-TAT

The phrase "tit-for-tat" might be new to you. Tit-for-tat is a behavioral rule or strategy that, if employed by animals, would support the evolution of reciprocal altruism. It involves doing to your partner whatever he did on the previous encounter. For example, if your partner gave you food the last time you saw him, you should give him food this time. But it needs to be just a bit more complicated. We need a way to get the tit-for-tat process started. If we begin with the premise that ordinary natural selection leads us to expect, then the first encounter would be nothing but selfish withholding: I give you no food; then the next time you give me the same: no food. In that scenario we are stuck in a selfish equilibrium. Therefore, the full tit-for-tat rule is as follows: Be altruistic on the first encounter and then do whatever your partner did. In other words, the kinds of advantages that Mald and Kleg reaped from reciprocity can be launched only if individuals are willing to take a chance on the reciprocal tendencies of new partners—as Mald did on Day 2 of the example.

Just as reciprocity needs this altruistic push-start, it also involves stern withholding from non-reciprocators. If Mald starts out altruistic, but on Day 9 Kleg eats herself sick instead of giving any food to her now-hungry neighbor, Mald should not offer any of her next surplus to Kleg. "Should not offer" is not intended as a moral rule; it is simply a clarification of what must happen if reciprocity is to become established in the population. It is easy to see from our simple example (above) that those who offer benefits without getting paid back end up with net losses. Only those who receive altruism in return will come out ahead. So, the only way to avoid net losses is to terminate relationships with non-reciprocators. Even better, try to get others to terminate relationships with non-reciprocators as well; and best of all, try to prevent others from offering that initial push-start of generosity to anyone known to be a non-reciprocator. "Don't bother to help him; he's a fair-weather friend." In this way, altruists take active steps to make sure that non-reciprocators cannot siphon benefits—cannot be what we might call "social parasites" or "free-riders."

COGNITIVE AND EMOTIONAL ADAPTATIONS UNDERLYING RECIPROCITY

By now you are probably realizing that for reciprocal altruism to take hold in a population, a particular set of *mental* adaptations is required. "Mental adaptation" may be a new idea for you but it should not seem radical. For example, when selection shapes the equipment of a predator, that shaping is not limited to fangs, claws, and speed. Selection also builds psychological adaptations for recognizing especially vulnerable prey, stalking into the wind and using all available cover, knowing when to start the final rush, and how to anticipate the prey's escape tactics.

Likewise, we can specify the mental adaptations that are likely to be found in any species that has undergone selection for reciprocity. Some of these adaptations are obvious. Reciprocal altruists must be able to recognize and remember the past actions of their neighbors. Jennifer is not just one of many adult female members of my species. Instead, I recognize her as a unique individual, I know

how much empathy she seems to have for the needs of others, and I see how often she shares the resources she has. But reciprocity is supported by more than a good memory for faces and gifts.

A growing body of research suggests that emotions are facultative psychological adaptations designed to guide our behavior. Think about that. A facultative adaptation (like sun tanning) has been designed by selection to monitor the environment and to "turn on" when it's needed. We know what the job of melanin is and therefore when it is needed (Chapter 5). But what job do emotions do? Notice that each emotion has either a positive or negative valence, making you feel good or making you feel bad; there are no neutral emotions. For this reason, emotions can be thought of as on-board reward and punishment systems. Positive emotions function to reinforce behaviors that, on average, promote fitness; and negative emotions steer us away from or help to correct behaviors or situations that are bad for fitness.

Let's make this more concrete for the case of reciprocal altruism. Most of us feel a little better—we get a little personal happiness reward—when we help someone in need; I assume that sounds familiar to you. This small happiness high fuels that altruistic push-start needed to initiate any reciprocal relationship. Likewise, the receiver of that altruism feels a surge of gratitude, which functions to motivate her to return the favor when she can. These alternating happiness and gratitude emotions in the two exchange partners will tend to keep the favorable exchanges flowing. On the other hand, an individual who does not reciprocate is likely to feel the negative emotion of guilt. Guilt often serves to trigger reconsideration and to motivate actions that will rebuild a partnership before it is too late. And what emotion do you feel when someone you have helped subsequently refuses to help you? Anger, perhaps even vengeance. The role of these negative emotions is to distance us from non-reciprocators and to reduce the future benefits we might spend on them.

Thus, for each possible outcome there is an emotion that serves either to motivate reciprocity or to prevent exploitation by social parasites. Here again science tries to go beyond merely *describing* the world (in this case the psychological world); it tries to *explain why* humans have this particular suite of emotions and why each is triggered in quite specific contexts related to opportunities for reciprocity. In Trivers' original formulation of reciprocal altruism (1971) he paid significant attention to the cognitive and emotion systems that regulate reciprocity. Trivers argued, as I do here, that humans evolved this pattern of emotional responses precisely because it facilitates an escape from zero-sumness via the avenue of reciprocity. A similar and highly readable perspective on the role of emotion in establishing and maintaining reciprocal relationships can be found in Chapter 3 ("Reciprocity with a Vengeance") of *The Happiness Hypothesis*, by the psychologist Jonathan Haidt.

COMPARING KIN SELECTION AND RECIPROCITY

Let's take the opportunity to solidify our understanding by comparing and contrasting the theories of kin selection and reciprocity. Both are evolutionary models (theories) intended to explain how alleles that induce altruistic behavior might become common. Since both are concerned with altruism, both models include the notion of fitness costs (borne by the altruist) and fitness benefits (accruing to the recipient of the altruism). The models differ on the hypothesized mechanism that could maintain such altruism in the population.

Kin selection does so via a "fitness swap" between genetically similar individuals; if the very same altruistic alleles that induce the altruism also reside in the recipient, those alleles may reap a net benefit. The necessary relationship is quantitative. If the altruistic allele is sufficiently likely to be in both the altruist and the recipient, and the benefit is large enough relative to the cost, the altruistic allele should replicate at a higher rate (through the increased reproductive success of the recipient) than a non-altruistic allele that promotes no such fitness swap. This quantitative relationship is more efficiently stated as Hamilton's rule ($rb > c$) but here I have expressed that rule in words for those who (think they) don't like math.

Let's notice several things. First, for Hamilton's rule to be satisfied (in other words, for altruism to be favored by kin selection) the benefit (b) always must be larger than the cost (c). This is required because r is always a fraction, something less than one. If a fraction times b must be greater than c, then b must be substantially greater than c. Note also that, in kin selection theory, it's the altruistic allele that (if conditions are right) gets a net benefit. For this to work, an altruistic allele must aim its altruism at other bearers of the very same allele; otherwise competing alleles get the benefit. As a corollary, the altruist (as an individual) always loses in Hamilton's model; only alleles profit.

What maintains altruistic alleles in the population according to Trivers' reciprocity model?

In this case it's because the altruist himself gets a compensatory amount of altruism back, at some point in the future. Each altruist accepts a small cost to give a larger benefit and is subsequently repaid a large benefit that has been provided at a smaller cost by another altruist. So there's a difference between the two theories: In kin selection, alleles benefit whereas in reciprocity individuals benefit (in the long run). Here's a second difference. As we just demonstrated, for kin selection to work the very same allele must be present in the altruist and recipient. There is no such requirement in the case of reciprocity. There is no r in that model because it doesn't matter if the altruist and recipient share genes; the only thing that matters is that altruists get paid back. Completely different genes at different loci on different chromosomes could be inducing the altruism in reciprocity partners; as long as they continue to get their pay-backs whatever altruism genes they have will be reaping the benefits.

So, the two models operate very differently and should build noticeably different adaptations. But they also have some common features, beyond the simple definitional one that they both deal with altruism. Both are models of what I like to call *phenotypic altruism*, one phenotype accepting a cost to benefit another phenotype. But both kin-selected and reciprocal altruism are, in fact, *genetic selfishness*. In reciprocity the returned benefit more than wipes out the cost, so a reciprocity partner is just a way of accruing more benefits. Put in a small cost and get out a large benefit? Sure, I'll do that all day long. In kin selection the benefit is to the altruistic allele. That's genetic selfishness too. The allele is using an individual to buy benefits for itself (the allele) in another individual.

I'll close out our exploration of how altruism evolves with one more comparison of these two models. Both kin selection and reciprocity should produce highly facultative altruism. Remember, facultative traits are expressed only in the environment where they produce positive fitness outcomes. Thus, neither of these models would produce indiscriminate altruism, with altruists broadcasting benefits constantly in all directions. Such indiscriminate altruism would generate fitness costs that would be uncompensated; uncompensated by benefits to the underlying allele and uncompensated by returned favors from other altruists. Thus, according to both models, altruism could only evolve if it were facultative. In the case of kin selection, altruism should be facultatively dependent on r, b, and c. In the case of reciprocity, altruism should be facultatively dependent on the reciprocal tendencies of individual social partners.

CHAPTER SUMMARY

Reciprocity provides a second evolutionarily plausible explanation for altruism. Reciprocal altruism is not nearly as widespread in the animal kingdom as is kin-based altruism, and it requires a set of specialized mental adaptations that are conspicuous in our own species.

CITED REFERENCES

Jonathan Haidt (2006). "Reciprocity with Vengeance," Chapter 3 (pages 45-58) from *The Happiness Hypothesis*. Perseus Books Group: New York.

Robert L. Trivers (1971) "The evolution of reciprocal altruism." *Quarterly Review of Biology 46*: 35-57.

CHAPTER 11

HOMOSEXUALITY

Homosexuality is an even a bigger evolutionary puzzle than altruism is because the homosexuality puzzle is not yet solved. Both are puzzles for the same reason: Because they reduce reproductive success, both altruism and homosexuality are expected to be eliminated by natural selection. Since they haven't been we need to see what amendments to the theory of evolution by natural selection are necessary. We did that in the previous two chapters for altruisms. Even though we don't have definitive answers yet we can certainly sketch out the range of possible explanations for homosexuality and examine the evidence for clues as to which explanation might be correct. At present, there is no single idea that explains all instances of homosexuality, but sketching the state of our present understanding is a worthwhile project, in part because it gives us another opportunity to explore the ways that evolution works. When we take on hard questions we often make significant breakthroughs.

In this chapter I'm going to focus almost exclusively on male homosexuality. That is because there have been many more studies of it than of female homosexuality, and thus more is known about it. That research "bias," if it is one, has been driven by the strong statistical association between male homosexuality and HIV-AIDS, thus making male homosexuality a candidate for medical research dollars—the lion's share of US federal research funding. This heavier research focus on male homosexuality means that we are in better position to explore its possible evolutionary basis.

There is some debate about the incidence of homosexuality in our species, but the more credible studies suggest that roughly 2 to 3% of men and 1 to 2% of women identify themselves as primarily homosexual. Note that we are not talking about the percentage of men or women who have had homosexual experiences or feelings; here we are focusing on those who prefer to couple exclusively with a same-sex partner. The key point is that figures like 2% are very far above the mutation rate. For reference, mutation rates are on the order of 0.0001%. In other words, homosexuality is not caused by new mutations every generation. To the extent that particular alleles influence sexual orientation, those alleles have apparently spread, because they now occur at frequencies too high to be explained by mutation alone. Let's explore some ways an evolutionist might explain the existence of male homosexuality.

PERHAPS HOMOSEXUALITY DOESN'T REDUCE FITNESS

The theory of evolution that we've developed so far says that selection will reduce the frequency of traits that lead to low reproductive success. A baseline assumption has been that exclusive homosexual mating preferences would lead to low reproductive success, and that's what lands homosexuality in the "puzzle" section of this book: Selection should have already eliminated it. This first explanation simply suggests that the assumption is incorrect and hence there is no puzzle. Perhaps gay men do produce as many kids as straight men. Obviously, if that were true, there would be no

selection against homosexuality. This "equal-fitness" explanation is a non-starter. The data show that, on average, homosexual men have far fewer children than heterosexual men have. You are probably not surprised by this finding, but scientists cannot rely on hunches; they have to collect and analyze the relevant data. OK, one down.

PERHAPS THERE ARE NO ALLELES FOR HOMOSEXUALITY

This explanation is at least theoretically possible and if it were correct it would cause the puzzle of homosexuality to evaporate. I don't expect you to immediately see why that is, so let's start at the beginning by saying what "alleles for x" might mean (where "x" is any phenotypic trait of interest to us, for example, homosexuality). It turns out that this phrase has several equally correct meanings and we should get familiar with them. You know that genes specify protein recipes, and that proteins coded by different genes interact with each other in building phenotypes. So, at that biochemical level, "alleles for x" means: alleles for a particular protein that, when present, makes the developmental process bend toward phenotype x. That's the molecular side of things and we now have quite good tools for studying it.

As you know evolutionists are interested in whether one trait can (or will) outcompete some alternative trait. For that to be possible these traits must be heritable (please review Figure 6-1 if you need to). They would be heritable if individuals who had trait x tended to have one allele and individuals who lacked trait x tended to have a different allele. So that's a second meaning of "alleles for x."

There are a variety of techniques for figuring out if there are "alleles for" a phenotypic trait. One is to recruit a bunch of people, sort them into two groups—those having and those lacking trait x—and then look at their genotypes. Of course there will be genetic differences among these people at many, many loci; every individual is unique. For example, some people will be tall because they carry more alleles for tallness. Right, but some folks *with x* will be tall and some folks *without x* will be tall, so alleles for tallness and alleles for shortness won't be concentrated in either group. The same should be true of other traits and their associated alleles; they should be equally represented in both groups. The only *systematic genetic differences* between the two groups should be...what? Right; the alleles affecting x!

A second technique for finding out if there are "alleles for x" invokes a key evolutionary concept: *heritability*. Heritability measures *how much of the population variation in a trait is caused by individuals having different alleles affecting the trait*. (Do you see that this is precisely what we have been discussing in asking whether there are 'alleles for x'?) Twin studies are a common way of assessing the heritability of a trait. (There is actually an array of twin study formats but here's one that's easy to understand.) Take a sample of identical twin pairs and a sample of fraternal twin pairs. For each individual determine if they have x. Now, for each pair of identical twins and for each pair of fraternal twins we want to record whether they match or don't match on x, and then we simply compare the degree of matching between the two types of twins.

There are three possible results of this comparison: Identical twins might be more similar, equally similar, or less similar than fraternal twins. The last result is quite rare and not especially interesting for our current purposes, so I'm going to ignore it. But if identicals are more similar than fraternals, what might that be telling us? We know that both kinds of twins share their mutual environments from the moment of conception, through gestation, childhood, and adolescence, until they leave their natal families. But there is a difference between the two kinds of twins, and it's a genetic difference. Identical twins are, of course, genetically identical, whereas fraternal twins share only ½ of their genes, no more than ordinary siblings. So if all twin pairs have shared environments but identicals are more phenotypically similar to each other, it must be because these twin pairs have been shaped by the same genotypes! Alternatively, if we found that identicals were no more similar to each other than fraternals are, we should conclude that greater genetic similarity makes no difference and therefore that shared environmental factors must account for the similarity between both kinds of twin pairs.

Two more points about heritability. I just categorized the interesting outcomes as "identicals more similar" or alternatively "identicals and fraternals equally similar." You know that the world is not generally black or white; everything tends to be a matter of degree. And the same is true of heritability; it too is a matter of degree. Thus, our estimate of heritability depends on *how much* more similar the identicals are than the fraternals. The greater the identical similarity is compared to the fraternal similarity, the greater the influence of genes is shaping individual differences on the trait. Now I turn to a minor point that you could probably intuit on your own. I gave an example where there were just two possible outcomes (x and no x). But we can just as easily compute heritabilities for any trait, including those like height or aggressiveness that vary along a continuous scale. Again, we would just compare the degree of similarity in identicals to the degree of similarity in fraternals. No problem.

Computed in these ways, heritability is a decimal number between 0 and 1. The higher the number, the more genes are shaping differences between individuals. I'll give you some examples to think about. The heritability of blood type is 1.0 (all the differences between individuals on this trait are due to genetic differences). The heritability of height is about 0.8; weight and IQ are both a bit lower, around 0.7. Many aspects of personality such as extraversion and agreeableness have heritabilities between 0.4 and 0.6. Of course it's also possible for a trait to have a heritability of 0.0 or close to it. Arm number would be an example. I know that is not what you expected but it is a helpful example. For most of the people you know, arm number is 2. Deviations from this number are occasionally seen, but what are they due to? To genetic differences or environmental differences? I don't think anybody is carrying alleles that say "make 3 arms" or "make 1 arm". No; differences from 2 arms (e.g., 0 or 1) are completely due to environmental causes (e.g., accidents). That's why the heritability is zero; because 0% of the arm-number differences between individuals are due to allele differences between them. Regardless of whether heritability is high (close to 1) or low (close to 0), genetic plus environmental effects must add up to 1. As we just saw for arm number, when allele differences explain none of the phenotypic differences then environmental effects explain all of them. To take height as another example, when allele differences explain 80% of the phenotypic differences, environmental differences must explain 20%.

It's finally time to get our payoff. Are there alleles for homosexuality? Yes, there are! Both of the two techniques I've shared with you have been used to answer that question, and they agree. The heritability of male homosexuality is about 0.5 (Pillard and Bailey, 1998). In other words, twin studies suggest that about half of the population variation in male sexual orientation is due to individuals having different alleles—alleles that push their sexual orientation in a particular direction. Remember, this conclusion means that the remaining half of the population variation (the part not explained by genetic differences) must be explained by environmental differences. I promise we'll return to that later. Also, the first technique has identified particular loci where gay and straight men tend to differ (Sanders et al., 2015), one at 8q12 and one at Xq28 (see Chapter 3 to remind yourself how to read locus addresses). Given that there are alleles for gayness, natural selection could raise or lower their frequency, potentially removing homosexuality from the population. So we now can see that explanation two is also wrong.

Let's recap. Selection can work only on traits that are heritable. But sexual orientation *is* heritable and homosexuality *does* decrease reproductive success. That means that homosexuality is still a puzzle because everything that we know about natural selection says that it should have eliminated homosexuality.

Really, everything? Think hard. Could homosexuality be altruistic? Let's consider that possibility.

PERHAPS HOMOSEXUALITY IS FAVORED BY KIN SELECTION

Remember, kin selection is an evolutionary process that maintains altruistic alleles in the population by systematically channeling benefits to other likely bearers of the same altruistic allele. Then, could kin selection keep alleles for gayness from being eliminated in the way that it keeps alleles for altruism from being eliminated? It could if (and only if) homosexual men disproportionately support the reproduction of relatives. By the meta-rules of science (Chapters 1 and 7) all candidate explanations stand or fall based on whether their predictions match our observations. By that standard I suggest that explanation three, (like one and two) is also wrong. While there may be individual exceptions, homosexual men do not systematically invest more resources in their nieces, nephews, brothers, and sisters *than do heterosexual men*. Both gay and straight men might be devoted uncles and brothers, supporting their relatives in various ways. But straight men are perpetuating their alleles for straightness via their own offspring. Because gay men have many fewer offspring, they would need to be more (probably much more) altruistic to their relatives for the gay allele to get passed on as often as the straight allele is. Over time the straight allele should replace the gay allele.

Where are we so far? Various methods strongly suggest that there are alleles for gayness, but that homosexuals tend not to pass them on. And they don't help their relatives pass them on either, at least not enough to make up for their own low numbers of offspring. Thus, our original puzzle still remains: Why do these alleles for homosexuality still exist? What other clues do we have? Well, we know that at least one of the gay alleles is on the X-chromosome (Xq28, mentioned above), the chromosome that men have one of but women have two of. I'll explain why that's interesting as I lay out explanation four.

PERHAPS ALLELES FOR GAYNESS ARE SEXUALLY ANTAGONISTIC

A sexually antagonistic allele is one that reduces reproductive success in one sex but increases it in the other. In general, the notion of a sexually antagonistic gene is not radical. Think of it this way: Natural selection is the ultimate statistician. If, *averaged over all the bodies* an allele is sitting in, it raises fitness, then the allele will tend to spread. This is definitionally true. Some of those bodies are older and some are younger; some are male and some are female. No matter. It could be that, on average, a particular allele—for example, a gay allele—reduces male fitness but increases female fitness by a larger amount. The positive and negative effects are not evenly spread over the whole population; they are clustered by sex, but so what? The average effect is positive, so the allele spreads. Are you skeptical?

Here is a noncontroversial example: nipples. Why do male mammals have them? They are nonfunctional in the sense that they do not nourish offspring, so they provide no obvious fitness benefits. Plus, they have a minus side; there are at least small metabolic costs to developing and maintaining nipples. So why don't males have featureless chests? Because the genes that produce nipples provide huge fitness benefits for females, benefits that far outweigh the relatively small fitness costs they produce in males.

But Xq28 has a special card to play. Ordinarily, any sexually antagonistic gene must produce a benefit in sex A that is larger than the cost it produces in sex B. Why did I say "ordinarily" instead of "always"? Because a gene on the X-chromosome (like Xq28) would not have to jump such a high hurdle. An X-chromosome gene has to produce a female benefit that is only half as large as the cost it inflicts on males. Why? Simply because, at each and every moment in evolutionary time, there are twice as many copies of any X-chromosome gene in female bodies as there are in male bodies (because females are XX and males are XY). In other words, females would be twice as effective at transmitting any X-chromosome gene as males would be, so a smaller female fitness benefit translates through them to a higher rate of gene transmission.

Let's study this possibility just a bit more. You know that, during evolution, mutation creates new alleles and selection evaluates them (Chapter 6). There are no rules or limits about what kinds of mutations can occur. Probably, in the billion or so years that sexual reproduction has existed, mutations for same-sex attraction have arisen many times in many species. Usually such genes would have been eliminated by selection because they lowered fitness. Somewhat less often, mutation produced a gene that caused homosexuality in one sex but provided a fitness benefit in the non-homosexual sex. How likely are those benefits to outweigh the fitness costs of homosexuality? Do you see that the answer to this question depends on what chromosome the gene is on? A mutation on an autosome would have to provide a female benefit at least as large as the male cost; but a mutation on the X-chromosome would have to provide a female benefit only half as large as the male cost. Thus, it was simply more likely that an X-chromosome homosexuality gene could meet the requirement of a net fitness benefit than it was that an autosomal homosexuality gene (one not on a sex chromosome) could.

If you are still with me, this is your next question: OK, but is that what happened in the case of Xq28? Specifically, how could we figure out if an Xq28-like genetic element predisposes male bodies to be homosexual but has nevertheless persisted in human populations because, when it occurs in female bodies, it elevates fitness? There have already been some ambitions attempts to answer that question (Camperio-Ciani et al. 2004) and I want to explain their methods and findings.

Before we review the details of their study, I want to clear up one small issue that can be confusing. Sometimes students have trouble imagining that an allele for homosexuality could increase the fitness of either sex. The assumption causing their confusion is the notion that the gene makes *both* sexes homosexual. That assumption is not at all required and is probably incorrect. Xq28, at least, clearly does not make both sexes homosexual. We know this from family studies; the sisters of gay men are not especially likely to be gay themselves. Here is a different way to think about how an Xq28-like gene might work. If you don't think of it as "a gene for homosexuality" but instead think of it as "a gene for liking to have sex with men," then you can see that such a gene could have opposite effects on male and female reproductive success. I am not claiming to know exactly how it works—nobody yet knows. I simply want to suggest how a "homosexuality allele" might express itself differently in men and women. OK, now let's see what Camperio-Ciani and his

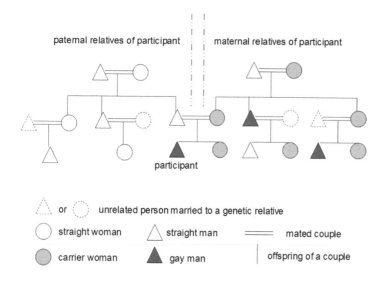

Figure 11-1. The diagram shows a homosexual male participant; his mother, father, and sister; one brother and one sister of each of his parents (the participant's aunts and uncles); the mates (shown dashed because they are not genetic relatives of the participant and therefore irrelevant) of these aunts and uncles; some of the aunts' and uncles' offspring (cousins of the participant), and the participant's mother's and father's parents. A man's X-chromosome comes from his maternal line. Why? Men have unmatched sex chromosomes, X and Y, and produce roughly equal numbers of X-bearing and Y-bearing sperm. Females have two X's, so all their eggs are X-bearing. When a mother's egg unites with a Y-bearing sperm, a son is conceived; when her egg unites with an X-bearing sperm, a daughter is conceived. This means that a male absolutely got his X-chromosome from his mother; if he had gotten an X from his father, he would be a female. These facts alone determine the pattern of X-chromosome sharing.

coworkers discovered in their northern Italian study population.

Their study began by recruiting both homosexual and heterosexual "participants," about 100 of each. But it is actually the relatives of these participants who provide the essential data for testing the hypothesis that Xq28 (or some other X-chromosome allele) *both predisposes male homosexuality and is sexually antagonistic.* To explore this hypothesis, we need to know which relatives of the homosexual and heterosexual participants are themselves homosexual, and we also need to know how many children each relative had. Thus, relatives of the participants were censused regarding their sexual orientation and their fertility (number of offspring). Next—and this step is critical—the relatives were grouped by how likely they were to have the same X-chromosome as the participant. All men, both homosexual and heterosexual men, have certain relatives with whom they are likely to share their X-chromosome and other relatives

with whom it is very unlikely that they would share an X-chromosome. (This sharing pattern is very predictable from basic genetic principles, and I will explain it soon.)

This approach allows the authors to test two key predictions of the sexually antagonistic Xq28 hypothesis. The first prediction involves the homosexual participants' male relatives, and the second involves their female relatives. First, if a gene on the X-chromosome is predisposing a man to be homosexual, then homosexuality should be more common among those male relatives who have the same X-chromosome he does, but not among those male relatives who do not share his X-chromosome. This natural contrast between the two types of relatives lets us see if something on the X-chromosome seems to be making a difference in sexual orientation. Likewise, the second prediction relies on this same kind of contrast, but it focuses on the homosexual participants' female relatives. If the hypothesized X-chromosome allele is sexually antagonistic, female relatives who have the same X-chromosome as a homosexual participant should have elevated fitness (more children). In contrast, women who have a homosexual male relative but do not share his X-chromosome should not have elevated fitness. These two predictions are both tested by Camperio-Ciani. To appreciate the tests, you will now need to understand which kinds of relatives are likely to share an X-chromosome and which kinds are not. Let's take a look at Figure 11-1.

Which men are most likely to share an X-chromosome with a participant? Certainly not the participant's father; his father gave him a Y, not an X. Every participant got his X-chromosome from his mother but, of course, his mother is not a man. The *men* who are most likely to have the same X-chromosome as a participant are his mother's brother (who most likely inherited it from the participant's mother's mother), and his mother's sister's son (his maternal cousin, who would have inherited it from the participant's mother's sister.) None of the men whom a participant is related to through his father (his paternal relatives) could have his same X-chromosome because, remember, his X-chromosome did not come from his father's lineage. Similar thinking will show that the female relatives likely to share a participant's X-chromosome are, again, his maternal relatives.

What can we do with these genetic patterns? The Xq28 hypothesis predicts that the male relatives of homosexual participants who share their X-chromosome (their maternal relatives) should be more likely to be homosexual than the male relatives who do not share their X-chromosome (their paternal relatives). But, because heterosexual participants presumably lack the X-chromosome allele for homosexuality, sharing an X-chromosome with them should not elevate the chance of being homosexual. Put another way, the maternal relatives of heterosexuals should be no more likely to be homosexual than their paternal relatives.

Participants	Elevated number of homosexual male relatives?		Female relatives fitter on average?	
	Maternal	**Paternal**	**Maternal**	**Paternal**
Straight	no	no	no	no
Gay	yes	no	yes	no

There is an equally important second prediction, about female relatives. According to the sexually antagonistic hypothesis, the female maternal relatives of homosexual participants (those who share their X-chromosome) should have higher fitness than their paternal relatives, *and* higher fitness than either maternal or paternal relatives of heterosexuals. All of these predictions are summarized in Figure 11-2. And all of these eight predictions were verified by the study. Eight out of eight is quite good.

At this point, do I dare to add another hypothesis? Well, I must, because we haven't paid any attention to the environmental side. Remember, the heritability of male homosexuality is about 0.5. That says that 50% of the variation in male sexual orientation is due to genetic differences between individuals, but that leaves the other 50% that must be due to environmental differences.

PERHAPS CERTAIN FAMILY COMPOSITIONS PREDISPOSE MALE HOMOSEXUALITY

Previous research by Ray Blanchard and A. F. Bogaert (1996) supports the idea that men with multiple older brothers

Figure 11-2. Predictions of the sexually-antagonistic-allele hypothesis. Elevated frequencies of homosexuality are predicted only among male maternal relatives of homosexual participants; elevated reproductive success is predicted only among female maternal relatives of homosexual participants.

are more likely to be homosexual. Note that, however we might imagine this happening, it must be an environmental rather than a genetic effect. Having more or fewer older brothers cannot possibly affect your genotype. The "older-brother effect" might operate after birth, growing up with those older brothers or, as Blanchard argues, it might operate in the womb. The data strongly suggest that it is a brother effect and not a sibling effect. Having a higher number of older brothers increases a boy's chances of becoming homosexual, while having a higher number of older sisters does not. Two facts strongly suggest what is called a uterine effect rather than a socialization effect. First, having a higher number of older step-brothers (or half-brothers related only through the father) does not increase the likelihood that a boy will grow up to be homosexual. On the other hand, even older brothers who do not grow up in the same household do, as long as they have the same mother. This older-brother effect is substantial. One older brother increases a boy's chance of being homosexual by about 33%, but be careful how you interpret this. We need to remember that the overall rate of male homosexuality is low (2% to 3%). So, if we use the 2% estimate, an increase of 33% will raise the likelihood of being homosexual from 2.0% to 2.7%. Each additional older brother would produce a similar increase, so three older brothers would essentially double the chance of being homosexual (from 2% to 4%). Just as older sisters do not seem to affect a boy's sexual orientation, neither older sisters nor brothers affect a girl's chance of being homosexual.

How might this kind of uterine effect operate? In other words, what process could allow the sex of your mother's previous fetuses

to affect your sexual orientation? Here is the mechanism that Blanchard suggested: Because a male fetus has a Y-chromosome, (and women don't) he will produce proteins (from genes on his Y) that are foreign to his mother's body. She in turn will produce antibodies (immunological defenses) against these proteins. And the amount of these anti-Y antibodies she produces will probably increase with each son she carries. These maternally produced antibodies might then interfere with the Y-derived proteins of subsequent sons during their fetal development. This maternal interference could affect the development of the male-typical traits that the fetus's Y-derived proteins are trying to produce. Whether or not it is caused by maternal antibody interference is not yet clear, but a brain region involved in the regulation of male-typical sexual behavior differs between homosexual and heterosexual men, with homosexuals' brains resembling those of heterosexual women. Thus, while we cannot say exactly how the older-brother effect operates, Camperio-Ciani and his team did observe it: Their homosexual participants had a preponderance of older brothers, but their heterosexual participants did not.

To summarize this study, two different biological factors could be shaping male homosexuality. A particular allele, apparently located on the X-chromosome, might increase the likelihood of being homosexual, and this allele may persist in the population because it is sexually antagonistic, increasing the reproductive success of female relatives who carry the same X-chromosome. In addition to these X-chromosome effects, men who have a higher number of older brothers are more likely to be homosexual than men with fewer older brothers.

As mentioned above, previous heritability studies indicate that about 50% of the variation in sexual orientation is due to genetic differences and 50% is due to environmental differences. In the Camprio-Ciani study the X-chromosome effect explained 14% of the differences and the older-brother effect explained 8% of the differences. This means that 36% (50-14) of the genetic effects and 42% (50-8) of the environmental effects remain to be discovered and measured.

PERHAPS ALLELES FOR GAYNESS INCREASE REPRODUCTION IN HETEROSEXUALS

This proposal is similar to the sexual antagonism hypothesis. Every allele needs some way of getting into the next generation, otherwise it won't be here for us to observe; natural selection will have already removed it from the population. The sexual antagonism hypothesis (above) suggests that the genes of gay men get into the next generation via the increased reproductive success of their female maternal relatives. This new hypothesis is indifferent about whether it's males or females who benefit from gay genes. Its logic depends on two assumptions, neither of which is at odds with what we know about genetics. First, it assumes that gayness is polygenic (Chapter 3), meaning that alleles at multiple loci jointly influence sexual orientation. Many traits are known to be polygenic and we already have evidence that alleles on at least two chromosomes are associated with sexual orientation so this assumption is plausible. Second, it assumes that (allow me to say it this way), to cross the threshold to being homosexual, one would need to have a gay allele at enough of the relevant loci (or at certain combinations of the relevant loci). This pattern is also plausible and has the name "dosage effect." The more loci carrying an allele boosting effect x, the more likely effect x is to show up in the phenotype. Combining these assumption we should expect that there will be more individuals who have *some* of those gay alleles (or allele combinations) but remain below the threshold (and hence are heterosexual) than there are individuals who have enough to cross the threshold (and hence are gay). The only other thing we need to make this all work is that the individuals who have these alleles but are below the threshold have higher than average reproductive success.

Brendan Zietsch (el al. 2008) put together a big team of researchers to test this hypothesis and found quite good support for it. Using a sample of almost 5,000 twins they found that "gender-atypical men" are more likely to be non-heterosexual. But, importantly, the gender-atypical men who are heterosexual have an elevated number of opposite-sex sex partners, suggesting they are unusually attractive to women. And, critically for the hypothesis, they were able to show that both effects (non-heterosexuality and increased attractiveness in heterosexuals) were due to the same genetic influences. This provides another route to the next generation for gay genes: When present in lower dosages they may increase attractiveness to opposite-sex sex partners.

CHAPTER SUMMARY

Just like altruism, homosexuality is an evolutionary puzzle. Male homosexuality has been more thoroughly examined than female homosexuality, so it is easier to address at present. Differences in male sexual orientation seem to be heritable, with roughly 50% of the variation explained by genetic differences between individuals. The locus with the best documented influence on male homosexuality seems to be Xq28. There is evidence from family studies that an allele at this locus is sexually antagonistic, predisposing both a homosexual orientation in males and elevated reproductive success in female carriers.

CITED REFERENCES

A. Camperio-Ciani, F. Corna & C. Capiluppi (2004) "Evidence for maternally inherited factors favouring male homosexuality and promoting female fecundity." *Proceedings of the Royal Society of London Series B-Biological Sciences 271*: 2217–2221.

R. Blanchard & A. F. Bogaert (1996). "Biodemographic comparisons of homosexual and heterosexual men in the Kinsey interview data." Archives of Sexual Behavior 25: 551–579.

R. Pillard & J. M. Bailey (1998). "Human Sexual Orientation Has a Heritable Component." *Human Biology, 70*: 347-365.

A. R. Sanders, E. R. Martin, G.W. Beecham, S. Guo, K. Dawood, G. Rieger, J. A. Badner, E. S. Gershon, R. S. Krishnappa, A. B. Kolundzija, J. Duan, P. V. Gejman & J. M. Bailey (2015) "Genome-wide scan demonstrates significant linkage for male sexual orientation." *Psychological Medicine, 45*: 1379–1388.

Brendan P. Zietsch, Katherine I. Morley, Sri N. Shekar, Karin J.H. Verweij, Matthew C. Keller, Stuart Macgregor, Margaret J. Wright, J. Michael Bailey, Nicholas G. Martin (2008). "Genetic factors predisposing to homosexuality may increase mating success in heterosexuals." *Evolution and Human Behavior, 29*: 424-433.

FIGURE CREDIT

11-2: Image created by Judith Geiger.

CHAPTER 12

CLASSIFYING ORGANISMS

People have been classifying organisms since at least the time of ancient Greeks, long before Darwin proposed his evolutionary views. In fact, the strong human tendency to think in categorical terms has been extensively studied by modern psychologists and has a plausible evolutionary basis. So it is not surprising that it feels natural to us to also group organisms together into more- and less-similar types.

We have already glimpsed two simplified biological classifications, of reptiles in Chapter 2 and of primates in Chapter 8. Now were going to consider how such groupings are created and to ask if some kinds of classification schemes are inherently more defensible than others. Does it make more sense to group together animals that have mammary glands than to group together animals that have stripes? Are both grouping schemes equally valid? Do we have any guidance besides our preferences and intuitions? Suppose I really like stripes; why shouldn't I use the presence/absence of stripes as my classification principle? Someone else might think that size would be the best criterion: Put everything less than 1 mm across in one group, everything bigger than 1 mm but smaller than 2 mm in another group, and so on. What's wrong with that? That is precisely the problem; we could have as many classification schemes as we have people dreaming them up. If everyone uses his own scheme we have no effective way of communicating.

CLASSIFICATIONS BASED ON EVOLUTIONARY HISTORY

In this chapter, we'll see that there is an objective principle to guide us: Our classification schemes should reflect what happened during evolution. All organisms are linked together over the history of life on Earth in a massive, branching tree. This tree defines their *phylogeny, their pattern of ancestor–descendant relationships.* An objective classification (one based on a real pattern in the world, rather than on personal preferences) would simply reflect those ancestor-descendant relationships: It would be based on phylogeny. It is important to begin our discussion by recognizing that all living organisms are related to each other. Why else would they all use the same molecules (DNA, RNA, etc.) to encode and interpret their hereditary material? Humans and slime molds and nematodes and algae are all descended from the original DNA-based life form. But how does relatedness help with classification? Do we just put all DNA-based life forms (all the life we know of) in one group and stop there? Actually, we can do much better. Because the tree of life is constantly branching, we can ask how old or new any given branch is; did it emerge early in the history of life, or did it appear just recently?

To think about this more concretely, let's consider the simplified example in Figure 12-1. This figure is arranged with form (phenotype) arrayed horizontally and with time running vertically. Species

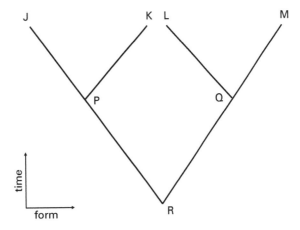

that are close together on the horizontal axis, for example K and L, look similar. Species that are close together on the vertical axis existed close in evolutionary time. For example, J, K, L, and M are all contemporary species, alive now. P and Q are both extinct but they lived at the same time in the past. R lived even longer ago.

What Figure 12-1 depicts is the order of branching that connects this set of species; it shows the phylogenetic tree for this group. R split into two lineages that eventually gave rise to P and Q, and then each of those split into two lineages. Thus R is the ancestor of all the other species. Likewise, P is the (more recent) ancestor of J and K, and Q is the (more recent) ancestor of L and M. The preferred classification method, phylogenetic classification, simply reflects the pattern of branching. Thus (this is important), J and K are put in one group because of their shared common ancestor, P; and L and M are put in a different group because of their different common ancestor, Q.

Figure 12-1. The vertical axis is time and the horizontal axis is form (morphology).

Of all the critters depicted in Figure 12-1, K and L are phenotypically the most similar to each other (reflected in how close they are on the horizontal axis). Nevertheless, classification based on phylogeny would *not* group them together. Mere similarity is not the deciding factor; what matters is ancestry. K belongs with J because they are both descendants of P. And, likewise, L belongs with M because of their shared ancestry. Here's an analogy (that's not really an analogy; it's actually the very same principle). You're in a certain family because of your ancestry, because of who your mother and father are. If you meet somebody who looks like you in your French class you can't suddenly be in her family no matter how similar you are. You have different parents and your parentage defines your family membership. Remember the idea of convergence from Chapter 8? Convergence can cause distantly related species to evolve similar adaptations. If we just use similarity to create our classification we could easily be fooled by cases of convergence and mistakenly group unrelated species together. For example, because of their similarity, Aristotle thought whales were fish. Now we recognize that the similarity between whales and fish is a result of convergence due to their similar environments. The order of branching on the tree of life tells that whales are not fish and that Aristotle's classification was incorrect.

When we base classification on phylogeny—on the order of branching—the groups we form must be *monophyletic*. A group is *monophyletic if all of its members are more closely related to each other than they are to any member of any other group*. A group could fail this test in either of two ways: by including members it should not

include or by failing to include members it should. Assume for purposes of this example that the phylogenetic relationships depicted in Figure 12-1 are correct, that it accurately represents the order of branching in the tree of life. Against that background let's suppose that, at present, species J, K, and L are all assigned to the genus *Paranthropus* and that species M is assigned to the genus *Australopithecus* (these are two genera that you'll meet in Chapter 14). In that case, is *Paranthropus* monophyletic? No, it is not, because L is more closely related to M (a species of *Australopithecus*) than it is to the members of its own genus, *Paranthropus*. The question is not whether or not *Paranthropus* (or any genus) *should* be monophyletic. All genera should be monophyletic! The question is, what species would need to be included or excluded to make each genus monophyletic? Given the phylogeny depicted in Figure 12-1, J and K would belong in one genus (say *Paranthropus*), and L would need to be placed in the same genus as M (say *Australopithecus*). That way both of these genera would be monophyletic. Then the members of *Australopithecus*, L and M, would be more closely related to each other than either is to any member of any other genus. And the same would be true of the members of *Paranthropus*, J and K. A genus is monophyletic if all of its member species have a single ancestor that has no descendants placed in a different genus. Please convince yourself that this requirement does not hold for the set of species [J,K,L], nor for the set [M], but that it does hold for each of the sets [J,K] and [L,M]. Of course monophyly is not just the gold standard for genera; it is the gold standard for every taxonomic level. Phyla should be monophyletic; kingdoms should be monophyletic; and so on.

WHY MUST EVOLUTIONARY CLASSIFICATIONS BE HIERARCHICAL?

Classifications based on the order of branching—on phylogeny—are inevitably hierarchical. Hierarchical simply means that smaller, more exclusive groups are nested within larger, more *in*clusive groups. Just as J and K form one group and L and M form another group at the same classificatory level, a larger group can be formed from all six (J, K, L, M, P, and Q) because they all share a more ancient common ancestor, R. What we have done in forming this more inclusive group is simply to trace back to a more ancient common ancestor, who necessarily links up more descendant species. When we form that larger group *all* the descendants of R must be included.

Figure 12-2 conveys the rationale for hierarchical classification with a tiny subset of the (perhaps 20 million) kinds of organisms on the planet. It shows two groups of vertebrates, mammals and birds (there are other groups of vertebrates not shown because of space limitations). For each of those major groups it shows some of their subgroups. Finally, for just a single subgroup of mammals—the primates—it shows some of its members. All of the subgroups have more members that could be depicted in a larger diagram. In the Figure smaller

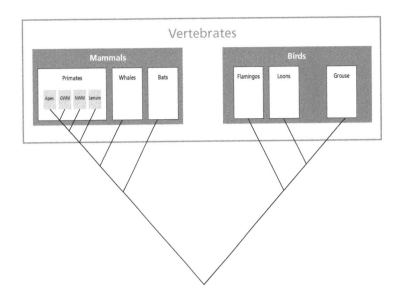

Figure 12-2. Less inclusive groups are nested within larger groups.

groups are nested within larger more inclusive groups. Superimposed on this classification we see the branching phylogenetic tree that produced all of these creatures. If this diagram is correct (which I believe it is), it can be interpreted as saying that lemurs, monkeys, and apes share a more recent common ancestor than any of those primates do with, say, bats. Similarly, it says that bats, whales, and primates share a more recent common ancestor with each other than any of them do with any bird. Finally, it says that all mammals and all birds share a more remote common ancestor than any of the ancestors just mentioned. The key idea to grasp in that the nesting of smaller groups within larger groups exactly matches the pattern of branching on the phylogenetic tree. Nesting is simply a reflection of the natural groups that are created as trunks split into major branches, and major branches divide into limbs, and limbs divide into twigs, and so on.

CLADISTICS: A TOOL FOR CREATING PHYLOGENETIC CLASSIFICATIONS

Phylogenetic approaches are not the only possible ways of doing classification. As I mentioned, people have been classifying organisms for centuries, long before they had evolutionary principles to guide them. Those older methods of classification are all based on what we could call "overall similarity." They group organisms together on the basis of how many traits they share. This approach can also produce hierarchical classification. Smaller groups would include those species that shared the largest number of traits, and our groups would naturally grow bigger and more inclusive as species that shared smaller numbers of traits were included. But problems would arise. For example, a platypus lays eggs and it has a bill and webbed feet, traits that make it similar to birds. Perhaps it should be grouped with the birds? How would you decide? Overall similarity can be inconclusive and different practitioners could disagree. Not good. We want an objective classification method.

The central tenet of the phylogenetic approach is that there is only one tree of life and it branched in a particular, idiosyncratic way as life evolved on our planet. The particular branching structure of that tree is therefore a theoretically defensible and objective way of classifying organisms. It's theoretically defensible because evolution by natural selection is the overarching framework within which we interpret and understand everything about organisms. And it's objective because there *is*

an actual tree of life which exists independently of any preconceptions we might have about which creatures are more and less similar. Let's return to our problematic platypus. Is it a bird or a mammal (Figure 12-3)? We can argue all day about whether it is more similar to birds or more similar to mammals, and still not agree. But in the history of life on earth, the platypus arose as a twig on one particular branch. Was it a twig on the bird branch (hypothesis B in Figure 12-3) or was it a twig on the mammal branch (hypothesis M)? It couldn't have been both anymore that your birthplace could be both Boston and Bogotá. You had one birthplace and the platypus had one "birth branch." If B is correct the platypus is a bird; if M is correct it's a mammal. Problem solved, sort of . . .

Thanks to the platypus, you now understand what a phylogenetic method *should* do. It should discover what actually happened as the tree of life pushed out new shoots and those shoots grew into branches that pushed out more shoots; it should discover the order and pattern of branching—and then reflect that branching arrangement in the classification it produces. The only trouble with the phylogenetic approach to classification is this: All that branching happened in the past and we were not there to see it! So, *if we knew the order of branching*, that information would be an ideal basis for a phylogenetic classification; but how can we know it? That is what *cladistic methods* are for, to *deduce* the order of branching from the similarities among species.

Wait a minute! Similarities? Didn't I just argue that relying on similarities as a basis for our classifications is problematic? I did, and it is, if we treat all similarities as equivalent. As mentioned above, old-school classifiers try to measure lots of traits—as many as they can—and group together the organisms that share the most traits. In contrast, cladists (scientists who use cladistic methods) intentionally ignore some similarities! You might wonder how throwing away some of the data could produce a more acceptable result. But it often can, and of course I have an analogy for you. If you want to hear what your friend is saying to you but there is a lot of background noise (for example traffic noise or your neighbor's loud music), you try to sort through all the sound reaching you ears and "throw away" all the parts that are not your friend's words; you try to edit out the background noise and just pay attention to the "signal" of your friend's voice. Cladists are trying to do the same—edit out the background noise in the pattern of similarity. To a cladist there are two kinds of similarities: *primitive* similarities and *derived* similarities. Derived similarities are the signal—the part that carries the useful information—and primitive similarities are the noise. Let's learn the difference.

PRIMITIVE AND DERIVED SIMILARITIES

As we begin I want to clarify one small issue of terminology: the distinction between traits and states. A trait is a feature and a state is one of several possible versions of the feature. Examples always help. "Eye number" is a trait and it has a variety of possible states: "two" is common, but we've also seen "zero" in many cave-dwellers. In most spiders its

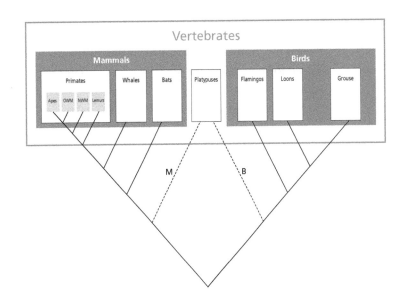

state is "eight." "Tail" is another trait and its states are just "present" or "absent". In other words, some traits we count or measure to determine their state; others we simply note whether or not they are present. In any case, when we look for similarities to create our classifications, the data are always states; we are looking for organisms that have similar states. But remember, a cladist is interested only in the derived similarities and ignores the "noise" of the primitive similarities. So how do we distinguish between primitive and derived similarities?

A primitive similarity is one that was present in the common ancestor of the entire group whose members you are trying to classify. A derived similarity is one that has evolved since the common ancestor of that group. Here's an example. Let's say we are trying to deduce the relationships among mammals; in other words, we want to discover the natural kinds of mammals based on their phylogeny. To get us started with our first cladistic exercise I

Figure 12-3. The problem of apparent intemediates. See text for fuller discussion.

am going to simply stipulate that having four legs is a primitive similarity for mammals (trust me for now; soon I'll show you how to figure that out that part). Saying that the state of having four legs is primitive simply means that the common ancestor of all mammals had four legs. What then would be a derived "leg state" for mammals? It would be having *anything but four legs*. As you know, there are some mammals that have flippers and a tail. Cladists would say that, because whales and dolphins share the derived state of having flippers and a tail, whales and dolphins are more closely related to each other than they are to the rest of mammals. Are there other kinds of mammals that also lack the primitive state of having four legs? Sure; some have two legs and two wings. Again a cladist would say these winged mammals (bats) should be grouped together because they share a particular derived state. Remember, sharing the primitive state of four-leggedness tells us *nothing* about the relationships among the rest of mammals. It's just the background noise retained from some earlier period in evolutionary history and thus gives no information about branching on the mammalian part of the tree we're studying at the moment. The fact that weasels and antelope and anteaters and chimpanzees all have four legs does *not* mean they are especially closely related; the common ancestor of all mammals had four legs, so the animals just mentioned (like most mammals) have simply retained that primitive state. If we wanted to finish classifying the remainder of mammals we could consider other derived leg states (like two, what we have) and we could also consider traits beyond legs, for example body covering. If the primitive mammalian body covering is hair, then mammals that have some derived covering, such as horny plates,

should be grouped together (pangolins; check them out!). And I can continue with various traits until I have found all the natural groups of mammals on the basis of their sharing some derived state with each other that they don't share with other mammals.

Now watch carefully. I have been searching for shared derived states to define various natural groups within the mammals. But how did I decide that mammals are a natural group? By the very same method. I used the trait presence/absence of mammary glands and determined that absence was the primitive state. That means that animals that do have mammary glands share a derived state and therefore form a natural group (mammals). So you see, the method is versatile in that it can be used to form more and less inclusive groups. Just remember that—and this is important—what is primitive and what is derived will change as you move up and down these levels. That's not a problem; it's required. Anything that is now primitive had an evolutionary origin farther in the past and was, at that point, derived. Let's quickly review our cladistic tour of mammals to exemplify this point: Compared to other terrestrial vertebrates (birds, amphibians, etc.), mammals share the derived state of having mammary glands; that makes mammals a natural group. But, within mammals, mammary glands are primitive, having been present in the common ancestor of the entire group.

For the purpose of getting started with cladistics, I stipulated that four-leggedness was the primitive state for mammals. Did you question my assumption? If so, you are right to recognize that we cannot just accept such assertions. To use cladistic tools *we need reliable methods for determining which of two (or more) states is primitive and which is derived for any given group.* Fortunately, cladists have three methods, since none of these methods is guaranteed to give the right answer every time. I'll list the methods and then explain them: 1) fossils, 2), development, 3) outgroup comparison.

The fossil method is the easiest if you're lucky enough to have the right fossils. This method says that the state present earlier in the fossil record is the primitive state. That makes sense, primitive states precede derived states. The development method is similar but instead of looking at sequences of fossils it looks at the sequence during development; this method assumes that the state present earlier in development is primitive. The justification for this approach is the observation that selection works in a cumulative way, layering new adaptations on older ones (Chapter 7), and that development reflects the temporal layering of these adaptations. Let me give an example that will not only illustrate this second method but will also usefully foreshadow a theme of the next two chapters. We know from the fossil record that our African ape ancestors walked on all fours, whereas we humans walk on two legs. If development correctly reflected the primitive and derived states then, during development, humans should walk on all fours before they walk on two legs. As you probably know, most humans do exactly that, crawling before they walk.

The out-group comparison method will require more words. This method says that the state present in

the outgroup is primitive. An outgroup is simply some creature that you are pretty sure does not belong in the group whose members you are trying to classify. To stick with our previous example, if I'm trying to find the natural groups of mammals, then the outgroup could *not* be a kangaroo or a sloth, since we think that both of these animals *are* mammals. The outgroup would have to be a non-mammal, something more distantly related to mammals like a bird, a lizard, or a frog. The assumption is that the trait state present in the outgroup was the one that was prevalent earlier in the evolutionary process. In this sense the outgroup comparison method treats the outgroup as a living fossil. It will

Figure 12-4. Using the ourgroup to define the primitive trait state, then using the derived trait state to define groups.

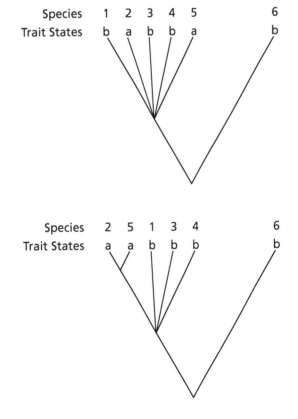

be helpful to see exactly how this method is applied (Figure 12-4).

In the top half of the Figure 12-4 we have five species (1–5) and we'd like to find the phylogenetic relationships among them so we can classify them. We also have decided to use another species (6) as the outgroup because we believe it is more distantly related to them than they are to each other. Finally we see that some species have trait state a, and some have the alternative trait state, b. This is all the information we need. What trait state does the outgroup have? Trait state b. From its presence in the outgroup we know that state b is primitive; hence we should *not* use its presence to determine which members of the 1-5 group are more closely related; b is noise, forget about it. The only useful thing about knowing that b is primitive is that it tells us that trait state a is derived. We can and should use the presence of state a to determine which members of the 1–5 group are more closely related.

In the bottom half of Figure 12–4 we see this solution. Because species 2 and 5 share the derived state, a, they are grouped together as closely related. The assumption is that they share a relatively recent common ancestor who was the first member of the 1–5 group to evolve state a, and who passed this derived state on to its descendants 2 and 5. What do we do with species 1, 3, and 4? Nothing, at present. This particular analysis didn't provide any information about how they are related to each other. They share the primitive state, b, which tells us only that they have probably retained it from a more distant ancestor who lived before the origins of the 1–5 group. The ancientness of state b is attested by its presence in the outgroup, species 6. To figure out how species 1, 3, and 4 are related to each other we

would need to apply the same procedure using different traits.

Let's come back to real animals and practice using our cladistic methods to find more groups of mammals. We can base our analysis on any trait we want as long as we begin by determining which state is primitive and which is derived. Let's choose the trait "mode of birth" and use outgroup comparison to determine the primitive state for mammals. We can pick any outgroup so long as it's not a mammal. How about a frog? Their mode of birth is egg-laying; ok, one vote for egg-laying being the primitive state. Let's pick another outgroup, say a lizard. Oh, egg-laying again. Let's try a bird as the outgroup; egg-laying again. We're getting a lot of votes for egg-laying; maybe that is the primitive mode of birth for mammals. Is there any evidence for that? Yes, there are some mammals that lay eggs—the platypus and the echidna—apparently retaining the primitive state. What did this exercise tell us about the relationships among various mammal species? First, it doesn't tell us anything about the relationship between the platypus and the echidna. Sharing the primitive state does *not* indicate closeness of relatedness. But the results of our outgroup comparison suggest that mammals that share the derived state, giving birth to live young, should be (and are) grouped together (Figure 12-5). They are called *therian* mammals.

Perhaps it would be useful here to revisit the status of the platypus, since it has reared its peculiar head again. Back in Figure 12-3 we asked a question that we never directly answered. Now that we're fully tooled-up as cladists we can. Is a platypus a bird or a mammal? Note that, to answer that question, we have to jump up one level. We're not asking about relationships *within mammals* (what are the proper groupings of mammals?). Instead we're asking about relationships *within vertebrates* (what are the proper groupings of vertebrates?). We're trying to decide what kind of vertebrate the platypus is: Does it belong in the bird group or in the mammal group? Every group is recognized and defined by *sharing the derived trait that appeared in the first member the group*. For example, within mammals bats are defined by their wings, and whales are defined by their fin/tail structure. But at the next level up in the hierarchy, what derived feature defines (and includes) all mammals? And in contrast, what derived feature defines (and includes) all birds? The answers, as you may know, are mammary glands for mammals, and feathers for birds. We now have our answer. The platypus has mammary glands but no feathers. The platypus is a mammal because of the particular derived trait it has (and not a bird, because the derived trait it lacks).

One more insight will bring your picture of phylogenetic (cladistic) methods up to date. Because we can now sequence entire genomes with relative ease, actual A,T,C,G sequences can be used as states. Outgroup comparison is typically used to determine which A,T,C,G sequence states are primitive and which are derived (although in Chapter 16, I'll explain that DNA can now be extracted from some fossils, so primitive states can now also be determined by the fossil method), and species sharing the derived sequences are grouped together. Of course, this method can be replicated with many different loci (since there are so many)

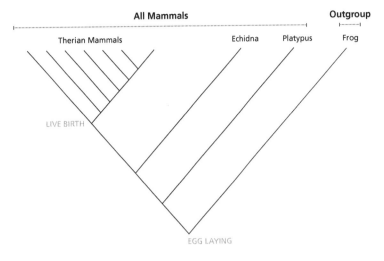

Figure 12-5. Cladistic grouping of mammals based on the mode of birth.

and different outgroups. This is genuine "big-data" research, given the size of genomes, and is producing some exciting (OK, exciting for phylogeneticists) revisions of older classification schemes based only on anatomy. For example, a recent DNA-based study involving most of the major groups of living birds revealed that falcons do not cluster with other raptors (hawks, eagles, and the like) but instead belong on the same evolutionary branch with parrots (Jarvis et al. 2014). (If they were on the same *physical* branch the parrots would be justifiably nervous.)

WHY IT IS ALWAYS MORE DIFFICULT TO APPLY CLADISTIC METHODS TO FOSSILS THAN TO LIVING FORMS.

Let me remind you what the cladistic method is trying to do. It aims to capture the pattern of branching on the tree of life. It recognizes those branches by assuming that derived states are evolutionary novelties and that the organisms sharing a derived trait must therefore lie on the same branch—the branch where that novelty arose. So far we've just been applying this technique to living animals. But we can and should use cladistic techniques to classify all organisms, whether they're living or extinct, because they were all produced by the same branching tree of life. True, some of those branches didn't reach the present (because of extinction), but they still have a specific placement on the tree and that placement should determine how we classify them.

That said, there are two reasons why it's more difficult to use cladistic methods with fossils, one obvious and one more subtle. The obvious reason is that we have less information about extinct creatures; we typically have few specimens and they are fragmentary and poorly preserved. The subtle one is depicted in Figure 12-6, where I've chosen to illustrate it with two genera, *Homo* and *Australopithecus*. There is one living species in the genus *Homo* but all the species of *Australopithecus* are extinct. All the evidence (Chapter 14) suggests that *Australopithecus* is the closest relative *Homo* (right, chimps are our closest *living* relatives, but we have closer relatives that are now extinct). Remember, my purpose is to demonstrate the special challenge of doing cladistics with fossil forms.

To see why, let's consider two hypothetical, recently discovered but still unnamed fossils that I'll call taxon j and taxon k. Figure 12-6 assumes we are omniscient and know their true evolutionary history. Taxon j branched off the *Homo* lineage long after *Homo* diverged from *Australopithecus*. Thus taxon j will probably have many of the derived traits that *Homo* has accumulated since it divergence from *Australopithecus*, and will therefore "obviously" be *Homo*. On the other hand taxon k branched off the *Australopithecus* lineage, but it did so very close to the divergence point between *Australopithecus* and *Homo*. Now, looking back from our vantage point in the present, we know that *Australopithecus* and *Homo* are going to become different enough that they won't just be different species; they'll be different genera. But close to the divergence point they will still be quite similar (remember the lessons of gradualism!). So even though taxon k belongs in *Australopithecus* just as much as taxon j belongs in *Homo* (because of where they each branched from), it will be *much harder to recognize* that taxon k belongs with *Australopithecus*. At the time that taxon k lived, the differences

Figure 12-6. Hypothetical diagram of the order of branching in part of the human lineage.

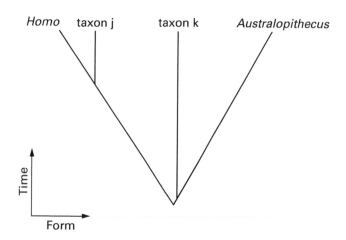

between *Homo* and *Australopithecus* were minimal. We will meet these challenges in a more-than-hypothetical way in the chapters that follow.

CHAPTER SUMMARY

Classification of organisms is based on similarities in states. An objective (based in external reality) classification scheme should reflect the branching pattern of the evolutionary tree that links all life on earth. Cladistics, by focusing on shared derived similarities, attempts to capture that sequence of branching. It groups species on the same branch together. Its methods can and should be iterated using many kinds of traits—including genetic traits—and many outgroups. Cladistic methods are applicable to both living and extinct creatures but can be more difficult to apply to species that lie close to the base of a branch.

CITED REFERENCES

E. D. Jarvis et al. (2014) "Whole-genome analyses resolve early branches in the tree of life of modern birds." *Science 346:* 1320-1331.

FIGURE CREDITS

12-2: Image created by Judith Geiger.

12-3: Image created by Judith Geiger.

12-4: Image created by Judith Geiger.

12-5: Image created by Judith Geiger.

CHAPTER 13

A DISTINCTIVE KIND OF APE: HOMININ BEGINNINGS

Thinking like cladists, we know that our own evolutionary history is going to be nested within progressively more inclusive groups of organisms who share progressively more ancient common ancestors with us. For example, we could start our inquiry into human evolution with our origins in the vertebrates. That would be an interesting journey but would take more time and space than we have. Even beginning with the primates is too ambitious for an introductory course that must also cover evolutionary theory and genetics. To have time for other critical topics, I have chosen to start several million years ago, when our lineage began to diverge from the rest of the African apes. I say, "from the rest of" because all the genetic and ana-tomical evidence—based on shared derived traits—points to the conclusion that humans are on the same branch of the evolutionary tree as the other African apes; we and our recent ancestors form a limb off that African ape branch. One commentator tried to capture the idea of our closeness to those apes by titling his book about human evolution *The Third Chimpanzee* (Diamond 1992).

In this chapter we will begin to explore the actual fossil record of human evolution. What were our ancestors like? What derived traits separate them from other kinds of apes? When and where did they live? How did they make their way in the world? It's astounding, breathtaking, to live in an age when we can offer some relatively concrete answers to questions like these! A short time ago when I was your age (well maybe not so short), such answers seemed beyond our reach. Although many puzzles and much confusion still remain, accelerating technological developments are bringing human evolution into progressively clearer focus. In this chapter I want to begin to sketch the outlines of what we anthropologists are more and less confident about.

To get our bearings, Figure 13-1 is a cladistic picture of our phylogenetic position within one group of living primates. Humans are apes (*hominoids*), more specifically, large-bodied "great apes" (*hominids*). A subgroup within the African great apes, we are called *hominins*. This phylogenetic tree, like all such trees in this book, reflects the timing and pattern of branching during evolution, in this case, during ape evolution. The closest outgroup to the apes, Old World Monkeys, is also shown for orientation and for comparison to other cladistic diagrams such as Figures 8-3 and 12-2. Please treat Figure 13-1 as a baseline reference as we proceed to unpack the details of human evolution.

In showing the pattern of branching, Figure 13-1 explicitly says that our closest living relatives are the chimpanzees, of which there are two species. I need to be very clear on this point. When anthropologists say that chimps are our closest living relatives, we do *not* mean that we are descended from chimps. We mean that, if

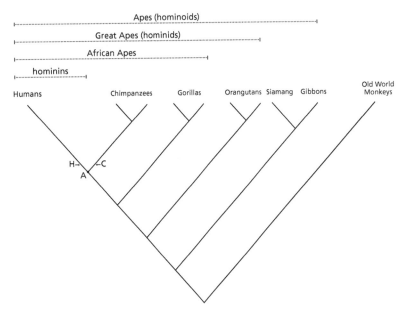

we look back in time to find the most recent common ancestor that we had with *any* living species, that creature would be the common ancestor that we share with chimps, at point A in Figure 13-1. That ancestor was *neither a chimp nor a human*; but some its current descendants are chimps and others are humans. Really; think about it. If that makes you a bit dizzy, here's your analogy (which again is not really an analogy but simply the same process at a smaller scale). You know that your cousin—for example, your mom's brother's daughter—is not your ancestor. Instead you are related to her because you share a common ancestor—for example a grandmother. Likewise, chimps are not your ancestors but your cousins, sharing a common ancestor with you. Chimps are clearly more distant from you than your mom's brother's daughter is, but that is *only* because your common ancestor with chimps lived *a lot* longer ago than your grandmother.

Figure 13-1. A cladogram of the living apes showing the order of branching. A designates the last common ancestor af humans and chimpanzees. H and C indicate the human and chimp branches, respectively.

Exactly how long ago the chimp-human common ancestor lived is the subject of intensive anthropological research. Much of that research is mathematical and heavily dependent on technical assumptions about mutation rates and population sizes (and well beyond the scope of this introductory text). But if we allow these assumptions to encompass all the plausible values, the resulting *divergence time* estimates range only from 5.5 to 12 million years ago. To my mind this 2-fold difference is not an embarrassing level of uncertainty; many key parameters in physics are estimated to a similar level of (im)precision. In addition, the fossil record imposes clear boundaries. We know that the common ancestor lived well before 1.5 million years ago because members of our own genus (*Homo*) were alive by then, and well after 25 million years ago because there were no apes at all then. Taken together these kinds of data suggest that we should look for the earliest hominins soon after the estimated time of the common ancestor, say between 11 and 5 million years ago. Remember, hominins are creatures who are demonstrably on the line to humans (H in the Figure 13-1) rather than on the line to chimps (C in the same Figure).

Let's start digging for fossils! Oh, but wait, how are we going to recognize the first hominin when we find it? Well, it's obviously going to have some human-like trait, a trait that is derived within the African apes, a trait that humans have that chimps and gorillas lack. The trait that all hominins will have (even the earliest hominin) will be the one that evolved *first*, as the hominin line (H) was just diverging from the chimp line (C). Was that trait a big brain, was it hairlessness, was it language, was it the use of fire, was it a chin, or the hand anatomy that permits a precision grip, or some

detail of the teeth? Our definition of hominins has to be based on actual phylogeny. It has to be based on the human-chimp difference that evolved first, since that one will be shared by subsequent members of the group.

The fossil record provides the answer. Of course, more fossil discoveries could change our opinion—science follows the evidence, the way good investigative reporters follow the money. But current evidence says that the diagnostic feature of hominins, because it was the first human-like trait to emerge some 5 or 6 million years ago, is bipedality: the habit of walking on two legs instead of four. Put another way, bipedality is for hominins what feathers are for birds and what mammary glands for mammals. Ok then, what is a hominin? It's a *bipedal African ape*; any bipedal African ape, even if you wouldn't go to the prom with it. In other words a hominin is not a "human". It's a creature that is more closely related to living humans than it is to living chimpanzees.

BIPEDALITY

For millions of years mammals, including most primates, have been quadrupedal; they walked on all fours. In fact mammals are descended from a group of reptiles whose members were also quadrupedal, so this mode of locomotion is quite ancient. We know that evolution can and does change things as it sculpts phenotypes to cope with new environmental challenges; and it clearly did orchestrate the change from quadrupedality to bipedality because chimps and most other primates are still quadrupedal while we're not. But the change from quadrupedality to bipedality involved a substantial redesign. Here's why a quadruped (your dog, say) can't just stand on its hind legs and make its way in the world.

In terms of what's called the biomechanics of walking, quadrupeds have things a bit easier than bipeds. Unless they are moving quite fast, quadrupeds have multiple limbs touching the ground at any moment. That's not true for a biped. To move, even quite slowly, a biped needs to lift one of its two legs, leaving (at most) one leg in contact with the ground. This creates balance problems with every single stride (problems that are exploited by a well known sobriety-check protocol). Let's think about bipedal walking from a physics viewpoint.

You'll need to stand up because you're going to be a subject in your own experiment; really. (Please don't merely read this section without doing the experiments because you won't get the essential point.) Stand at rest with both feet on the ground. Now, lift your left leg and stand on your right foot only. You'll notice that your upper body shifted (leaned) to the right when you did that. Stand on your left leg and you'll see the same compensation, but this time to the left. Why is that happening? When you're standing normally your mass is naturally centered over your two feet. But when you lift your right leg your mass is unbalanced. The mass on your left side is not so well supported, and that's why you lean to the right: to realign and center your mass over your solitary right foot.

Now for phase two of the experiment. Again, stand on your right foot only, but *without* leaning to the right. That's much harder, isn't it? Practice a bit and you'll probably get better at it. Can you say what you're doing to compensate for the fact that you're not leaning? I can't see you but I predict you're tensing certain muscles on the right side of your body, muscles whose contraction is keeping your body from tipping and falling towards your lifted left leg. If you probe with your fingers about 2 inches below your waist band on your right side, you can probably feel those muscles tensing up (and, if you stand on your right leg for 30 seconds or so, they'll start to twitch because they're getting tired of doing that much work). These muscles are collectively called leg abductor muscles, the most important being the gluteus medius, followed by the gluteus maximus (Figure 13-2). In relation to these muscles Figure 13-2 shows a rear view of the lower part the human spine, the upper leg bone (the femur), and

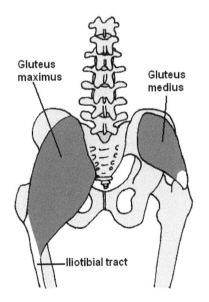

Figure 13-2. Sketch showing the principal leg abductor muscles. Both muscles are present on both light and left sides, but shown separately here to make their position and extent clear.

the bony girdle that links the spine to the legs (the pelvis). Since you're symmetrical, you have a gluteus medius and gluteus maximus on your right side, and a gluteus medius and gluteus maximus on your left. But, because these muscles overlap each other, the Figure shows the gluteus maximus on the left and the gluteus medius on the right, so you can more clearly see their extent. Notice that they attach to the upper end of the femur to the pelvis. As a result, when they contract they prevent the body from tipping toward the lifted leg. In fact, if you did that part of the experiment, you were feeling the contraction of the gluteus medius just below your waist band! Try it again if you want, now that you know what you're looking for.

These biomechanical issues are illustrated in Figure 13-3, for humans and for chimpanzees. Taking humans first, with the left leg raised (e.g., to take a stride), gravity tips the body towards the left. The contraction of the right abductors, especially the right gluteus medius, exerts a force that counterbalances the force of gravity. This counterforce is as efficient as it can be because the angle of pull, as the gluteus medius contracts, is *precisely opposite* to the tipping force. This level of efficiency is achieved because of the relative positions of the two attachment points of the gluteus medius. As can be seen in both Figures 13-2 and 13-3, this muscle runs from the greater trochanter on the femur to the pelvis. Natural selection can alter the shape of bones during evolution and it has clearly operated to make this anti-tipping force more efficient during hominin evolution, as evidenced by the very different positioning of these attachment points in chimpanzees.

Figure 13-3. A comparison of hindlimb biomechanics in a bipedal human and a quadrupedal chimpanzee. See text for a full discussion.

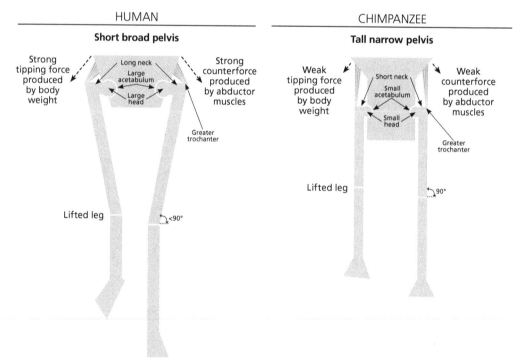

The human pelvis is short (in the vertical dimension) and broad. The chimpanzee pelvis is tall and narrow. Another difference between these two species is the length of the neck of the femur, much shorter in the chimpanzee than in the human. When combined, these differences place the greater trochanter and the pelvis in a very different spatial relationship to each other in these two species. When the human gluteus medius contracts it generates a force that *directly* counteracts the tipping force of raising the opposite leg. In the chimpanzee, a muscle with the same attachment points produces little anti-tipping force because it pulls in the wrong direction. But of course the anti-tipping function isn't necessary since the chimpanzee is a quadruped, not a biped. (There is no suggestion here that Chimpanzee anatomy is poorly adapted. It is as efficient as human anatomy, but for a different mode of locomotion involving quadrupedal locomotion on the ground and a great deal of vertical climbing.)

It would be wrong to leave the impression that non-hominin apes absolutely cannot walk bipedally. They can do so for short periods. When they do they have a shuffling, side-to-side gait and walk with their knees bent. It's not a very efficient mode of locomotion for them, given the organization of their pelvis, leg, and associated muscles. Nevertheless, it's interesting to ask when they tolerate this inefficiency and walk bipedally anyway. The consistent answer is, when they have items they want to carry, typically preferred foods. Bipedality frees the hands for other uses.

This lesson in functional anatomy serves two purposes. As always, examining the design of organisms gives powerful insights into the ways in which different environments—different selection pressures—favor different adaptations, in this case anatomical adaptations for two different models of locomotion. But more importantly for our present purposes, it shows us that we don't need a time machine to figure out which extinct animals were bipedal; their fossilized bones will tell us how they walked—if we're lucky.

While we *can* read behavior from bones, the murky reality is that fossils are both rare and fragmentary. The vast majority of creatures that have lived on the planet didn't get fossilized; they just decomposed back into the soil. And when we do find fossils, we don't find whole skeletons; we find bits and pieces. The most common find is a single tooth. (Teeth are harder than bone and so are more frequently fossilized.) But if we were lucky enough to find a significant chunk of a pelvis or a complete femur neck, we'd be fairly confident about how that creature got around. Are there any other parts of the skeleton where the mode of locomotion (bipedal versus quadrupedal) leaves its imprint? Yes, there are several.

Two more of them are also depicted in Figure 13.3. First, in quadrupedal apes like the chimpanzee the body weight is distributed across four limbs, but in bipedal hominins two legs must carry the weight. As a consequence, the weight-bearing structures must be more robust in a biped than in a similarly sized quadruped. For example, the ball-and-socket joint (where the head of the femur mates with the *acetabulum* of the pelvis) is larger in bipeds. And the same general increase in robusticity should show up in the knee and ankle joint of bipeds. Second, in a quadruped the legs descend from the pelvis straight to the ground. But bipedal apes necessarily have a different arrangement. The longer femur neck—that allows the gluteus medius to pull in the right direction—inevitably extends the top end of the femur outward, far from the midline of the body. So, to get the feet under the body the femurs must angle inward to meet the more centrally placed lower leg at knee. As a result, the articulatory surface at the lower end of the femur will not form a 90° angle to the shaft, as it does in quadrupeds. A biped will have an oblique *valgus angle*.

Bipedalism shows up in other parts of the skeleton as well. In bipeds the skull is balanced on top of the vertebral column. Thus the large hole (*foramen magnum*) at the base of the skull where the spinal cord exits the brain is centrally located, and there isn't a lot of heavy musculature to support the head because of its balanced position. In quadrupeds the skull is cantilevered off the end of the vertebral column, the foramen magnum has a more rear-ward position, and there is much heavier musculature connecting the back of the skull to the vertebrae. Muscles don't fossilize but the size of muscles is directly reflected in the areas of attachment of the bone: Large muscles require more attachment area. Figure 13-4 shows a gorilla skeleton, with the extensive areas of neck (nuchal) muscle attachment to the base of the skull and the large, backward-projecting spines on the first several vertebrae. The gorilla skeleton also shows the tall narrow pelvis that was diagrammed in Figure 13-3.

Now we know that bipedality is the first derived feature to appear in the hominin line. And we have a pretty good idea about the kinds of features that might indicate bipedality in the various fossils that we're lucky enough to find.

Figure 13-4. Gorilla skeleton showing a tall pevis and substantial areas of attachment for the neck muscles.

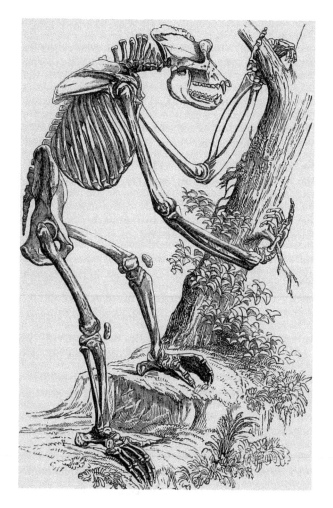

ADAPTIVE RADIATIONS

Before we start sorting through the many kinds of hominin fossils I want to orient you to what you should expect, or more precisely, what you should not expect. Human evolution could be a neat, linear story. You know: Once there was an ape that was just a tiny bit human and, generation by generation, its descendants became more and more human until, after millions of years, we arrived at our present fully human form. In this scenario, natural selection was consistently favoring any mutation that made an ape more human-like and it just took a long time for all the right mutations to come along. That's partly correct; for example, we don't see very human-like creatures six million years ago. But it's also true that all the known hominins *do not* simply lie at different points along a single ancestor-descendant lineage. (Figure 13-1 might give that impression, but remember, it shows the phylogenetic relationships among the *living apes* only.)

Anthropologists believe that there are some (to many) side branches along the hominin line. There were many bifurcation points where, under the influence of some local selective regime, a group of hominins evolved traits that were not more human-like. These side-branch populations were evolving their own unique, hominin but non-human, sets of adaptations. The least controversial example of such a side branch would probably be the genus *Paranthropus* which we will discuss in the next chapter. In other words, there was no single set of "humanizing" selection pressures operating over the past five million years. Instead, selection was always probing multiple new adaptive possibilities. Some of these evolutionary experiments lasted so briefly we've never seen a trace of them in the fossil record. Others spawned lineages that lasted a million or more years before dying out. And yes, at least one has descendants who are reading this book.

There is no reason to think that human evolution is at all unique in regard to the number of extinct lineages. Lineage proliferation followed by lineage extinction is a much-repeated pattern in the fossil record. The proliferation phase is called an adaptive radiation. *Adaptive radiations occur when selection creates diverse kinds of creatures from a single ancestral type.* This might sound mysterious, but adaptive radiations are caused by precisely the same kind of natural selection you've already learned about. Adaptive radiations can be viewed as "bursts" of allopatric speciation. This may be more likely

to occur following the emergence of a new adaptation that opens up a range of previously unavailable ecological niches. Populations carrying this new adaptation fan out into new territory, experience new selection pressures and continue evolving in response. For example, bipedality—the defining characteristic of hominins—may have been just the kind of evolutionary innovation that would open up a range of new environments and thus expose the bipeds to new selective regimes (Foley 2002).

I think the processes outlined in the previous paragraph are fully consistent with the picture of evolution we have developed so far, but I want to add one important note of circumspection. Above, I suggested that adaptive radiations could be understood as "bursts" of allopatric speciation. I felt it would have made the prose too dense, but what I wanted to say was that I think they represent the *same kinds of processes that are involved in allopatric speciation*. In other words, yes; different environments and selection pressures will cause populations to diverge and evolve different adaptations. But it won't necessarily push them all the way to being separate species. Of course it can do so; but depending on the amount of time, how much interbreeding there is between the populations, and how different the selection pressures are, they may travel some way down the road to becoming different species, but not get all the way there—like lions and tigers (Chapter 7). So, as hominins spread out across first Africa and later the planet, they did evolve different traits. But, looking into the past, we usually cannot apply our "interbreeding test" to see whether any two types are the same or different species. I want to emphasize caution here because of very recent discoveries; we now know with a high degree of certainty that some hominins previously considered separate species could and did interbreed! See Chapter 16 for more information about that.

Like all of evolution, adaptive radiations are fueled by two things: new raw material for selection to sort through (mutations) and new opportunities (e.g., new habitats or ecological niches). We know that, because DNA has very high copying fidelity, mutations are rare. But because there are so many loci in the genome and so many individuals in natural populations, there will be some new mutations in every generation. Likewise climate change, geological forces, colonizations, and extinctions of predator or prey species will sporadically offer new avenues to reproductive success. So, new mutations and new opportunities inevitably arise. It's true that being in the right place with the right mutation is just luck, but selection will capitalize on any such luck, spreading the beneficial mutation through the population. Adaptive radiations are simply the cumulative sum of many such events, as selection steers populations through previously uncharted regions of adaptive space.

FOSSIL NAMES

Before we jump into the lion's den of fossil hominin research, we should spend a bit more time with naming issues. We've used a few scientific species names earlier in the book, for example we saw the scientific names of several lizard species in Chapter 2. As I mentioned at that time, a full species name includes two parts: The first part is the genus (which is always capitalized) and the second part is the species (which is never capitalized). Both genus and species are italicized, or underlined if you can't italicize. If you want to refer to a subspecies, you add a third part after the species name, and that too is italicized.

Naming conventions are directly linked to our system of biological classification. As you know, that system is hierarchical: Species are nested within genera (the plural of genus); genera are nested within families . . . and phyla are nested within kingdoms. So, naturally, there are also scientific names for larger, more inclusive groups. For example *Mammalia* is the scientific name for mammals.

Any named biological group, at any level in the hierarchy, is a "taxon" (plural: "taxa"). All the levels in the classificatory hierarchy are taxa. Animalia (a kingdom) is a taxon, but so is *Pan troglodytes verus* (a subspecies of the common chimpanzee). It's useful to have a term, like taxon, that includes all classificatory levels because sometimes we change our mind about where a taxon should be placed in the hierarchy. For example, some anthropologists have argued that "Neanderthals" are a subspecies of *Homo sapiens*, in which case they would be called *Homo sapiens neanderthalensis*, but others have argued that they are a separate species, which would be called *Homo neanderthalensis*. But regardless of that disagreement, (which is now settled, see Chapter 16) pretty much everyone agrees that "Neanderthals" represent a valid taxon, sufficiently distinct and recognizable compared to other populations of *Homo* to be worthy of its own name. Having a word like taxon, which is noncommittal about placement, lets us distinguish two questions: 1) are the forms distinct (and hence different taxa), and 2) if so, at what classificatory level should they be separated from other similar taxa?

This is the main reason anthropologists sometimes defy the two-part naming convention and use only partial names, such as "*rudolfensis*." It's because there's disagreement about what genus *rudolfensis* belongs to, some folks preferring *Homo rudolfensis* and others arguing for *Australopithecus rudolfensis*. Using *rudolfensis* by itself is saying "hey look; for the moment I don't want to fight about whether this taxon belongs in *Homo* or in *Australopithecus* but I do have quite a few things I want to say about these creatures (their anatomy, when and where they lived, etc.) and I need to make it clear what creatures I'm talking about."

That's fine. But there is an even better way to handle this kind of uncertainty: Use specimen numbers, for everything. Every discovery, no matter how tiny, has an associated specimen number based on the cataloguing system of the particular museum that houses it. This specimen number will never change no matter how many times scientists decide to move it to a new taxon. "KNM-ER 1813" (Kenya National Museum, East Rudolph site, 1,813th specimen) will never change, although some people might claim it's *Homo* and others will assert that it's *Australopithecus*. At least we know what we're arguing over and we can all measure and remeasure its various features. Taking this approach, people are free to reassign these specimens to various taxa as they try to meet the standards of cladistic classification.

This agnostic approach is sensible and it has allowed quite a bit of useful research to get published and discussed. But I should mention one other naming issue that is probably not so sensible or helpful. That is the tendency for each fossil discoverer to give every discovery a new scientific name. In other words, every unearthed specimen is claimed to represent a previously unknown species (or one previously named by the current discoverer). That might be correct. But remember that our key test of whether two populations represent one or two species—ability to interbreed and produce fertile offspring—is not going to work for fossils

(but see Chapter 16). So I suggest that we need to be somewhat skeptical about how many different hominins have graced our planet.

FOSSIL DATING

A sensible interpretation of the fossil record would be impossible if we couldn't determine how old the various fossils are. The most accurate methods for determining the age of fossils, called *radiometric dating*, are based on the decay of naturally occurring radioactive isotopes. For example potassium (K in the periodic table) has one unstable isotope, ^{40}K, which decays at a known rate (its half-life) to an inert gas, ^{40}Ar, that does not form chemical compounds with other elements. Potassium, including predictable amounts of its unstable isotope, occurs naturally in rocks and soils. When rock is heated, for example during a volcanic event, any previously accumulated ^{40}Ar is released. But when the lava cools sufficiently ^{40}Ar begins to accumulate again. Neat; that resets the clock. So by measuring the ratio of ^{40}K to ^{40}Ar we can calculate when a particular sample of rock cooled. This method can be used to determine the age of fossils by dating the volcanic layers found above and below the fossil. Of course that doesn't work if there are no volcanic deposits in the area where the fossil was found. Given ^{40}K's moderately long half-life it takes considerable time for a measurable amount of ^{40}Ar to accumulate. Thus the K-Ar method is more reliable for rocks that cooled more than 100 thousand years ago (100 KYA).

Fortunately there is another radiometric method that can be used with younger materials, and it can be used on the fossils themselves. Carbon is a major constituent of life on earth and it has a radioactive isotope, ^{14}C, that decays to ^{12}C at a known rate. Because ^{14}C is constantly being created in the earth's atmosphere living animals, which are taking in carbon from their food, reach an equilibrium with the atmosphere. But when they die they stop accumulating carbon and the ratio of ^{12}C to ^{14}C begins to increase. So measuring the ratio tells how long ago the animal died. Because the half-life of ^{14}C if fairly short, 5,730 years, it is not accurate for fossils older than about 50,000 years, since there is too little ^{14}C remaining.

Beyond these radiometric techniques, fossils can be assigned relative ages, older and younger, based on layering of the strata where they are found. Also, if the hominin fossils in question are too old for the radiocarbon method and occur where there are no volcanic layers, they can sometimes be assigned approximate ages based on other fossils found with them. Various extinct animals and plants are well known and the time range when they existed has been determined, for example by the K-Ar method, from other sites. The hominin is then assumed to have been a contemporary of these dated animals or plants.

EARLIEST POSSIBLE HOMININS

In looking for early hominins we'll be looking for evidence of bipedality. The anatomical nature of that evidence was laid out earlier in this chapter. Here I want to consider how the transition from quadrupedality to bipedality might have occurred, because we should expect to eventually find fossils that represent those transitional states.

Natural selection doesn't create new alternatives. Selection has as grist for its mill whatever

worked in previous generations (and therefore got passed on) plus a sprinkling of new mutations. It's very difficult to imagine a quadruped-to-biped transition without some kind of intermediate, transitional form or forms. For reasons extensively discussed in Chapter 7, we'd expect this transition to be gradual. What might it have looked like? Fossil African apes seem to have been arboreal—living in the trees. Monkeys live in trees and they walk quadrupedally on top of branches. A larger animal like an ape might climb trunks—vertical supports—as much as or more than it walks on branches. That climbing mode of locomotion naturally favors a vertical rather than horizontal orientation of the spine. (This is an example of the kind of small, intermediate step towards bipedalism that I think we should look be looking for early in hominin evolution.) Once that horizontal-to-vertical re-organization was established, an animal with an upright posture might then walk bipedally when it did walk on branches, especially if it had a big, powerful grasping toe. The next cumulative step could then have been a shift to terrestrial bipedalism—walking on the ground—as well as, or eventually, instead of walking in the trees.

Calculations based on mutation rates mentioned earlier in this chapter suggest that the chimp-human divergence time (point A in Figure 13-1) might be as early as 12 million years ago (MYA). In spite of that estimate, the oldest fossils claimed to be hominins date to about 7 MYA. Let's see what is known about those fossils.

Sahelanthropus tchadensis; 7 MYA (Figure 13-5). This fossil was found in Chad's Djurab Desert in an area of North-central Africa that has produced very few hominin fossils. Unfortunately the skull is crushed, broken, and distorted in multiple dimensions. A fragment of a femur was supposedly found nearby but there have been no publications describing that leg bone. Thus, the claim that *Sahelanthropus* is a hominin has been controversial. Some argue that the foramen magnum is central while others disagree, a range of interpretations permitted by the poor condition of the fossil. Other features of the skull are primitive in the cladistic sense of resembling the outgroup—in this case the chimpanzee. For example, there is a massive bony brow ridge above the eyes, the canine teeth are large, and the brain is very small (less than 350 cubic centimeters). More material, especially post-cranial material (bones below the head) will be needed to determine if *Sahelanthropus* was actually bipedal, and hence a hominin. Because there are indications that this fossil was redeposited (not found where it died), habitat reconstructions would not be informative.

Orrorin tugenensis; 6 MYA (Figure 13-6). This taxon is represented by about 20 fragments that include some finger bones, bits of a jaw, single teeth, the lower part of the humerus (the upper-arm bone) and three pieces of the femur. Fortunately the femoral fragments include the head and neck, which suggest bipedality. On the other hand, the finger bones are curved which is a typical adaptation in climbing species. Of course these two conclusions are not automatically incompatible. Orrorin may have spent a lot of its time in the trees but may have walked bipedally when on the ground. Based on the associated plant and animal fossils, it apparently lived in a

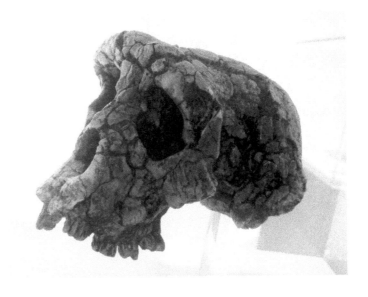

Figure 13-5. *Sahelanthropus tchadensis* skull.

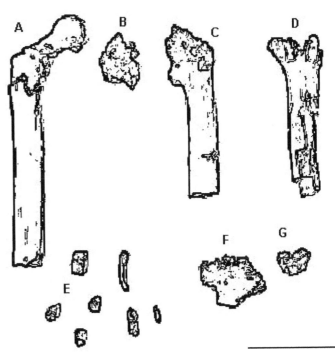

Figure 13-6. A sketch of the fragmentary material assigned to *Orrorin tugenensis*.

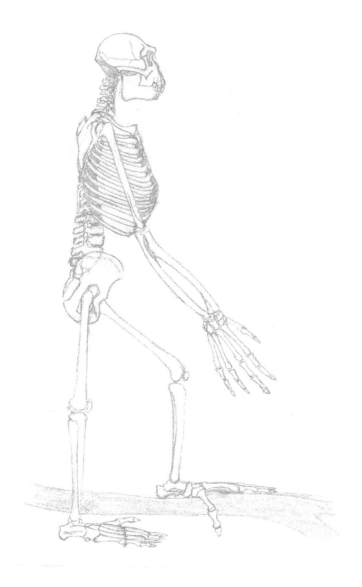

Figure 13-7. A sketch of the reconstruction of an Ardipithecus ramidus skelton from the fairly complete remains of a single individual.

discovered that together represent more than 45% of what is believed to be one individual. When mirror-imaged to allow right-side fossils to stand in for missing left-side elements (and vice-versa) a rather complete reconstruction can be accomplished, as shown in Figure 13-7. *Ardipithecus* seems to have lived in a mosaic environment with forests, savannas, and swamps nearby. This taxon still presents many primitive traits including a brain size less than 350 cc. While the discoverers argue that *Ardipithecus* was bipedal it has clear features related to climbing. These include huge hands and feet, with curved fingers and toes, a grasping big toe on the foot that could oppose the other digits in the way that your thumb opposes your fingers, and a rather tall pelvis. Unfortunately the head and neck of the femur have yet not been found. As suggested for Orrorin, Ardipithecus may have spent considerable time in the trees. How it moved if and when it came to the ground is unclear. But *Ardipithecus ramidus* may represent the kind of transitional creature we described above. (There are fragments of somewhat older material that have been assigned to *Ardipithecus kadabba*, another species in the same genus, but the quantity and quality of evidence seems insufficient to make that judgment.)

dry evergreen forest. The canines are large (primitive) but the enamel layer of the teeth is thicker than in modern chimps; thick enamel is a derived trait of hominins. Thus Orrorin displays an interesting mosaic of traits and may have been at least facultatively bipedal when on the ground.

Ardipithecus ramidus; 4.4 MYA (Figure 13-7). A large number of cranial and post-cranial fragments have been

CHAPTER SUMMARY

The fossil record of human evolution reveals that we are bipedal African apes.

We can recognize fossil hominins because bipedality and quadrupedality impose different biomechanical constraints, and these constraints are reflected in various parts of the skeleton. Many kinds of hominins have existed over the past several million years but few of them have living descendants. Between 7 and 4.4 MYA there are creatures that may represent different stages in the transition to bipedality, but they are still primitive in many other respects, notably their very small brains.

CITED REFERENCES

Jared Diamond (1992). *The Third Chimpanzee*. New York: Harper Collins.

Robert Foley (2002) "Adaptive radiations and dispersals in hominin evolutionary ecology." *Evolutionary Anthropology 11*: 32–37.

FIGURE CREDITS

13-1: Image created by Judith Geiger.

13-2: Copyright © Beth ohara~commonswiki (CC BY-SA 3.0) at https://commons.wikimedia.org/wiki/File:Posterior_Hip_Muscles_3.PNG.

13-3: Image created by Judith Geiger.

13-4: https://commons.wikimedia.org/wiki/File:Carpenter%27s_principles_of_human_physiology_(1881)_(14594642947).jpg. Copyright in the Public Domain.

13-5: https://commons.wikimedia.org/wiki/File:Sahelanthropus_tchadensis_skull_-_Naturmuseum_Senckenberg_-_DSC02104.JPG. Copyright in the Public Domain.

13-6: Copyright © it:User:Lucius (CC BY-SA 3.0) at https://commons.wikimedia.org/wiki/File:Orrorin_tugenensis.jpg.

13-7: Copyright © Tobias Fluegel (CC BY-SA 3.0) at https://commons.wikimedia.org/wiki/File:Ardipithecus_Gesamt.jpg .

CHAPTER 14

THE AUSTRALOPITHS AND THE TRANSITION TO *HOMO*

The fossil record is tantalizingly fragmentary. Many extinct populations are surely not represented at all. And those that are may be represented by a few bone fragments from just one individual. The job of paleoanthropologists is to extract as much valid information as they can from that very fragmentary record. To do so, they need to walk a tightrope between creativity and scientific rigor. Each researcher will find his or her own unique balance point. The range of available techniques is growing rapidly and they are allowing us to coax more and more information out of the material we are lucky enough to find.

THE FOOTSTEPS OF OUR ANCESTORS

I'll begin this chapter with a fossil find that has no scientific name attached to it. That's because it's not a bone or tooth. It's a hardened layer of volcanic ash. I'm telling you about it because, before the ash hardened, some creatures walked across it; and three of them were bipedal apes (Figure 14-1). It's true that we don't know what creatures made these tracks, but we do know (from K-Ar techniques) that they date to 3.7 MYA. We also know that the track-makers did not have a thumb-like big toe (as *Ardipithecus* did), and that their stride was similar to ours. Their heel struck the ground first and then weight was transferred onto the ball of the foot before push-off, and they walked with an extended leg as we do, not with the bent-knee shuffle that chimps use when they (occasionally) walk bipedally (Raichlen et al. 2010). These fossilized footprints provide a clear benchmark for when extended-leg bipedality was established, and it was only about 700,000 years after the time of *Ardipithecus*. What kinds of hominins were alive 3.7 MYA who could have made those footprints?

Figure 14-2 is intended to help you organize your thinking about the various hominins we'll be discussing. For each taxon, the bar indicates its estimated first and last appearance in the fossil record, to provide a temporal frame of reference about which hominins existed when. This Figure is *not* intended to show ancestor-descendant relationships among the various fossil types. Our best guess at that is in Figure 16-1.

You may find it useful to organize your time line of human evolution into three somewhat unequal periods. Let the first of those periods be the one covered in the previous chapter, from the chimp-human common ancestor to about 4.0 MYA, a time that spawned some possible transitional (perhaps facultative) bipeds but apparently no modern-style ones. The second period is the focus of this chapter. It is the time of the australopiths, beginning about 4 MYA and ending with the emergence of our own genus, *Homo*. Exactly where that end point is will depend on which hominins we decide to put in *Homo* but,

regardless of how inclusive or exclusive we decide *Homo* should be, the boundary will be between 2.3 and 1.8 MYA. The third period is, of course, the time of *Homo* and it is the subject of Chapter 16. So now, based on the fact that they are 3.7 million years old, you know that some kind of fully bipedal australopith was the likely footprint maker at Laetoli.

THE AUSTRALOPITHS

The australopiths include two major types that are generally regarded as separate genera: *Australopithecus* and *Paranthropus*. The fossils that are assigned to these two genera come from eastern and southern Africa, with a single exception (*Australopithecus bahrelghazali* from Chad). Their restriction to Africa makes sense because cladistic analysis tells us that hominins are African apes. Australopiths are small compared to modern humans. In many cases we don't have any postcranial bones, but some finds include as much as 50% of the skeleton, and these individual hominins can be reconstructed to estimate their stature. Both *Australopithecus* and *Paranthropus* seem to include smaller individuals who were about 1.1 m (3.5 feet) tall, and somewhat larger individuals who were about 1.5 m (5.0 feet) tall.

Figure 14-1. Photograph of museum replica of 3.7 million year old bipedal footprints from Laetoli. Tanzania.

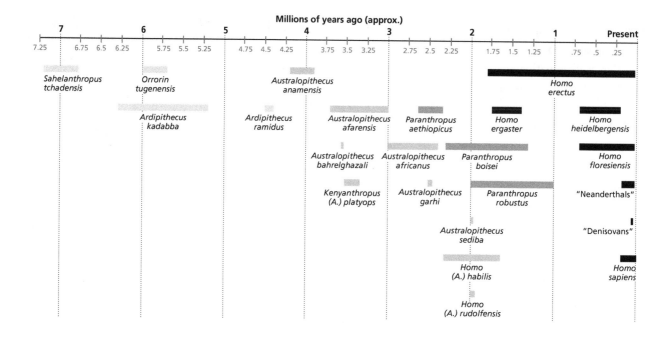

Millions of years ago (approx.)

Figure 14-2. A time line of hominin fossils. Length of bars marks the first and last example of each taxon. This graphic does not show ancestor-descendant relationships.

This bimodal distribution (two distinct sizes with no intermediates) suggests what biologists call *sexual dimorphism*—distinct male and female phenotypes. On analogy with what we know about modern humans, other apes, and other mammals, the smaller individuals are assumed to be females. It turns out that the *amount* of sexual dimorphism is a good predictor of the *mating system* of a species, so I will return to this issue in later chapters.

Where we can judge from the associated plant and animal fossils, these creatures typically lived in or adjacent to open, savanna-like habitats, often in lakeside or streamside settings. In contrast, the very first member of this group, *Australopithecus anamensis*, seems to have inhabited a less open, woodland setting. This is interesting because pre-australopith hominins (Chapter 13), as

well as the non-hominin apes, are all associated with forest or woodland settings. So significant movement into and exploitation of savanna habitats seems to be a derived trait that first emerged in the Australopith period.

Despite being modern in their mode of locomotion the australopiths were still primitive in many respects. They had small brains ranging in size from 350 to 550 cc. For comparison your brain is about 1300 cc. Likewise, their limb proportions resemble those of non-hominin apes in that their arms are as long as or longer than their legs (Figure 14-3). You have the opposite pattern with your legs longer than your arms. These chimp-like limb proportions of the australopiths are somewhat surprising, because they were bipeds. We might expect natural selection to extend the stride by lengthening the leg, as it did do in *Homo*. Perhaps that didn't happen because the australopiths were also subject to opposing selection pressures related to tree climbing. This is a reasonable speculation because they have other anatomical features that suggest a significant amount of climbing, such as curving finger bones, the upward inclination of the shoulder joint, and a funnel-shaped rib cage that narrows towards the head (also visible in Figure 14-3). So these australopiths were quite competent bipeds but tree climbing was also a component of their lifestyle.

The australopiths' dental features present a more complex story. In some ways their teeth too are primitive. The canine teeth provide a good example of this. Look back at the gorilla skeleton in Figure 13-4. Note that the canine teeth, both upper and lower, project beyond the others. The gorilla can still close its mouth because there is a gap in the upper jaw (the canine diastema) to accommodate the lower canine, and because the premolar behind the lower canine is dramatically reshaped to accommodate the upper canine. Chimpanzees show a very similar dental arrangement to gorillas. But in modern humans, and in all members of the genus *Homo*, the canines are much smaller; they are level with the rest of the teeth and there is no trace of a diastema. This canine reduction and associated shrinking of the diastema occurs gradually, from earlier to later australopiths. The earliest, such as *Australopithecus anamensis* have fairly large canines and a diastema, whereas

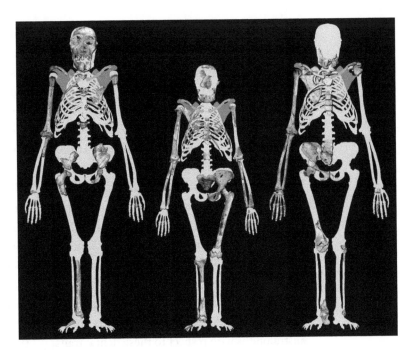

Figure 14-3. Illustration showing actual fossil material and reconstructions for two *Australopithecus sediba* individuals and one *Australopithecus afarensis* individual (center).

later ones approach the condition in *Homo*.

On the other hand, several dental traits of the australopiths are derived relative to chimps and gorillas, but are not particularly *Homo*-like. Consider relative tooth sizes. In chimps and gorillas (Figure 13-4) the front teeth (incisors and canines) are quite large, as large as or larger than the chewing teeth (molars and premolars). In australopiths the incisors are quite small in some species, but the molars and premolars can be huge, especially in *Paranthropus*. But with the transition from the australopiths to *Homo*, *all* of the teeth shrink in size, and the reduction is more dramatic in the molars and premolars. Enamel thickness shows a similar reversal. Enamel is the hard, protective outer layer of the tooth. Chimps have relatively thin tooth enamel, australopiths have very thick enamel (again, especially in *Paranthropus*), and Homo has enamel that is intermediate in thickness. So, there seem to be selection pressures—probably related to diet, since the teeth are involved—that are operating in the australopiths to move them away from the primitive condition, but that don't simply continue with the transition to *Homo*. If they had, we would have tiny incisors and canines, but molars and premolars each one the size of a quarter, and enamel so thick your dentist would need little sticks of dynamite to get through it!

My point is not that any of those things would be bad; if natural selection had built them it would have done so because of the benefits they provided. No; my point is simply that, whatever natural selection was favoring among australopiths with respect to these dental traits, it began favoring something *different* with the transition to *Homo*. These shifting dental traits exemplify what I said in Chapter 13 when I stressed that human evolution has been nonlinear. There was no single suite of "humanizing" selection pressures operating over the last 6 million years; instead, selection explored many different hominin niche opportunities.

MATERIAL CULTURE

Material culture refers to physical items that animals make and use. I chose the more inclusive term "animals" rather than "humans" because we are not the only animals that have material culture. Put another way (to continue reinforcing cladistic concepts), material culture is not a derived trait for hominins; it is primitive. Notably, chimps make and use tools. Admittedly, some tools used by chimps are unmodified objects simply picked up in the environment. Chimps are mainly

frugivores (fruit eaters) but they get a smaller fraction of their diet from other sources: nuts, insects, and some meat. Some of the nuts that chimps eat have shells that are too hard for them to break open with their teeth. They lay these hard nuts on an exposed boulder, pick up a hand-sized rock, and use it as a hammer-stone, to crack them open and expose the edible parts. They typically do not modify the hammer-stone in any way, but they may show some foresight in collecting an appropriate rock and carrying it to the boulder, since rocks are not common in the forest environments where they live.

In other instances some actual tool manufacture regularly occurs, for example when they "fish" for termites. (Remember that fruit provides a lot of carbohydrates but very little protein, and insects are a good source of protein.) Termites build large mound nests of mud, plant tissue, and their own secretions. In fishing for termites chimps exploit the fact that termites are hydrophilic (they like moisture). Chimps find a twig of appropriate stoutness, break off any side branches, lick it (applying the moisture "bait"), and insert it into the tunnel system of the termite mound. The termites grab onto the wet twig with their jaws. When the twig is withdrawn the termites can simply be licked off. Yummy. Chimpanzees also use stouter sticks to dig for roots and tubers (Hernandez-Aguillar *et al.*, 2007).

The tools used and then discarded by chimpanzees can be recognized by astute primatologists, but they would not be recognizable as tools by archaeologists millions of years later. For this reason we don't know how long African apes have been using tools made out of perishable materials such as wood. But, during the australopith period, we do see the first evidence of more durable stone tools. For many years we believed that the earliest stone tools dated to about 2.6 MYA (Figure 14-4). The style (or more technically, the *industry*) represented by these early tools is known as *Oldowan*, not because the tools are old but because they were first found at a site called Olduvai Gorge in Tanzania. They are made by smashing together rocks of the appropriate composition, driving off sharp flakes. Both the "core"—the larger rock from which flakes are removed—and the flakes themselves have sharp edges that make them useful as tools. Quite recently, however, tools that are a full 700,000 years older, dated to 3.3 MYA, were found near Lake Turkana in Kenya (an area that has regularly yielded hominin fossils). These tools are different from the younger Oldowan tools—for example, they typically employ a different fracturing technique—and are thus classified as *Lomekwian*, a distinct industry (Harmand et al. 2015). Independent evidence that stone tools were being made and used by hominins at this early date comes from stone-tool butchery marks on the fossilized bones of prey animals, dated to 3.39 MYA (McPherron et al., 2010). This not only verifies the existence of stone tools, but it also establishes at least one of the ways they were used: obtaining meat.

At present, no one believes the genus *Homo* yet existed 3.3 MYA. (Very generous estimates would place the origins of *Homo* around 2.3 MYA. More conservative estimates would cluster around 1.7 MYA. This uncertainty is not

Figure 14-4. Example of Oldowan (Mode 1) stone tools. Only a few flakes have been removed, thus much of the original coble remains.

a result of unreliable dating techniques. As mentioned above it's a result of disagreements about which taxa belong in *Homo*.) So, regardless of how we define *Homo*, we have no alternative but to conclude (based on available evidence), that techniques of stone tool manufacture and use, as well as some degree of carnivory, predate our genus. Just as we don't know which hominin made the Laetoli footprints, we don't know which one(s) made the tools. It's time to examine the two kinds of australopiths in a bit more detail.

AUSTRALOPITHECUS AND PARANTHROPUS

I remind you that Figure 14-2 is a complete time-sorted list of all the (possible and certain) hominins mentioned in this book. It includes the taxa covered in Chapter 13, the australopiths who are the focus of this chapter, as well as various members of the genus *Homo* dealt with in more detail in later chapters. I thought it would be more useful to have them all gathered into a single reference.

Australopithecus is older than *Paranthropus*. *Australopithecus* spans the time period from about 4.0 to about 1.8 MYA. *Paranthropus* arises and persists considerably later, appearing in the fossil record from about 2.5 to roughly 1.2 MYA. *Paranthropus* is widely thought to be a descendant of some kind of *Australopithecus* because they share so many anatomical features, especially their bipedally adapted post-cranial anatomy. We know that *Australopithecus* and *Paranthropus* were not geographically separated types. Both genera occur in eastern and southern Africa and, for about 700,000 years—from roughly 2.5 to 1.8 MYA—they overlapped temporally and spatially and probably met each other with appreciable frequency.

When two species co-exist in this way for such an extended time period, ecologists believe that they must have been exploiting somewhat distinct ecological niches. If their ecologies overlapped too much one type would have been better adapted and would have out-competed the other and replaced it.

A significant clue to their ecological differences can be seen in their skulls and teeth. As mentioned above, both kinds of australopiths have quite small incisors but large chewing teeth—the molars and premolars. And all of their teeth have very thick enamel which is a protection against wear. Of course large chewing teeth need large jaws to accommodate them, and significant chewing muscles to work those jaws. The key difference between *Australopithecus* and *Paranthropus* is that everything I just said about the australopiths is more extreme in *Paranthropus* than in *Australopithecus*. *Paranthropus* has a really massive chewing apparatus. Sometimes anthropologists prefer to talk in terms of "gracile" and "robust" australopiths. Remembering that these comparative terms refer mainly to differences in the skull, jaws, and teeth, then the gracile ones are *Australopithecus* and the robust ones are *Paranthropus*.

Let's do another anatomical experiment to demonstrate how chewing works; you can stay sitting down for this one although you might want a mirror. Put your fingertips on the sides of your head, a little above and in front of your ears. Now open and close your mouth in an exaggerated chewing motion. As you close your jaw you will feel a muscle

Figure 14-5. Diagram showin the extent of the temporalis muscle in modern humans. The temporalis is the main chewing muscle.

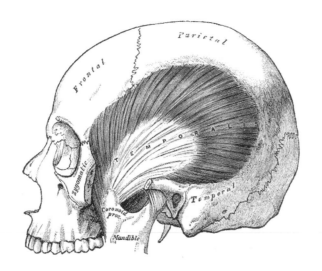

contact (if you're using a mirror you can see it make a small bulge on the side of your head). That's your *temporalis* muscle (Figure 14-5) and it's the major chewing muscle in mammals. Next, place your hands a couple of inches below your eyes and feel the bony arch that runs from your nose around to the side of your head about the level of your ear lobes. Got it? That's the *zygomatic arch* and it's shown cut away in Figure 14-5, so you can see the temporalis muscle which runs underneath it. The zygomatic doesn't move when you chew; its job is to provide structural bracing.

Please make a prediction about the size of the temporalis muscle and zygomatic arch in a hominin that does significantly more chewing than you do. More work should favor a bigger temporalis muscle and more bracing, right? How would you recognize that kind of change? More bracing would be obvious in the form of a larger, more massive zygomatic arch. Muscles don't fossilize but a bigger temporalis muscle needs a larger area of attachment (as we noted for the substantial neck muscles of the gorilla in Figure 13-4). Perhaps you haven't thought about this problem, but muscle can't attach to muscle; it has to attach to bone at both ends. As you know, the temporalis attaches to the jaw at one end and to the skull at the other, so that it pulls the jaw closed when it contracts. Now, if the skull is small (because the brain is small) and the temporalis is quite large, there might not be enough skull surface area for the temporalis to attach to. What would happen then? Selection would favor an expansion of the skull surface area. Take a look at the Paranthropus skulls in Figure 14-6. Wow, mohawks! Of course that's not hair; it's a bony extension of the skull called a *sagittal crest*. The crest would not have protruded from the skin. Instead, the entire volume between the skull and the top of the crest and almost all of the volume between the heavy zygomatic arch and the skull would have been filled with a muscle as big as your bicep! This is probably easiest to visualize on the *Paranthropus boisei* specimen, since it's most complete. Also note the very small incisors and canines and the huge molars and premolars. These folks lived to chew.

Now let's compare the other members of our rogues' gallery of australopiths (Figure 14-6). (I'm going to begin using a standard biological convention of abbreviating the genus name to a single letter such as *A. afarensis*.) Beginning about 3 MYA with the oldest australopiths for which there are suitably complete skulls, we can see a series of taxa—from *A. afarensis* through *A. africanus* to *A. sediba*—that become progressively more gracile over time, with a less and less massive chewing apparatus. But about 2.5 MYA some of the *Australopithecus* species seem to move in the opposite direction: A. platyops (sometimes called *Kenyanthropus platyops*, a genus-level designation that seems unwarranted) and *A. garhi* both have small sagittal crests. In fact, in the *A. garhi* photo the extent of the temporalis muscle is evident from "crease" line that starts behind the eye and extends up to the crest. Leaving aside the question of how many australopith species there were previously, by 2.5 MYA there was an adaptive radiation underway that involved significant dietary differences among the lineages. Some lineages started to specialize in easier-to-chew foods and others went in the opposite direction. That's allowed; evolution is often non-linear.

Before we leave our *Australopithecus* versus *Paranthropus* comparisons we should dig just a little deeper on these diet-tooth issues. Large

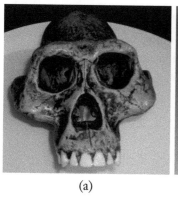 (a)

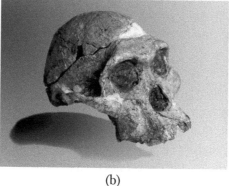 (b)

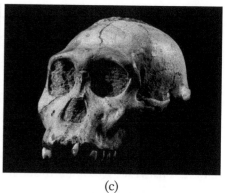 (c)

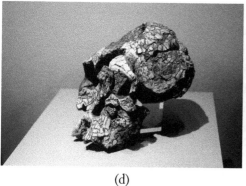 (d)

 (e)

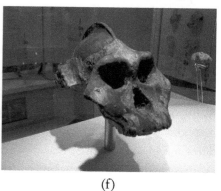 (f)

Figure 14-6.

a. *Reconstructions of various australopith skulls:* a. Australopithecus afarensis; 3 MYA

b. Australopithecus africanus; 2.5 MYA

c. Australopithecus sediba; 2 MYA

d. Australopithecus (Kenyanthropus) platyops; 2.5 MYA

e. Australopithecus garhi; 2.5 MYA

f. Paranthropus aethiopicus; 2.5 MYA

g. Paranthropus boisei; 1.7 MYA

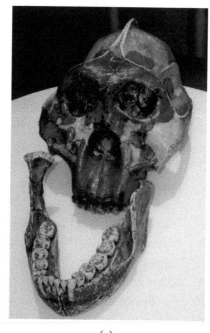 (g)

teeth, jaws, and temporalis muscles suggest food that was difficult to chew, requiring a lot of mastication to break it down—tough, perhaps fibrous food. Thick enamel means something different. It suggests food that was abrasive in some way. This could be because it was gritty—think about roots and tubers, for example. Or it could have been because the food itself included raspy elements, for example the silica that many grasses incorporate into their leaves. This suggests that the robust australopiths—perhaps including some transitional forms such as *A. garhi*—where eating food that was both tough to chew *and* abrasive. The foods of the gracile australopiths were apparently less demanding in these particular ways.

THE TRANSITION TO *HOMO*

One of the few conclusions that anthropologists *won't* disagree about is that the genus *Homo*—the genus to which all living people, but no other living species belong—was an offshoot of the genus *Australopithecus*. This conclusion is based on the simple observation that we share more derived features with *Australopithecus* than with any other known genus. However, extensive debate surrounds questions about precisely where in Africa and when the genus *Homo* arose, and about which member of the genus *Australopithecus* gave rise to *Homo*. Some argue for nearly lineal descent through the gracile (*Australopithecus*) line, from *A. afarensis*, to *A. africanus* (perhaps though *A. sediba*), to the first species of *Homo*. At another extreme there are claims that *A. afarensis* is the only know fossil ancestor of *Homo* and that all the other australopiths are on phylogenetic side-branches. How should we think about this question? Cladistically of course. Just as we identified lactation as the first derived trait of mammals, and bipedality as the first derived trait of hominins, what we want to do now is identify the first derived trait of the genus *Homo*.

We know the ways that modern humans and modern chimps differ. When we list those traits and look around in the fossil record for the first one, we have no difficulty because bipedality occurs so much before all the others. If we now think about the ways that modern humans differ from *Australopithecus*, again we have a substantial list, so we do know what traits to look for. *Homo* has a larger body size and a larger brain size than *Australopithecus*, but the size difference is not merely proportionate. The body of *Homo* is somewhat larger but the brain of *Homo* is much larger. In other words, the brain size/body size ratio (the standard way biologists compare brain size across species) is substantially larger in *Homo*. The limb proportions are different, with *Homo* having legs longer than arms and *Australopithecus* having the reverse pattern. *Homo* also lacks the climbing-related adaptations of *Australopithecus*, such an upward facing shoulder joint, a funnel-shaped rib cage, and curved fingers. *Homo* has proportionately larger incisors and proportionately smaller molars and premolars than *Australopithecus*. Let's review what's known about the various candidates for first member of our genus, to see what derived features they're sporting.

Homo (*Australopithecus*) *habilis*, 2.35-1.65 MYA, Figure (14-7). Fossils currently assigned to this taxon have been found in both southern and eastern Africa. It had both the short stature of 1.3-1.5 m (4.25-5.0 feet) and

Figure 14-7 Reconstructed skull of *Homo (Australopithecus) habilis*.

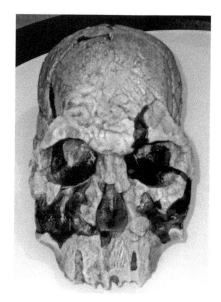

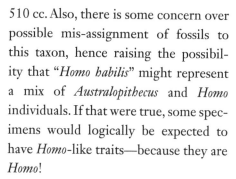

Figure 14-8 Reconstructed skulll of *Homo (Australopithecus) rudolfensis*.

Figure 14-9 Extensive fossils of *Homo (Australopithecus) naledi*.

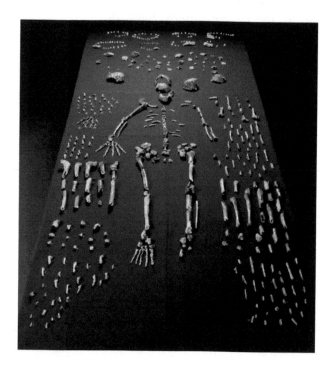

long arms characteristic of *Australopithecus*. Oldowan tools are often found in association with *H. (A.) habilis* remains but stone tools are known to pre-date the genus *Homo*, so this evidence is not definitive. The molar teeth of *H. (A.) habilis* are somewhat smaller than those of earlier hominins such as *A. africanus*, but still much larger than those of modern humans. Its primary claim to inclusion in *Homo* is its brain size thought to average around 600 cc, though estimates are controversial and varied because of the fragmentary nature of most fossils attributed to *H. (A.) habilis*. The best specimen (KNM-ER 1813, Figure 14-7) has a brain size of only 510 cc. Also, there is some concern over possible mis-assignment of fossils to this taxon, hence raising the possibility that "*Homo habilis*" might represent a mix of *Australopithecus* and *Homo* individuals. If that were true, some specimens would logically be expected to have *Homo*-like traits—because they are *Homo*!

Homo (Australopithecus) rudolfensis, 2.0-1.95 MYA, Figure 14-8. This is a poorly known taxon with few specimens, all from eastern Africa. They suggest a creature that is somewhat larger and more robust than *H. (A.) habilis*. Discoverers emphasize its less-projecting lower face, making it more similar to later *Homo* than to earlier *Australopithecus* (whose large jaws and teeth necessarily projected well in front of their eye sockets). They also argue that it had a larger brain than *H. (A.) habilis*. This claim is controversial because the best specimen (Figure 14-8) was found in fragments and has been reconstructed several different ways, yielding brain-size estimates that range widely, from 526 to 752 cc. Moreover because it was larger than *H. (A.) habilis* it may actually have had a smaller *relative* brain size (McHenry and Coffing, 2000). A few leg bones are sometimes attributed to *H. (A.) rudolfensis*, and they do suggest a larger body size than that of *H. (A.) habilis*, but they were not found together with *H. (A.) rudolfensis* skulls so the attribution is questionable.

Homo (Australopithecus) naledi, no date, Figure 14.9. This recently described taxon is represented by more than 1500 fragments from at least 15 individuals all found in a deep natural cave in southern Africa. There are no datable volcanic deposits and virtually no associated animal fossils, hence the complete uncertainty about the age of this hominin. These fossils have a number of australopith-like features. They were short in stature, the tallest being only 1.5 m (5.0 feet). Their brains were small, between 465 and 560 cc (based on four partial skulls). They possessed a shoulder joint, funnel-shaped rib cage, and curved fingers all suggestive of significant climbing. Many details of the teeth are also primitive. Some features of the wrist and fingertip resemble later *Homo*, and the legs appear to be somewhat longer than is typical of *Australopithecus*. The various individuals span a wide age range which is helpful for understanding patterns of growth and development in ancestral hominins. Overall, the taxon present few *Homo*-like traits, so why did its discovers assign it to *Homo*? I believe it was their interpretation of how the fossils came to be in the cave: The geological circumstances suggest that they could not have simply fallen in or been washed in by water after death. There are essentially no other animal fossils, not even much in the way of fossilized pollen, and no evidence of water flows that could have transported the fossils. To get to the chamber where the bones were found one must descend for quite a distance, then climb a steep ridge before making the final descent to fossil site. The argument is that only active, intentional transport could have gotten the hominins into the chamber. Since there are no traces of carnivore chewing on the bones, the discoverers contend that living *H. (A.) naledi* must have "buried" their dead in the chamber. In other words, they are using inferences about behavior to suggest a particular level of awareness in this taxon.

Homo ergaster 1.78-1.4 MYA, Figure 14-10. Note that there is no parenthetical "*Australopithecus*" embedded within this name. That reflects the general agreement that this taxon unequivocally belongs in *Homo*, and that is because *H. ergaster* is demonstrably more derived than any of the previously mention taxa. Its cranial capacity is 700–900 cc. It is large bodied—the most complete skeleton has been reconstructed to suggest a stature of 1.8 m (6.0 feet)—and its limb proportions are modern, with legs longer than arms. The climbing related adaptations of curved fingers, upward-facing shoulder joint and a funnel-shaped rib cage are gone. Compared to *Australopithecus* its incisors are enlarged and its molars and premolars are reduced, again more closely approaching the pattern that we see in modern humans. Except for its cranial capacity and other details of the skull, *H. ergaster* is significantly "modern."

By way of summarizing the features of these taxa we see that *H. (A.) habilis* probably has a larger brain size/body size ratio and somewhat smaller chewing teeth than most australopiths, but it is primitive in its small body size, apelike limb proportions and climbing-related

Figure 14-10 Reconstructed skull of *Homo ergarster.*

traits. *H. (A.) rudolfensis* may have been larger bodied than *H. (A.) habilis* and it had smaller jaws and teeth resulting in a less-projecting lower face. But its relative brain size was not especially large, and we don't have sufficient material to confidently reconstruct its body proportions. *H. (A.) naledi* is challenging to fit into our phylogenetic picture because we have no idea when it lived. It was decidedly small-brained and had typical *Australopithecus*-like climbing adaptations. Some features of the hand, somewhat longer legs, and the possibility that they buried their dead are *Homo*-like. Because these three taxa possess so few derived traits, many anthropologists not involved in the actual discoveries are inclined to regard all of them as belonging in *Australopithecus*. On the other hand, *H. ergaster* presents nearly the full suite of derived traits we were looking for and clearly belongs in the same genus with us.

What the traits of these four taxa jointly suggest is that, between 2.4 and 1.8 MYA there was a fairly vigorous adaptive radiation (Chapter 13) of australopiths. In the process, some lineages were beginning to exhibit *Homo*-like traits. At present, the fossil record does not allow us to recognize an earlier member of our genus than *H. ergaster* although—as the *H. (A.) naledi* discovery demonstrates—extremely rich new finds are possible. We should continue looking for the earliest *Homo* in deposits that are roughly 2 million years old, but it may remain difficult to identify the very first members of the *Homo* lineage because (all together now) evolution is gradual.

I want to close this chapter with an ecological perspective. When *Homo* does unambiguously emerge—in the form of *H. ergaster*—all known members of *Australopithecus* rapidly disappear from the fossil record. However, *Paranthropus* persists for at least another half a million years, in similar habitats with *Homo*. What do these observations suggest? As mentioned earlier, when two species are ecologically similar, one tends to displace the other. On the basis of their anatomical similarities, we suggested that *Homo* evolved from some *Australopithecus* species. The prompt extinction of *Australopithecus* suggests it was also *ecologically* similar to its successor, *Homo*.

CHAPTER SUMMARY

The second major phase of hominin evolution stretches from about 4.0 to around 1.8 MYA. That time period was dominated by the australopiths, including the more gracile *Australopithecus* and the more robust *Paranthropus*. One or both of these taxa began to make and use stone tools during this period. Despite being fully bipedal the australopiths did significant amounts of climbing and retained some other primitive (chimp-like) traits such as long arms and short legs. Our genus, *Homo*, almost certainly arose from earlier populations of the genus *Australopithecus*, probably between 2.3 and 1.7 MYA in savanna habitats in Africa. At that time horizon there are multiple taxa exhibiting some variation is the direction *Homo*-like derived features, probably in the context of an adaptive radiation of australopiths. However, until *H. ergaster* at 1.7 MYA, there are none that exhibit all the cranial, dental and locomotor traits that characterize later *Homo*.

CITED REFERENCES

Sonia Harmand, Jason E. Lewis, Craig S. Feibel, Christopher J. Lepre, Sandrine Prat, Arnaud Lenoble, Xavier Boës, Rhonda L.Quinn, Michel Brenet, Adrian Arroyo, Nicholas Taylor, Sophie Clément, Guillaume Daver, Jean-Philip Brugal, Louise Leakey, Richard A. Mortlock, James D. Wright, Sammy Lokorodi, Christopher Kirwa, Dennis V. Kent, & Hélène Roche (2015). "3.3-million-year-old stone tools from Lomekwi 3, West Turkana, Kenya." *Nature, 521*: 310–315.

R. Adriana Hernandez-Aguilar, Jim Moore, & Travis Rayne Pickering (2007). "Savanna chimpanzees use tools to harvest the underground storage organs of plants." *Proceedings of the National Academy of Sciences, USA, 104*: 19210–19213.

Henry M.McHenry & Katherine Coffing (2000) "*Australopithecus* to *Homo*: Transformations in body and mind." *Annual Review of Anthropology 29*: 125–146.

Shannon P. McPherron, Zeresenay Alemseged, Curtis W. Marean, Jonathan G. Wynn, Denné Reed, Denis Geraads, René Bobe, & Hamdallah A. Béarat (2010). "Evidence for stone-tool-assisted consumption of animal tissues before 3.39 million years ago at Dikika, Ethiopia." *Nature, 466*: 857–860.

David A. Raichlen, Adam D. Gordon, William E. H. Harcourt-Smith, Adam D. Foster, Wm. Randall Haas, Jr. (2010). Laetoli Footprints Preserve Earliest Direct Evidence of Human-Like Bipedal Biomechanics. *PLoS ONE, 5*: e9769.

FIGURE CREDITS

CHAPTER 15

WHY HUMANS ARE NOT CHIMPANZEES

Natural selection sculpts each kind of organism to meet the demands of its environment. Thus, humans (*Homo sapiens*) are not chimpanzees (*Pan troglodytes*) because of the different selection pressures that operated on our respective lineages and caused human and chimp adaptations to diverge. This chapter explores some of those selection pressures, concentrating on what is different about humans compared to our African ape cousins.

BIPEDALITY

None of our great ape relatives—chimpanzees, gorillas, or orangutans—move the way we do. Orangutans use all four of their limbs to clamber around the canopy of tropical forests. Chimpanzees and gorillas walk quadrupedally on the ground, carrying their weight on the soles of their feet and the knuckles of their hands. Chimpanzees also do a lot of climbing. Humans are striding bipeds, using only our hind limbs for locomotion. As discussed in the preceding two chapters, bipedality is the first derived trait of hominins, and we saw some of the anatomical changes that made it possible. Exactly when it evolved is unclear because there is dispute about whether or not the pre-*Australopithecus* forms are bipedal. But certainly by 3.7 million years ago (MYA) bipedality was well established.

The obvious question that we have left aside until now is, *why* did our lineage become bipedal in the first place? What benefits might it have provided? Paleoanthropologists have several plausible ideas and all of them ultimately trace back to the effects of a long-term climate change. Beginning in the Miocene Epoch, roughly 20 million years ago, the earth's climate began an accelerating series of cooling and drying cycles that continued until the end of the Pleistocene, a mere 12,000 years ago. In Africa, where almost all of human evolution occurred, this cooling and drying caused dramatic habitat changes. The forests shrank, and there was an expansion of more open habitats dominated by grasses and scattered trees. These more open habitats, called savanna and woodland, differ in many ways from forests; they are hotter, sunnier, drier, and support more large game animals, especially ones that form herds. They also have more large predators such as lions, leopards, cheetahs, hyenas, and the dreaded cape hunting dog.

The other great apes are all primarily forest dwellers, and their fortunes shrank along with the forests. There are an estimated 300,000 chimpanzees in the wild versus 7,441,000,000 people (as this book goes to press). We humans are the apes who left (or were pushed out of) the dwindling forests and began to exploit new niches in the expanding woodlands and savannas of a progressively cooler and drier Africa. So, our question about the advantages of bipedalism should probably be framed in terms of this new niche, especially since bipedality does not become clearly established until hominins—in the form of *Australopithecus*—colonized those savanna environments.

Here I'll discuss four hypothesized advantages of bipedalism, and they are not in any way mutually exclusive; in other words, multiple selection pressures could have simultaneously pushed our ancestors toward bipedalism. The first possible advantage concerns getting around in an extensive two-dimensional habitat (as compared to forests which are three-dimensional). Resources can be far-flung and patchy in savanna and woodland habitats, and therefore early hominins may have needed to forage over long distances. Bipedalism seems to have been an energetically efficient way to cover these long distances. Sockol (et al., 2007) used treadmill studies and showed that bipedally walking humans use 75% fewer calories than chimpanzees to cover the same horizontal distance. Second, bipedalism is cooler, literally. It exposes less body area to the hottest perpendicular rays of the sun—just the top of the head and the shoulders, as compared to the entire trunk in quadrupeds—and additionally it raises more of the body farther from the ground where the temperatures are lower and there is more cooling wind. This cooling function would have been more useful for a savanna-dwelling than for a forest-dwelling species. Third, by extending the vertical reach, bipedalism allows foraging from the smaller trees and bushes that are common in these open habitats. Finally, bipedalism frees the forelimbs for other purposes, such as carrying food or other resources, and for wielding tools and weapons that could have aided in hunting herd animals or in fending off predators. Note that chimps will walk bipedally—though inefficiently—if they are carrying an armload of some favorite food.

EXTRACTIVE FORAGING

There is a saying (rooted in physics) that nature abhors a vacuum. Ecologists have a similar saying, that evolution abhors an empty niche. If there is a way to make a living in a particular environment, selection is likely to find it. Our ancestors didn't make their living the way many of us do today—earning a salary and buying what we need from people who earn a salary provisioning us. Like other "wild" animals our ancestors had to find all of the resources they needed in their environment. Thus, an animal's ecology defines a very prominent set of selection pressures acting on it. Our ancestors were dependent on balancing their energy budgets every day, making sure they got enough nutrients to support their growth, maintenance, and reproductive needs. Make the right choices and you survive; screw up and you're dead—either from starvation or because you poison yourself. Evolutionarily, it's important to get this right, every day.

Our ancestors' had no grocery stores, but does that mean their diets were like those of modern chimpanzees? Or are dietary differences another set of factors that pushed chimp and human adaptations in different directions? The problem may seem overwhelming because human diet is so variable: People eat different foods in China or in Morocco than you do. But those cultural differences are relatively superficial and recent; we want to know what kinds of diets predominated over the big sweep of human evolution. Anthropologists have several ways of reconstructing what our ancestors ate. One is to sift the fossil and archaeological records for food remains or for indications of how foods were processed. Another is to study existing hunter-gatherer populations. Hunter-gatherers do not have any domesticated animals or crops. Domestication is less than 10,000 years old, so, for several million years before that, humans had to get all their food from naturally occurring plants and animals. Thus, existing hunter-gatherers provide a glimpse into the pre-agricultural past that prevailed for 99.9% of the time our lineage has been on the planet.

By studying existing hunter-gatherers, and the ecology of our ape cousins, we have learned that human diets are very different from those of our close primate relatives—chimpanzees, gorillas, or orangutans. Each of these apes has a unique diet, to be sure, but they are all heavily based on collected foods. Collected foods are ones that you just pick up and eat. If you have ever picked and eaten berries on a hike, then you have made use of a collected food. But collected foods are not the mainstay of hunter-gatherer diets. Humans rely instead on extracted foods. Extracted foods cannot simply be plucked and eaten. They need at least some additional processing or handling. A soft fruit can be collected, but a nut, surrounded by a hard shell, must be extracted. Likewise, tubers or roots must be dug up, and large animals must be pursued, killed, and butchered, so these are all extracted food. Chimpanzees, our closest living relatives, have diets that are about 95% collected and about 5% extracted. In contrast, human hunter-gatherers are at the opposite end of the spectrum, relying on extracted foods for more than 90% of their intake. This is a dramatic difference, but one that lets us see what adaptations emerge to support even small amounts of extractive foraging. Studies of chimpanzees in their natural habitats reveal not only what they eat; they reveal how chimps procure these foods. One consistent observation across multiple chimp populations is that they spontaneously make and use tools to facilitate their extractive foraging, but do not when they are relying on collected foods.

TOOL MANUFACTURE AND USE

Because extracted foods cannot be simply picked up and eaten, tools are often useful in accessing and processing them. This is not limited to human extractive foraging. Chimps use wadded up leaves as a sponge to extract water from crevices, twigs to extract edible termites from their mounds, and the combination of hammer and anvil stones to crack hard nuts. Chimpanzees are predominantly forest-living animals but, as for most species, there is some variability in the habitats they exploit. In the most open (savanna-woodland) habitats where they occur they use tools to dig for roots and tubers (Hernandez-Aguilar et al., 2007). This association between tool use and extractive foraging is not limited to our closest relatives. For example, tools are used in extractive foraging by California sea otters and by New Caledonian Crows.

As our ancestors moved out of the forest, they encountered many fewer fruits—the mainstay of the modern chimp diet. Many of the new food sources they did encounter, including underground roots and tubers and potential large animal prey, required significant extraction. These dietary shifts thus triggered a greater reliance on technology, for example, hammer and anvil stones in the case of nut extraction, digging implements for roots and tubers, and sharp implements for killing and butchering animals. Fortunately we do not have to rely on guesses and plausible arguments. The tools and the scars of their use can be highly durable and many have been discovered by archaeologists.

Humans have been making stone tools for at least 3.3 (recently extended from 2.6) million years, and the archaeological record offers evidence in the form of use scars suggesting they were used for digging tubers and for butchering animals—two kinds of extractive foraging. Remember that 3.3 million years ago there were apparently no members of the genus *Homo*, so the tool makers and users must have been some kind of relatively small-brained *Australopithecus*. If a large brain is not required (chimps have roughly *Australopithecus*-sized brains), it's likely that hominins used tools even earlier than 3.3 MYA, but tools that were made from more perishable materials than stone. Such earlier tool use is very likely, because some basic tool-making and tool-using abilities seem to be primitive (in the cladistic sense) in the chimp-human group. In other words, because humans and chimps both possess these abilities to some degree, the simplest explanation is that our common ancestor did as well.

Due to an expanding reliance on extracted foods in the human lineage, selection for the ability to make and use tools was stronger in our ancestors than it was in the ancestors of modern chimpanzees. Even the earliest hominin-produced stone tools (of the Lomekwian and Oldowan types) are more sophisticated in design and execution than tools made by modern chimpanzees—either in the wild or in experimental settings where chimps were explicitly trained to make such tools (Toth and Schick (2009).

BRAIN EXPANSION

Extracted foods are not just *physically* difficult to acquire. Accessing them also requires *knowledge, technique, and expertise*. What kind of shriveled leaf signals a fat tuber below; what is the best way to stalk a wildebeest on a cloudy day; what distinguishes the tracks of a wounded animal; what techniques leech the toxins out various foods; what are the best materials to make each type of tool and where can those materials be found? Thus extractive foraging imposes mental demands on the forager that can generate selection pressure for increased brain size. And we do see a dramatic increase in brain size over the course of human evolution.

It can't be emphasized enough that chimpanzees are *not* our ancestors. They are our cousins; they share a common ancestor with us. So when we observe that both chimps and human use tools, for example, we incline toward the parsimonious assumption that both species inherited that habit from a tool-using common ancestor.

Returning to brain size, we see that the earliest hominins were no more brainy than modern chimps, both having cranial capacities on the order of 350 cc. (The brain size of fossils is estimated from the size of the region of the skull that contains the brain, and is thus measured as volume, in cubic centimeters. Brain size of living creatures is typically measured as weight in grams. However, since 1 cc of brain tissue weighs very close to 1 g, these numbers are easy to compare). So, we might profitably guess that the brain size of the chimp-human common ancestor was also in the 350 cc range. Chimps' brains have not budged from there since our divergence. What happened to brain size in the hominin lineage? By the time of *Australopithecus afarensis* (roughly 4.0-3.0 MYA) brains had increased in size by about 10% from the assumed ancestral

baseline, to about 440 cc. Over the next million years there were a variety of *Australopithecus* species, which as you know from Chapter 14, differed somewhat in brain size ranging up to about 700 cc (though that estimate for *H. (A). rudolfensis* is controversial and has been challenged). The first *undisputed* member of the genus *Homo*—*Homo ergaster*—had a brain size of about 700–900 cc, more than twice the australopith baseline. The average brain size for *Homo sapiens*, our species, is about 1,300 cc, 3 times larger than that of our assumed common ancestor with chimps.

Of course we can puff up our chests and be proud of our gigantic brains. But an evolutionary perspective suggests further questions. Adaptations exist because of the reproductive benefits they provide but they also have costs—costs that must be outweighed by those benefits for selection to favor them, but costs nonetheless. This perspective is especially salient because it turns out that brain tissue is extremely costly. You already know how needy brains are: Even brief interruptions in oxygen supply will kill a brain (so-called brain death) well before the rest of the body dies. That's because the brain uses a lot of metabolic resources, much more that its proportionate share, as we'll see below. These cost considerations emphasize just how substantial the benefits of brain expansion must have been, but they also lead to the interesting question of how those costs were paid. Leslie Aiello and Jonathan Wells (2002) have offered an intriguing answer to that question.

Here is their core idea. An animal's body size is an important determinant of its total metabolic needs but some kinds of tissue are more expensive to operate than others. In other words, body size alone does not tell the whole story; it matters how much of that body is made up of cheap or expensive tissues. To evaluate "cheap" or "expensive," we need some kind of scale and Aiello and Wells elected to use kilocalories per day, at rest (RMR for "resting metabolic rate"). On this RMR scale, the cheapest kind of tissue is fat. Next comes muscle, but this is a big jump. At rest, muscle is a bit more than four times more expensive to maintain than fat. But most expensive of all is organs, things like intestines and brains. The human brain amounts to about 2% of total body weight, but consumes roughly 20% of RMR; in other words, *ten times* the consumption rate of the body as a whole.

All these caloric bills need to be paid; otherwise the organism dies. How do hominins pay for such big brains? Aiello and Wells have argued that there is a trade-off among different kinds of similarly costly tissues. You could not save enough calories to pay for a bigger brain by reducing the amount of some cheap tissue like fat; that would be like trying to pay for your rent by drinking less coffee. (In fact, there are good reasons, which we will come to later, why fat must *increase*, not decrease, when brains increase.) The only way to pay for a big brain is by significantly cutting back on some other costly tissue. Following that line of thinking, Aiello convincingly argues that big hominin brains were paid for by a reduction in hominin guts—digestive tissue. Of course, you cannot blithely delete your digestive system because that is how you extract calories from your food. So, if you want to reduce caloric expenditures on guts in order to afford a bigger brain, you would need to switch to a higher quality—more calorically dense—diet. That way, you could still extract lots of calories, but do so with less digestive processing, with less gut.

This is a clever argument, and it probably is at least partially correct. For example, we do have evidence—both from fossil teeth and from fossilized food remains—that our hominin ancestors were moving away from an almost completely vegetarian diet, like that of our chimpanzee cousins, to a diet that included more animal prey. We also have evidence that the expanding tool kit of early hominins was used in acquiring these new foods. Thus, there may have been a kind of ongoing feedback system, with brain evolution supporting tool use, and tool use supporting a shift to higher-quality foods, thus allowing the brain to be paid for by digestive savings. All of this would have had to occur gradually, in small steps; but that's how adaptive evolution generally occurs—incrementally, gradually.

We can get pretty good estimates of brain size for fossil taxa, because the brain more or less fills the skull. But what about gut size estimates? Aiello and Wells have an interesting perspective. You may remember that there are body-shape differences between *Australopithecus* and *Homo*. *Australopithecus* had a funnel-shaped rib cage, narrow at the shoulder and wide at the gut, but *Homo* generally has a barrel-shaped thorax, without the widening toward the waist. Aiello and Wells suggest that these shape differences are a direct consequence of *Homo*'s smaller gut. The *Australopithecus* rib cage had to flare out at the waist to accommodate its larger digestive system.

CONTROL OF FIRE

Most animals run from fire, but humans find it mesmerizing. People will stare into a fire as willingly as they'll watch a sitcom. We're not repelled by fire; we're attracted to it. Why should our brains be wired that way? Perhaps it's because fire was an important tool for our ancestors.

Because time destroys everything, early fossil evidence—of anything—tends to be scarcer than recent fossil evidence. There is good evidence for the use of fire by humans 300,000 years ago, but poorer evidence before that. Richard Wrangham, a Harvard-based anthropologist, acknowledges that, because fire occurs naturally (e.g., lightning-caused fires), the earlier we look, the more difficult it is to tell natural fires from human-built hearths. But he suggests in his book, *Catching Fire* (2009), that hearth fires burned hotter and longer in one place than natural fires. Archaeological evidence supports the presence of hearths back to about 1.5 MYA (James, 1989). In other words, members of the genus *Homo* may have been using fire since their origins.

The benefits of fire are many. It decontaminates food. It makes more of the nutrients in plant foods available for digestion by breaking down their tough cell walls (remember the challenges faced by the lizards forced to switch to a plant-based diet). And it makes it possible to consume much more meat by rendering it chewable. If you have ever eaten raw meat—steak tartare, for example—I guarantee that it had been heavily processed by grinding, pounding or extremely thin slicing. This is because raw unprocessed muscle meat is almost impossible to chew (large carnivores such as lions do not chew it; they tear it and swallow it in large unchewed chunks and let their guts do the work). Wrangham argues that fire is what made meat an efficient source of nutrients for hominins. His ideas mesh well with those of Aiello and Wells because fire would make nutrients available with less expenditure on digestion, thus allowing reductions in gut size with the savings channeled to brain expansion, which in turn would allow more successful extractive foraging.

Wrangham's ideas also have implications for hominin social structure. At least at the beginning hominins probably weren't very good at making fire. It's much easier to keep a fire going than to start one. And it's probably easier to keep it going in one place than to carry it around. This line of thinking, if valid, suggest the emergence of "home bases" where foragers maintained a fire, returned to cook, and perhaps share the results of their labors. In line with this, the archaeological record suggests that some sites were intensively used and contain accumulations of animal-prey remains that could not be the result of a single visit.

BODY FAT

Body fat adds to the costs of locomotion, because every pound of it has to be lugged around. You have surely noticed that heavier people tend to get out of breath climbing up stairs. Nevertheless, for some reason selection has favored fat accumulation in a wide array of species. In agreement with other anthropologists, Aiello and Wells believe that reason is insurance against periodic food shortages. They suggest that fat is like a savings account where occasional foraging surpluses can be banked, to be later burned for calories during periods of food scarcity. This is certainly *part* of the story, because it is a pattern we see in a wide variety of animals; they put on a little fat in the good season and use it up when times are tough. But it cannot be the whole story, because humans are nearly unique among land mammals in how much fat they store. And I am not referring to the obesity epidemic; I am talking about normal, healthy people—even hunter-gatherers. Let's look at some numbers.

The way to measure this is simply to express fat as a percentage of total body weight. For men this number is around 14%, and for women it is 26–28%. If you weigh 150 pounds and you are an average man, about 21 of those pounds would be fat; if you are a woman of the same weight (150), roughly 40 pounds would be fat. The fact is that humans are *much* fatter than other animals. Appropriate comparisons might be other mammals that live in savanna habitats like those where australopiths and *Homo* evolved. For example, ungulates (hoofed mammals)—whose ancestors' bones we find in hominin butchery sites—have 2–3% body fat (a 150-pound ungulate would have roughly 4 pounds of fat). Open-country primates such as baboons have 3–5%. On the view that fat represents a caloric savings account, one would need to explain two facts: 1) why humans face so much greater food scarcity risks than other animals living in the same habitat, and 2) why women face so much greater food-scarcity risk than men. The first challenge seems daunting. Regarding the second, one could argue that the caloric demands of pregnancy and lactation dictate that women must have more stored resources. But if this were true, all mammals should exhibit sex differences in body fat—but only humans do!

Ok then, why are humans so fat? There are clearly other functions of fat beyond guarding against starvation in tough times. For example, the brain—there it is again—is the fattiest organ in the body. Fat is essential to the operation of every nerve cell in the brain. This is true of all brains, not just human brains. But because we have such big brains, we need more fat to build and maintain them than other animals. Now you see why women are fatter than men. Over their reproductive careers, women will build multiple large brains. So the pregnancy-and-lactation argument was sniffing up the right tree, but for the wrong reason. Women do need extra calories to pay the energetic costs of baby making, but they also need (particular kinds of) fat as an essential material for constructing that quintessential hominin adaptation, a huge brain. Chapter 19 will show how modern diets are restricting our access to these critical brain-building fats.

RECIPROCITY

In Chapter 10 we explained that reciprocity can take hold where there are opportunities to trade small costs for large benefits. If one were regularly dealing with large spoilable resources, for example a recently killed animal, there would be many opportunities for such trades. Because of satiation—because of the limits to what a person can consume and metabolize on any given occasion—each successive pound of meat is less valuable than the one before it. (You'd pay $10 for your first burger, and maybe your second, but not your fifth or sixth; it wouldn't be worth it because you're already full.) What a hominin hunter *could* do with excess meat is to invest it in the prospect of returned favors from other hunters. Another certainty about hunting is that it's *uncertain*; you can work hard, spend a lot of time following game trails and stalking animals, and still come up with nothing. This means that, sooner or later, even the best hunters are going to be hungry, so everyone has an interest in establishing and maintaining reciprocal relationships of food sharing. All of these considerations suggest that a shift from a chimp-like diet of fruit to one with substantial dependence on the meat of grazing animals would create more intense selection for reciprocity.

Of course humans are not the only animals to share food. In many species of mammals and birds parents share food with their own off-spring—an observation which is not at all puzzling from an evolutionary perspective. Food sharing among adults is less common in other species, but it does occur in certain contexts. In an excellent recent review of food sharing in humans and other primates Adrian Jaeggi and Michael Gurven (2013) conclude that the same factors are at work:

"The majority of foods shared among humans and primates come in relatively large packages that are difficult to monopolize and yield diminishing marginal returns to consumption. Also, there is asynchrony in acquisition, resulting in food possessors and nonpossessors." Jaeggi & Gurven (2013, p. 186).

It is also notable that, among contemporary foraging peoples, whose behavior we can observe directly, all resources are not shared in the same way. Gathered plant foods tend to be kept within the nuclear family (just the mom, dad, and kids, and maybe grandparents), but the meat of hunted animal prey is shared outside the family; and larger prey are shared more widely than smaller ones. Again, all of this is in line with simple predictions from reciprocity theory. Meat—more precisely meat's large packet size (a giraffe), diminishing marginal returns (how many burgers can you eat?), and unpredictability (it's easy to come home empty-handed)—would strongly favor reciprocity. So, what is the evidence that hominins did significantly depend on meat? The answer is knowable because archaeologists can recognize the fossilized bones of animals that were hunted by the stone-tool cut marks on those bones. Such evidence is first seen at 3.4 MYA (Chapter 14) and is abundant after 1.8 MYA. Recent work has turned up three large assemblages of such hominin-processed animal bone from about 2.0 MYA (Ferraro et al. 2013). It seems hominins have had opportunities to benefit from reciprocity for at least 20,000 centuries.

SEXUAL DIVISION OF LABOR

Studies of contemporary foragers have contributed many insights about the selection pressures on our hunting-and-gathering ancestors; and we have already seen several. From studies of contemporary foragers we know that, with very few minor exceptions, there is a very strong sexual division of labor: Men hunt larger animal prey and women forage for immobile plant foods. Interestingly, this same difference is found among chimpanzees. Chimps only derive about 1% of their total food intake from animal prey—most of it being monkeys. But this hunting is almost exclusively done by males, who cooperate with each other to close off the escape routes of their intended prey. When chimps are successful in capturing a monkey, the resulting meat is shared among the males who cooperated in the hunt and with females who happen to be ovulating at the time—and thus able to conceive. Yes, chimps regularly trade meat for sex, but in general, males get more of the meat, and thus female chimps spend considerably more time fishing for termites and cracking nuts (two good alternative sources of protein) than males do.

A related and very interesting question in human evolution is whether or not enduring male-female bonds—families—grew out of a mutual dependence on the products of each other's hunting and gathering efforts. In other words, did ancestral men and women pair up so she could provide the calories and he could provide the protein? Does the fact that males share their foraging gains more widely argue against this view? Or is it just a consequence of the need to insure against uncertain hunting yields? In any case, this sexual division of labor is highly consistent across a wide array of foraging societies, but its evolutionary origins are still uncertain.

ENDURING MALE-FEMALE BONDS

We will consider this trait in more detail in Chapter 22 but it deserves some mention in our survey of human "peculiarities." Marriage is essentially a human universal, occurring in virtually all described societies. In many tribal societies there are no licenses, and rituals may be minimal or absent, but the marital bond is recognized and it carries certain rights and obligations. Our cousins the chimps have no such relationships; in fact their mating systems are among the most promiscuous of any primate. Female chimps have a fertile span of a few days every month, right around their ovulation—just as human females do. But the differences stop there; chimp females typically mate with all of the males in their social group during each of their monthly fertile windows.

Why are human mating bonds so stable? One possible explanation was mentioned above: They are essentially economic partnerships—protein/calorie alliances—that arise out of the sexual division of labor. Without a mate you'd be missing essential nutrients. That may have some explanatory power; it may describe some of the glue that keeps men and women together. Note that, like any scientific hypothesis it makes testable predictions. For example, each sex should be more likely to initiate divorce where the mate is not delivering his/her share of the bargain. But there may be other forces favoring stable mateships. This idea is linked back to another derived hominin feature: bipedality.

This shift in mode of locomotion is the first derived hominin trait to appear in the fossil record, and it produced a variety of changes in the anatomy of the trunk and limbs. Unless they are running very fast, quadrupedal animals have two or three feet in contact with the ground at all times. But even when walking rather slowly, bipeds often have only one foot touching the ground. Thus, there are dramatic weight-bearing and balance differences between these two modes of locomotion, which in turn require different sets of muscular connections between the pelvis and the hind limb. The anatomical aspects of bipedality were covered in more detail in Chapter 13; here we consider a related consequence. As a result of the biomechanics of bipedality, the hominin pelvis has become twisted and compressed compared to the arrangement we see in the other apes. This kind of evolutionary modification is not at all unusual; as you know, selection modifies existing structures to meet new demands. But the pelvis is not only involved in balance and weight-bearing; it is also involved in the birth process—human infants have to pass through the pelvis as they are born (or had to, for the vast span of human evolution before Caesarian section was available). The same pelvic twisting and compression that was necessary for bipedalism has also constricted the birth canal (Rosenberg and Trevathan 1995). Anthropologists call this the "obstetrical dilemma."

To make the point more strongly, our ape cousins face no such dilemma. Being quadrupedal their pelvic structure was not compromised by the structural needs of bipedality. And being small-brained, their infants slip out easily. Consequently a non-human ape might even sleep through the birth of her infant. Not so for women. Bipedal moms and big brained babies make a bad team. The skull must be large enough to accommodate the infant brain and that same skull needs to pass through the birth canal without damage to the skull's precious contents, or to the mom. It might seem odd that selection would saddle women with such a risky birthing arrangement where some infants die from being unable to fit through their mother's birth canal. But remember the sequence of derived traits. Bipedality evolved millions of years before hominin brains expanded significantly. And when they did expand, that expansion was gradual. Selection is a great tinkerer, retaining any bit of junk—any mutation—that happens to improve the design. Two types of mutations seem to have been favored as bigger brains began to collide, quite literally, with bipedal pelves (the plural of pelvis).

The first type of mutation adjusted the timing of birth. If selection is favoring large brains but the birth canal cannot be expanded because of locomotor constraints, a possible solution is to bring the infant through the birth canal earlier, before its brain has finished growing. Of course, this tactic produces less-developed

infants who may have a harder time surviving the first weeks and months after birth. But this is one route that selection took, and, as a consequence, we humans have very helpless—the technical word is *altricial*—newborns. Human babies are much less mature than, for example, chimpanzee infants; newborn chimps can ordinarily walk, climb, and cling to their mothers without help or support. Partly because of our "hind-start," we humans grow up much more slowly than the other great apes.

A second type of mutation also helped in addressing the big-brain-versus-bipedal-pelvis problem. Altricial, hind-start infants are at great risk, especially out on the savanna. A mother chimpanzee can care for her well-developed infant on her own. But hominin mothers have their hands full with altricial infants. This situation might favor hominin dads who offered some material help. Because male mammals never gestate or lactate, they have potentially much higher reproductive rates than female mammals (see Chapter 21 for a fuller discussion of these issues). This leads to the generally correct prediction that male mammals will compete to fertilize as many females as possible and not bother much with any resulting offspring. That is precisely what we see in chimpanzees, gorillas, and orangutans.

But consider this hypothetical situation: Imagine, for example, that because her offspring was so helpless, a mother absolutely could not rear it alone. In such a case, a male who fertilized females and then went off to search for additional mating partners doomed each and every one of his offspring to death. My intention is not to suggest that the human case is, or ever was, that extreme. No, I just want to suggest that early *Homo* males hurt their offspring's survival chances when they abandoned their mating partners. More precisely, they hurt those survival chances more than a similarly abandoning chimpanzee father does. That is the kind of selection pressure that could drive the evolution of paternal care. This argument—which is intended to explain why humans are among the tiny minority of mammals that have enduring male-female bonds and paternal care—is discussed more fully in Chapter 22.

One additional derived human trait—language—is so unique that I have dedicated an entire chapter to it.

CHAPTER SUMMARY

Many of the selection pressures discussed in this chapter are portrayed as a flow chart in Figure 15-1. Cooling and drying conditions reduced the amount of African forest and correspondingly expanded the amount of more open savanna and woodland habitat. At least one lineage of apes colonized that open habitat and began exploiting new resources. This colonist adopted a bipedal mode of locomotion, which was more efficient for the extensive travel needed to harvest dispersed savanna resources, and slowly moved into a more extractive foraging niche since few readily collectable foods were available. Tool use, probably already weakly developed in the common ancestor of humans and chimpanzees, became even more advantageous as the amount of extracted food increased. Brain expansion was likewise favored as it supported tool-using and

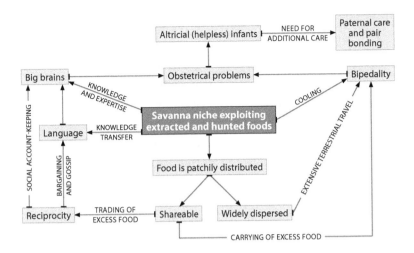

-making abilities, as well as the extensive knowledge and expertise needed to be a successful extractive forager. The controlled use of fire allowed more nutrients to be extracted from both animal and plant foods. Cooking, and a focus on higher-nutrient foods, allowed a decrease in gut size which at least partly "paid for" increases in brain size. The combination of large packet size, diminishing returns of consumption, and highly variable success rates made reciprocity among hunters an effective strategy for preventing starvation. Sexual division of labor and long-term bonds between individual males and females emerged, perhaps in response to the helpless infants that were selection's compromise to the opposing demands of bipedality and large brains.

Figure 15-1. Possible selection pressures arising out of a shift to extractive foraging in savanna habitats.

CITED REFERENCES

Leslie C. Aiello & Jonathan C. K. Wells (2002) "Energetics and the evolution of the genus *Homo*."

Joseph V. Ferraro et al. (2013) "Earliest archaeological evidence of persistent hominin carnivory" *PloS One 8*: e62174

R. Adriana Hernandez-Aguilar, Jim Moore & Travis Rayne Pickering (2007) "Savanna chimpanzees use tools to harvest the underground storage organs of plants." *Proceedings of the National Academy of Sciences of the USA 104*: 19210–19213.

Adrian V. Jaeggi & Michael Gurven (2013) "Natural cooperators: Food sharing in humans and other primates." *Evolutionary Anthropology 22*: 186–195.

Steven R. James (1989). "Hominid Use of Fire in the Lower and Middle Pleistocene: A Review of the Evidence". *Current Anthropology, 30*: 1–26.

Karen Rosenberg & Wenda Trevathan (1995) 'Bipedalism and human birth: The obstetrical dilemma revisited. *Evolutionary Anthropology 4*: 161–168.

Michael D. Sockol, David A. Raichlen & Herman Pontzer (2007) "Chimpanzee locomotor energetics and the origin of human bipedalism." Proceedings of the National Academy of Sciences of the USA 104: 12265–12269.

Nicholas Toth & Kathy Schick (2009) "The Oldowan: The tool making of early hominins and chimpanzees compared." *Annual Review of Anthropology 38*: 289–305.

Richard Wrangham (2009) *Catching Fire*. Basic Books; New York.

FIGURE CREDIT

15-1: Image created by Judith Geiger.

CHAPTER 16

THE SPREAD OF HOMO

Now that we have a framework for understanding the selection pressures that may have been important in shaping humans, let's return to the fossil record. The genus *Homo* emerged in Africa roughly between 1.8 and 1.7 million years ago (MYA). Depending on which taxonomic scheme one follows, there might be as many as eight species in the genus; perhaps more remain to be discovered; or maybe, as some recent discoveries suggest, there are fewer. Where did they live? What are the plausible ancestor–descendant relationships among these species? Did multiple species of *Homo* ever coexist—either at the same time in different parts of the world, or perhaps with overlapping geographic ranges but distinct habitats? How did a single species—*Homo sapiens*—come to occupy the whole planet? Questions like these are the focus of this chapter.

Of course, the basic evidence is the fossils themselves, their anatomical features and the locations where they are found. This evidence shows that particular fossil types (candidate species) are 1) limited to certain areas, or 2) found in some areas first and only later appear elsewhere. For example, forms attributed to *Homo neanderthalensis* fit the first pattern because they are restricted to western Eurasia between roughly 140 thousand years ago (KYA) and 30 KYA. Characterizing the second pattern, *Homo sapiens* appeared in Africa perhaps as early as 195 KYA and subsequently dispersed to all continents except Antarctica.

While there are many species to keep track of, this part of the story is not so difficult to follow. To review what you learned in Chapters 13 and 14, and to link it to our current focus on the genus *Homo*, Figure 16-1 summarizes one view of the ancestor-descendant relationship among the various hominin taxa. The vertical axis is time, with the present at the top of the diagram and our common ancestors with the other African *apes* at the bottom.

HOMO ERGASTER AND HOMO ERECTUS

I'll be dealing with the most recent two million years of human evolution in temporal order, from the earliest, so we'll begin where we ended Chapter 14, with the first undoubted member of our genus, *Homo ergaster* some 1.78 MYA. Just as there is debate about whether some of the later *Australopithecus* (such as *habilis* and *rudolfensis*) should be placed in *Homo*, there are also naming issues concerning the more recent kinds of *Homo*. The first of these concerns *Homo ergaster* itself. Here the issue is whether *Homo ergaster* is sufficiently distinct from another taxon, *Homo erectus*, that was first discovered on the island of Java (part of Indonesia) in the late 19th century. By international convention, the names attached to earlier-described forms have priority, so if *H. ergaster* and *H. erectus* are really a single species, that species has to be called "*H. erectus*." This is not a terribly big deal. Since

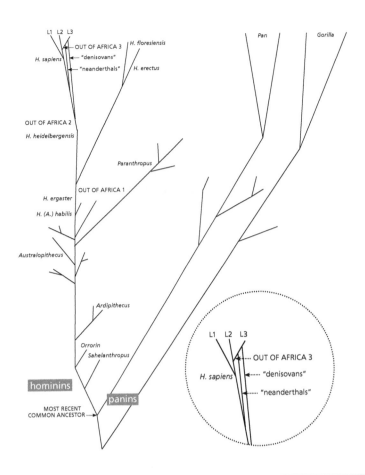

we're unlikely to discover whether these two taxa interbred, many anthropologists dodge the problem by calling *H. ergaster* "African *erectus*." No harm done. Everybody knows what specimens we mean, so we can separate these taxa again in the future if that seems justified. An African form (KNM-WT 15000) is shown in Figure 14-10 and a Javan example (Sangiran 17) is shown in Figure 16-2. The reason I don't want you to get bogged down in that debate is because there are much more interesting issues to steal our attention, like Java! What the heck? How did those hominins get way over there? Up until now we haven't discussed any fossil sites outside

Figure 16-1. Appoximate ancestor-descendant relationships among hominin (and possible hominin) taxa. Sister groups of African apes are shown.

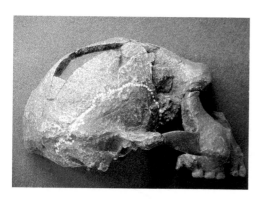

Figure 16-2. An Asian *Homo erectus* skull from Java.

of Africa, because there aren't *any*. All of that changes with *Homo*.

The original Javan *H. erectus* finds, augmented by subsequent material from multiple sites on the island, have been challenging to date. Recent work suggests that some of these specimens may be as old as 1.49 MYA, but that is not the end of the story. There are similar fossils from Dmanisi, Georgia in west-central Asia that are dated to around 1.8 MYA, as old as or perhaps slightly older than the African *H. ergaster* specimens. In addition there are classic *Homo erectus* fossils from China, Viet Nam, Turkey, Hungary, and Spain (The Spanish ones are sometimes put in a separate species, *H. antecessor*.) In most of the Old World, including Africa, *Homo erectus* types seem to continue for about a million years in Africa and then disappear after about 0.7 MYA (700 KYA). They persist somewhat longer in Europe, until about 450 or 400 KYA. But one of the most surprising aspects of the *H. erectus* saga is that, in China, they continue to appear in the fossil record until less than 30 KYA! This makes *H. erectus* the longest-lived hominin taxon, enduring from about 1.8 MYA to about 27 KYA, a span of 1.75 million years (Wood and Boyle 2016).

When I said "classic" *Homo erectus* in the preceding paragraph I was referring to fossils that are quite modern (like us) in terms of their body size, post-cranial skeleton and teeth, but that still retain some primitive features of the skull, including a smaller cranial capacity (between 850 and 1100 cc), quite heavy brow ridges and zygomatic arches, and a forehead that slopes backward from the brows, rather than rising vertically as yours does. Of all the geographically scattered *H. erectus* fossils, the ones that fit this classic description *least* well are the oldest ones, from the Dmanisi site in Georgia. The Dmanisi specimens seem somewhat more primitive than the rest of the fossils currently assigned to *Homo erectus*, and they also seem more primitive than those assigned to *H. ergaster* in Africa. In particular the Dmanisi fossils have smaller cranial capacities (from 545 to 730 cc) and smaller body sizes. One individual judged to be a male on the basis of facial robusticity was estimated to stand between 1.45 and 1.65 m (4.8 and 5.5 feet) tall. From an objective perspective, these Dmanisi hominins seem to share more diagnostic features with the last australopiths, such as *habilis* and *rudolfensis*, than they do with *H. erectus* (or with *H ergaster*). The implications of these observations are currently producing shockwaves in anthropology.

For the last several decades the fossil record has seemed to suggest that most of the landmarks of human evolution were attained in Africa: the first hominins evolved there, the first members of the genus *Homo* evolved there and then spread into Eurasia, and the first members of our own species, *H. sapiens*, evolved there and then spread around the world. The first and last of these three African landmarks are not currently under attack, but the middle one may be. The primitive traits of the Dmanisi fossils raise the possibility that they may *not* actually be *Homo*, and that it was pre-*Homo*, late australopiths (of the *habilis* and *rudolfensis* types) who were the first hominins to spread beyond Africa. If that did happen there are two possible scenarios for the evolution of the first true members of the genus *Homo* (of the *ergaster* and *erectus* types). *Homo* could have evolved in Africa (from the *A. habilis* or *A. rudolfensis* who remained there); in this scenarios *Homo* would have then migrated to Eurasia (where they may have encountered relict australopiths). Alternatively, the first true *Homo* might have evolved in Eurasia from the australopiths who migrated there, and some of these *Homo* would then have migrated back Africa, where we find them at 1.78 MYA. At present we don't know which of those two scenarios is correct. Whichever hominin it was who first entered Eurasia, that migration is referred to as "Out of Africa 1."

I will return to those late examples of *H. erectus* in China, but one more taxon from this same time period needs to be discussed: *Homo floresiensis*, which has been nicknamed "the Hobbit" (Figure 16-3). These creatures are known only from the small island of Flores a few hundred miles east of Java, where the very first *H. erectus* fossils were found. They were tiny, standing about 1.1 m (3.5 feet) tall, and they had very small brains, probably less than 400 cc and thus in the size range of australopiths. Even more bizarre is their apparent persistence on Flores from 700

KYA to a mere 17 KYA. That's only two times as old as agriculture. We practically met these hominins! While many interpretations have swirled around these unexpected fossils, the emerging view is that they represent a dwarf species derived from *H. erectus*. So-called island dwarfism is a well know biological phenomenon; for example there were dwarf mammoths (an oxymoron I guess) on the Channel Islands just 25 miles from where I'm typing these words. This kind of dwarfing is thought to result form a combination of factors including a reduction in both the numbers of predators and the availability of food in island habitats. The more we learn about human evolution, the more non-linear the story becomes.

Figure 16-3. Reconstructed skull of *Homo floresiensis*.

HOMO HEIDELBERGENSIS

H. erectus seems to disappear in Africa by about 700 KYA. They don't leave a vacuum, however. There *H. erectus* is replaced by a species called *Homo heidelbergensis* based on the region where the first example was found, even though the African forms have turned out the be older. (Sometimes the African representatives are put in a different taxon, *H. rhodesiensis*; I give you these alternative names to keep you from being confused if you

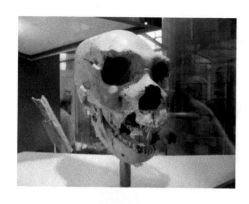

Figure 16-4. A European *Homo heidelbergensis* skull from Spain.

ever read the primary scientific articles.) Beginning about 500 KYA hominins of the *heidelbergensis* type start to appear in Europe and their appearance is generally considered to represent a migratory event, called Out of Africa 2. Following that exodus we see examples of *H. heidelbergensis* in Germany, England, France, Italy, Greece, and Israel, and in a particularly rich site called Sima de los Huesos in the mountains of northern Spain Figure 16-4).

We have discussed ring species, where adjacent populations can interbreed but terminal ones cannot (Figure 7-1). I want to revisit that gradualist perspective to help you picture what the *erectus-heidelbergensis* transition might have been like in Africa (or wherever it occurred).

GRADUALISM REVISITED

You know that evolution doesn't generally proceed by big jumps because mutations that make a big change in the phenotype are almost always harmful (Figure 7-2). The mutational changes that selection is most likely to hold onto, as opposed to discarding, are the ones that make quite small changes. That's not to say that evolution can't have dramatic effects. For example, we think it made whales out of land mammals; but it did so gradually, small change layered on small change. No mother caribou ever gave birth to a dolphin. The changes in each generation were imperceptible; only when we look back over many generations do we see the cumulative sum of all those small changes. Here I am going to use yet another analogy to help you think about the gradual transformation of one species into another. I thought I had borrowed the analogy from Richard Dawkins, the famous British evolutionist, but he tells me it's mine. OK, Richard, if you say so.

Imagine you attend an event in a large circular or oval-shaped stadium. You go in and take your seat. You also bought a ticket for your mother, who sits in the next seat, immediately to your right. She thoughtfully bought a ticket for her mother (your grandmother) who sits to your mother's right. Your grandmother bought a ticket for her mother and so on, all the way around the stadium! (I know, most of them are no longer alive; it's a thought experiment, not a real one.) They all come in and sit down. Here's my question: Whom do you see when you look to your left? Well, obviously you see your great, great, great, great . . . (enough "greats" to get all the way around the stadium) grandmother. But if this is a big enough stadium, with enough seats, then you are in for a surprise: The "woman" sitting on your left—your ancestor—will *not* be a member of your species.

This is not a trick. If we accept modern evolutionary theory, this is what we should expect to see from a hypothetically perfect fossil record. Now let's drive home a key aspect of this thought experiment. You and your mother are members of the same species; likewise, your mother and her mother belong to a single species; and that same claim is true for the occupants of every adjacent pair of seats (except yours and the one to your left)! No mother ever gave birth to an offspring that was a member of a different species from her. Mother and offspring are always a little bit different because they have different genotypes, but not nearly different enough to be members of different species. The daughter could not be a member of a different species given that her genotype was assembled from the recombined genes of her mother and father, who themselves were genetically similar enough to mate.

So this creates an apparent paradox. Each adjacent pair shows only minor differences, but if we add up the small mother-child differences all the way around the stadium, we have accumulated enough differences that the end points of the continuum could not interbreed. Think about why this is similar to the real-world example of ring species. The thought experiment in the stadium is a ring species in *time* rather than in space.

The notion that many accumulated small changes add up to a big change is not hard to understand. You grew from a tiny infant to the adult you are today. Looking in the mirror on any two consecutive days you would see no noticeable change; but the sum of those daily changes is large. Many other examples could be given. The highest peaks in Himalayas are roughly five miles above sea level but that towering height has grown at a rate of about 5mm (about one-fifth of an inch) *per year* as the Indian plate crashed into the Eurasian plate.

We don't need abrupt changes to explain evolution. You and the "person" on your left are *not* members of the same species. But everyone else *is* a member of the same species as the person on her right, her mother. So, as we move

around the stadium, where are we going to draw the species dividing line? We know that we have (at least) two distinct species, so some individuals must be in one species and some in the other. Where is the boundary? The apparent paradox comes from this: Evolution is dynamic, always shifting and changing the traits of organisms. But the names we give to species imply fixed, sharply bounded pigeonholes. The problem is not with the dynamic theory. The problem is that we haven't yet figured out how to capture the shape-changing process of selection in a static classification system. So don't lose any sleep over that. Just don't fall prey to the false conclusion that, because the species names are separate, the adaptive changes are abrupt. They aren't; gradualism dominates the evolutionary process.

Returning to the *erectus-heidelbergensis* transition (or any transition that interests us, such as *Australopithecus-Homo* or *heidelbergensis-sapiens*) we need to keep this gradualist perspective in mind. As the fossil record improves, with more and more discoveries, it should become *more difficult* to sort the fossils into two discrete types (the ones before and the ones after the species boundary) because *there is no species boundary*. We should expect to see a relatively smooth and incremental accumulation of derived features, with ancestral species grading into descendant species because (as in the stadium), generation by generation, that's what actually happened.

HOMO SAPIENS AND OTHER DESCENDANTS OF *H. HEIDELBERGENSIS*.

Like *H. heidelbergensis*, *H. sapiens*, the species to which you and I belong, seems to have evolved in Africa. The earliest evidence, from the Omo

River Valley in south-western Ethiopia, dates to 195 KYA. Over the next 50,000 years *H. sapiens* spread throughout Africa. For example there are *H. sapiens* sites dated to 160 KYA in Morocco and to 164 KYA in coastal South Africa, marking the extreme corners of the continent. Genetic evidence (below) suggests that *H. sapiens* evolved into (at least) *three distinct African races* during this time period. The earliest *H. sapiens* fossils outside of Africa are from closely adjacent areas of Israel and date to about 100 KYA, but this population of migrants apparently died out. However, between 70 and 60 KYA a later and much more successful wave of *H. sapiens* began colonizing the rest of the world in what is called Out of Africa 3. But who did these *H. sapiens* find when they started their big expansion out of Africa? In other words, what had been happening in Eurasia while *H. sapiens* was evolving in apparent isolation in Africa?

Remember that after about 450 KYA *H. heidelbergensis* was widely distributed throughout the Old World. African *heidelbergensis* are the presumed ancestors of *H. sapiens*. But in Eurasia *heidelbergensis* gave rise to at least two other recognizable lineages, the "Neanderthals" (from Europe and western Eurasia) and the "Denisovans" (whose geographic range is poorly understood). First let me explain that I have placed these two names in quotes because they are clearly not separate species from *H. sapiens*. Fully named these two would be *H. sapiens neanderthalensis*, and *H. sapiens denisova* to indicate that they are subspecies, not species. In the same terms, the contemporary African population would be labeled *H. sapiens sapiens*. I will explain in more detail below, but anthropologists are convinced that Neanderthals and Denisovans were subspecies of *H. sapiens*

because of evidence that they interbred—the definitive evidence, after all.

There is quite a lot of Neanderthal fossil material spanning the period from about 130 to 40 KYA, and extending from Wales in the northwest, throughout Europe and the Balkans and into central Asia. Importantly, there are no Neanderthal remains from Africa. We have a very good idea of what the Neanderthals looked like. They were shorter with shorter legs and a longer trunk than modern humans; males were about 1.66 m (5.6 feet) tall and females were about 1.54 m (5.0 feet) tall. They had bulkier more muscled bodies and these various shape differences were likely adaptations to cold conditions since they inhabited high-latitude areas during a period when glaciers extended considerably farther south than they do today. As Figure 16-5 shows, Neanderthal skulls differed from ours. They had larger jaws and teeth, producing a more forward projecting lower face; and this effect was amplified by the relative position of the braincase, which sits more behind the eyes in Neanderthals. Earlier estimates suggested that Neanderthals might have had larger brains than modern humans. However, a rather comprehensive recent study concludes that they were actually slightly smaller and, moreover, were organized somewhat differently (Pearce et al., 2013). In particular, as suggested by the observation that Neanderthal eye sockets are about 15% larger than those of modern humans, they probably had more brain tissue dedicated to vision than we do, perhaps another consequence of life at high latitudes with lower light levels and seasonally short days.

The Denisovans are a much greater mystery. There are three fossils consisting of a fragment of a finger bone (Figure 16-6), a toe bone, and a molar that were all found in a single cave in the Altai Mountains in south-central Russia. The bone fragments suggest a heavily built hominin, as robust as the Neanderthals. The evidence that they are not actual Neanderthals is genetic (below). These fossils date to about 50 KYA.

By way of summary, during the last 500,000 years, various regional populations of *H. heidelbergensis* evolved into at least three somewhat distinctive populations: *H. sapiens sapiens*, *H. sapiens neanderthalensis*, and *H. sapiens denisova*. As a result of Out of Africa 3, these three populations all eventually met. Stay tuned to see what happened when they did.

TOOL TRADITIONS AS INDICATORS OF POPULATION RELATEDNESS

Besides the fossils themselves and their geographic distributions, there are two additional kinds of evidence that can be used to reconstruct the history of *Homo*: cultural data and genetic data. I'll take them in that order. The cultural data are mostly, but not exclusively, based on stone tool technology. In Chapter 14 you learned about the Lomekwian and Oldowan (also called Mode 1) industries, with earliest dates of 3.3 and 2.6 MYA, respectively. Based on their dating it is tempting to associate the Lomekwian industry with earlier gracile australopiths such as *A. afarensis*, and the Oldowan with later, more advanced members of that genus such as *A. habilis* and *A. rudolfensis*, though these ideas

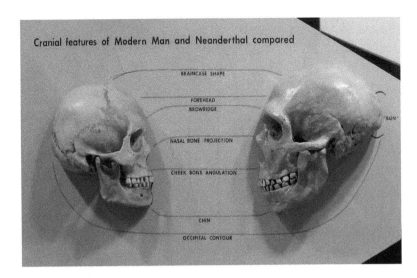

have to remain speculative until sites are found that show clear associations between particular fossils and particular industries.

Acheulean (Mode 2) tools first appear about 1.75 MYA, in Ethiopia (Beyenea et al. 2013) and in Kenya (Lepre et al. 2011), which is temporally and geographically correlated with the emergence of a new

Figure 16-5. A comparison of the skulls of a "Neanderthal" and a modern *Homo sapiens sapiens*.

Figure 16-6. An example of the fragmentary remains of "Denisovans".

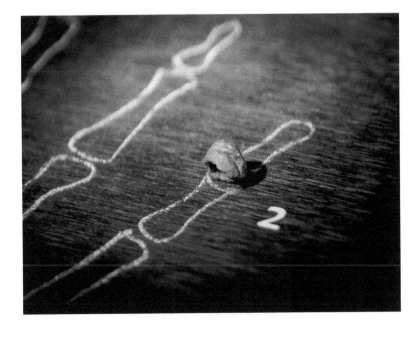

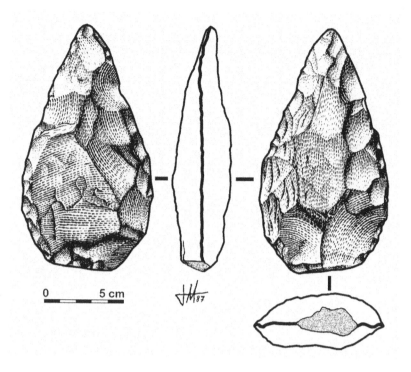

Figure 16-7. Drawing of an Acheulean handaxe showing the extensive bifacial flaking.

taxon, *Homo ergaster* (or "African *erectus*" if that is your preferred terminology). The quintessential Acheulean tool is the so-called handaxe (Figure 16.7). The name seems to imply that we know the tool's purpose. In actuality handaxes, like modern screwdrivers, were probably used in many different ways. In any case, a handaxe is considerably more sophisticated than any Oldowan tool. Like large Oldowan choppers, handaxes are typically made from cobles; but unlike choppers they tend to have nearly their entire raw surface removed by flaking. Moreover, as material is chipped away, a relatively uniform tear-drop shape is produced that is pointed on one end, rounded on the other, and lenticular in cross-section. The tools are described as "bifacial" because flakes are removed from both sides to make the tool relatively symmetrical. Of course

there wasn't an abrupt transition from Oldowan to Acheulean tools. Early Acheulean tools are less fully worked and less regular than later examples, and Oldowan-style tools continue to be mixed in with Acheulean handaxes for hundreds of thousands of years. Although the Acheulean seems to have originated with *H. ergaster*, it remained the primary industry of *H. heidelbergensis*, throughout its range.

Mode 3 stone tools come still later. They are associated with the descendants of *H. heidelbergensis*: with *H. sapiens* in Africa, and with Neanderthals in Europe. Their two versions of this technology differ somewhat, but what Mode 3 tools have in common is their *prepared-core technology*. To make a prepared-core tool, many flakes are initially removed from a coble, not to make it into a tool, but to prepare it so that a single flake of predetermined size and shape can be struck from it. Figure 16-8 shows a European-style (Neanderthal) Mode 3 tool.

Mode 4 tools are also prepared-core tools. In this case the coble is initially worked so that not just one, but many long blades of similar size and shape can be struck from it. These Mode 4 tools are associated with the Out of Africa 3 wave of *H. sapiens*. Thus we see that different species—in some cases different populations of a single species—tend to make different tools. These associations between particular taxa and particular industries help us unravel the mysteries of human prehistory.

GENES AS INDICATORS OF POPULATION RELATEDNESS

The last category of evidence is genetic, and this evidence comes in a variety of forms and from a variety of sources. I'd better explain that last comment immediately. You would think that all genetic evidence has to come from genes, and of course you'd be right. But there are different categories of genes that are transmitted in different ways. First, there are the "normal" autosomal genes (genes on the non-sex chromosomes). They make up the large majority of our genome and they are transmitted the same way for males and females; men and women carry them in equal proportions and are equally likely to pass any allele they carry to either sex of offspring. There's nothing tricky here.

Second, let's consider Y-chromosome genes. Because of the way sex determination works in mammals, only males have a Y-chromosome. Roughly half of a man's sperm carry an X-chromosome and half carry a Y-chromosome. If an X-bearing sperm fertilizes an egg, the result is a daughter; conversely, fertilization by a Y-bearing sperm will make a son. Plain and simple: A man can't give a Y-chromosome to a daughter. What this means is that Y-chromosomes, and the genes they carry, get passed strictly down the male line. As a further corollary of this arrangement, the X- and Y-chromosomes do not ordinarily recombine with each other during meiosis. (A little secret: There are very few "facts" in biology that don't have interesting

Figure 16-8. A Mode 3 (prepared-core) tool.

exceptions. So, I'll tell you that there are two small *pseudo-autosomal* regions of the Y-chromosome that do recombine with the X. Rare recombination errors near this region led to the discovery of the Y-chromosome gene that is responsible for male sexual development—but that story is beyond the scope of this book.)

The third source of genetic evidence comes from mitochondrial genes. Mitochondria are complex structures, each enclosed in its own membrane that is very much like a cell membrane or the membrane that surrounds the cell nucleus. So far as is known, all mitochondria are found outside the nucleus (in the cytoplasm) of the cell. Mitochondria are recognized as essential because they generate the chemical power that cells use for fuel. That's interesting and important enough for us to pay attention to them, but the reason I need to talk about them here is that mitochondria have their own genes—their own DNA that they pass to their offspring! Let's make sure we get this. Your genes are in the nuclei of your cells. Living in the cytoplasm outside the nucleus, your mitochondria have their own, very different, DNA that never mixes with yours. What the heck? (For comparison, other essential cytoplasmic structures like ribosomes don't have their own genes.) We can't be certain about why mitochondria have their own DNA, but the base sequences of their genes (the ordering of A's, C's, T's, and G's), as well as their circular arrangement, most closely resemble those of an ancient group of bacteria (called proteobacteria). The implication is somewhat mind-bending: that the ancestors of mitochondria once lived independently, but long ago become so-called *endosymbionts*, living inside cells and paying their way by generating chemical energy. Whatever their origins, these mitochondria (and the genes they carry) are passed down only from the mother; eggs include the parent's mitochondria, but sperm don't. This is not simply the opposite of Y-chromosome genes; they are passed only from father to son. Mitochondrial genes are passed from mothers to *both* sexes of offspring. Genetic information from the Y-chromosome is called Y-DNA and genetic information from the mitochondrial genome is called mt-DNA.

Any of these tree types of DNA (nuclear DNA, Y-DNA and mt-DNA) can be used as traits to work out the phylogenetic relationships among various living human populations. How? With the very same cladistic methods you learned in Chapter 12. These methods work especially well with pieces of the genome that don't recombine, for example Y-DNA and mt-DNA. In fact, it turns out that examinations of the male-transmitted and female-transmitted genes have been central in untangling the thread of human ancestry. Let's see why.

Remember that cladistics is concerned with identifying the sequence of lineage branching. To illustrate this approach, Figure 16-9 shows a very simplified version of the human mt-DNA tree. Here, L1 is the oldest (ancestral) kind of mt-DNA. Mutations in the base sequence of L1 gave rise to two daughter lineages, L2 and L3. We can keep track of the descendants of L2 and L3 because they each preserved their distinctive L type (2 or 3) as later mutations occurred at other loci in the mitochondrial genome. For example, a mutation called M occurred in an individual with the L3 allele (but not in any individuals with L1 or L2), and a different mutation called N arose in a different L3 individual. Because both M-bearing and N-bearing individuals have L3 (rather than L2 or L1) we know that their lineages branched off the L3 lineage. Still later, an individual with the M allele experienced a mutation called G, at a different locus; likewise a subsequent mutation known as I occurred in some member of the N lineage. These mutational events establish yet more branches on the human tree. Because the

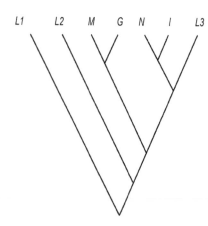

Figure 16-9. A cladogram based on mt-DNA. All the clades have many more descendants than are shown here.

L1   L2   M   G   N   I   L3

G-bearers also have L3 and M, we know their ancestry. And likewise we can deduce that I-bearers derive from the L3-N lineage. The lack of recombination makes us relatively confident about these inferences; because paternal and maternal contributions can never mix, the mutations simply accumulate, revealing the sequence in which they occurred. The actual human mt-DNA lineage is much more complex than Figure 16-9, but the full tree can be deduced, laboriously, by these same principles.

Probably the most exciting result of constructing mt-DNA (and Y-DNA) trees is that the lineages they reveal have strong geographic associations. For example L1 and L2 are almost completely limited to Africa. L3 occurs both in Africa and throughout the world. Most African L3 individuals have neither M nor N, so these mutations probably arose after members of the L3 lineage had left Africa. M is common throughout Asia and Australia; its descendant, G, is found in northeastern Asia and Japan. In contrast, N is found throughout Eurasia, but its descendant, I, is most common in Eastern Europe and adjacent areas of western Asia. If we combine the cladistic gene trees with the allele-distribution data, we get maps that show the spread of *H. sapiens* from Africa to the rest of the world (Figure 16-10). The combined evidence is hard to refute. Three lineages arose in Africa, but only one left that continent. As that departing lineage spread around the world, it accumulated many new mutations, and the distribution of these mutations lets us track the progress of their expansion. Older mutations (L3, M, N) tend to have wide distributions, and more recent ones (G, I) have smaller distributions, having had less time to spread. The same principles can be used to construct Y-DNA trees and they suggest a similar pattern of expansion out of Africa.

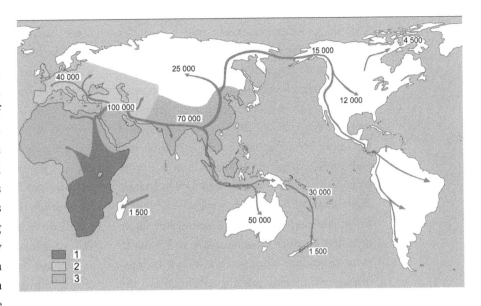

Figure 16-10. A map of the spread of L3 Homo sapiens (Out of Africa 3) and their approximate arrival dates in various regions.

ANCIENT DNA

The most exciting aspect of science is that it's never finished; it's a process of continually trying to reduce the distance between the actual world and our theories about that world. Thus, another surprising fact—and the reason genes are being discussed in this chapter—is that all three kinds of DNA can now be extracted from fossils. DNA can be quite a stable molecule, especially under cold, dry conditions. Given current methods of DNA extraction and processing, usable DNA might be obtained from fossils up to half a million years old. *H. sapiens neanderthalensis* went extinct a mere 32 KYA. So in 2010 a draft sequence of the entire Neanderthal genome was published and more complete data are continuing to emerge. Now that Neanderthal DNA data are available there has been an explosion of recent work; and that work reveals significant interbreeding between Neanderthals and modern "Out-of-Africa 3" humans. But it's not a simple black-or-white case and the subtleties are the most interesting part. Here is a summary of this break-through science.

Laying Neanderthal genomes side-by-side with modern human genomes we can see many DNA-base differences, but there are more base differences between Neanderthals and modern Africans than there are between Neanderthals and modern Europeans or Asians. Specifically, the L1 and L2 lineages of *sapiens*, both of which remained in Africa, have very little Neanderthal DNA, about 0.08%. In contrast, the L3 lineages which left Africa—Asians and Europeans—have an order of magnitude more: 1.38% and 1.15%, respectively (Sankararaman et al., 2014). This strongly suggests that, when (L3) *sapiens* and *neanderthalensis* met, they did interbreed. Otherwise why would L3 individuals have more Neanderthal DNA than L1 and L2 individuals?

I know: This means that *sapiens* and *neanderthalensis* are not different species. But there more subtle points to be gleaned; stick with me. If we look at which Neanderthal genes have persisted in modern humans there are distinct differences depending on what those genes do. Neanderthal genes affecting skin color (surprise, surprise) have not only persisted but have been driven to relatively high frequency in both Asians and Europeans. In other words, Neanderthals, having been in non-equatorial environments for longer had evolved some traits that turned out to be useful to the newcomer *sapiens*. But Neanderthal genes affecting testicular function (sperm production) have mostly been eliminated. Remember that L3 individuals have roughly 1% (I'm rounding) Neanderthal genes; but among genes affecting testes function the percentage is roughly 0.01%—two orders of magnitude lower (Sankararaman et al., 2014). The authors believe that these, and other patterns they see in the genetic data, suggests that at least the male offspring of *sapiens-neanderthalensis* matings tended to have low fertility. I think this is exactly what we should expect to see: If two populations have traveled some way down the road to allopatric speciation (but not yet completed that process) the hybrid offspring should show reduced fertility. Why? Because reproductive incompatibility should evolve gradually, not suddenly.

Interestingly, this gives us a kind of bench mark. Human populations that were allopatric for half a million years did not quite become separate species. One implication of this finding is that all of those named *Australopithecus* fossils may also not represent different species. Don't panic; questioning is the main job of all scientists.

Finally, what about those fragmentary Denisovan fossils found in central Asia? Although we have virtually no idea what they looked like, their DNA has been extracted and sequenced. On the basis of their derived base sequences, they are not *H. sapiens sapiens* and they are not *H. sapiens neanderthalensis*. And they are not a separate species because they too interbred with the Out-of-Africa-3 humans. Thus, they represent a third subspecies of *H. sapiens*, all apparently derived from *H. heidelbergensis*. Neanderthal genetic material seems to represent a bit over 1% of modern human DNA; and that percentage is fairly constant in most non-Africans, being a bit higher in east and south Asians. On average, Denisovans contributed *much* less to modern human DNA, on the order of 0.05% in most populations. But the Denisovan contribution is much less uniform; it reaches a peak of 0.85% in Oneania (Ermini et al. 2015, Sankararaman et al. 2016). On this and other grounds, our ancestors' interbreeding with Denisovans seems to have occurred later than their interbreeding with Neanderthals.

At this point genetic data from East Asian *Homo erectus* and *Homo floresiensis* populations would be extremely useful in resolving uncertainties in our ancestry but, so far, they have not been available. Regardless, these new techniques of ancient DNA extraction and "big data" statistical analyses are going to significantly shape our picture of human evolution in the future.

Homo erectus and *H. floresiensis* as well as the Neanderthals and Denisovans all survived until quite recently (Figure 14-2). The exact causes of their demise are unknown at present, but the first three disappeared soon after the arrival of *H. sapiens* in their part of the world. (The same might true of the Denisovans as well but the data are too sparse to say at present.) Correlation is not causation, as good scientists know, but ecological competition and possible outright aggression are not implausible.

CHAPTER SUMMARY

With the first members of the genus *Homo* (or perhaps just before) hominins begin to spread beyond Africa for the first time (Out of Africa 1). *H. erectus* types became widespread throughout the Old World but about 700 KYA in Africa they begin to be replaced by *H. heidelbergensis*, which then spread to Eurasia about 500 KYA (Out of Africa 2). Again in Africa, we see the first *H. sapiens* around 195 KYA. These hominins differentiate into at least three geographic races within Africa and one (L3) begins a successful dispersal from Africa between 70 and 60 KYA (out of Africa 3). Throughout hominin evolution particular hominin taxa tend to be associated with particular stone-tool industries. Minor variants in DNA between contemporary populations and among various fossil taxa are providing a rich and detailed picture of human population history. These genetic data support the African origins of *H.sapiens* but also indicate that several subspecies, including Neanderthals and Denisovans have contributed DNA to contemporary human gene pools. As can be seen from Figure 14-2, a number of hominin taxa went extinct only recently.

CITED REFERENCES

Yonas Beyenea, Shigehiro Katoh, Giday WoldeGabriel, William K. Hart, Kozo Uto, Masafumi Sudo, Megumi Kondo, Masayuki Hyodo, Paul R. Renne, Gen Suwal, and Berhane Asfawm. (2013). The characteristics and chronology of the earliest Acheulean at Konso, Ethiopia." *Proceedings of the National Academy of Sciences, USA, 110*: 1584–1591.

Ian McDougall, Francis H. Brown & John G. Fleagle (2005). "Stratigraphic placement and age of modern humans from Kibish, Ethiopia." *Nature, 433*: 733–736.

Lepre, C. J., Roche, H., Kent, D. V., Harmand, S., Quinn, R. L., Brugal, J.-P., Texier, P.-J., Lenoble, A., & Feibel, C. S. (2011). An earlier origin for the Acheulian. Nature, 477, 82–85

Luca Ermini, Clio Der Sarkissian, Eske Willerslev, Ludovic Orlando (2015) "Major transitions in human evolution revisited: A tribute to ancient DNA." Journal of Human Evolution 79: 4–20.

E. Pearce, C. Stringer, R. I. M. Dunbar. "New insights into differences in brain organization between Neanderthals and anatomically modern humans." *Proceedings of the Royal Society B: Biological Sciences, 2013*: 280–286.

Sriram Sankararaman, Swapan Mallick, Michael Dannemann, Kay Prüfer, Janet Kelso, Svante Pääbo, Nick Patterson & David Reich (2014) "The genomic landscape of Neanderthal ancestry in present-day humans." Nature 507: 354–357.

Sriram Sankararaman, Swapan Mallick, Nick Patterson & David Reich (2016). "The Combined Landscape of Denisovan and Neanderthal Ancestry in Present-Day Humans." Current Biology, 26: 1241–1247

FIGURE CREDITS

CHAPTER 17

DESIGNED FOR LANGUAGE

Human language is so ubiquitous—all around us, like the air—that we tend not to think much about it. But natural human languages are marvels of complexity, arguably more intricate than the vertebrate eye. Think of the size of dictionaries, or the maze of grammatical rules. All of that knowledge gets into kids' heads just through hearing ordinary speech, really; studies show that there is minimal "instruction." I contend that you could speak into a computer for a hundred years and it would never learn your language. Yes, there is speech-recognition software that can type out (with some hilarious errors) what you're saying; but it can't answer you intelligently (as even a child could) because it doesn't *understand* what you're saying. It has vocabulary but nothing else.

Another surprising discovery is that, although they sound quite different to us, all natural human languages have the same deep structure. That is why infants adopted into other cultures grow up speaking perfectly the languages of their adoptive parents. The claim I want to advance—the reason language is in a book on human evolution—is that humans have *evolved adaptations* for learning and using language. I'm going to begin with a mini-lesson on linguistics—the science of language—so you can appreciate the complexity of human language and understand what functional elements all languages, no matter how "different," have in common.

In this chapter I am discussing only spoken language; in fact, most human languages are only spoken and have no writing system whatsoever. We know that writing is a relatively recent invention, no more than a few thousand years old. Thus, it's much more plausible that spoken language—which we believe has been around much longer—would be supported by evolved adaptations. Nevertheless, in order to communicate in a book I will have to write out material that I want you to think of as spoken. Ready?

THE STRUCTURE OF LANGUAGE

All languages are hierarchical systems with distinct kinds of units that do separate jobs at different levels of the hierarchy. That's mouthful. Let me take it apart for you. At the lowest level we find what linguists call *phonemes*. They are sounds that don't carry any meaning on their own but do serve as markers that distinguish meanings. That sounds contradictory, so here's an example. In English, /b/ (the "buh" sound), and /p/ (the "puh" sound) are two different phonemes. Do you see that neither /b/ nor /p/ has any meaning? Of course they don't. But if I say /b//a//t/, that has a different meaning from /p//a//t/, different because you may not care if I pat you on the head but you probably will object if I bat you on the head. The only thing that changed was the substitution of /b/ for /p/, so these two phonemes *distinguish meaning*, without having any meaning of their own. That's what phonemes do. Continuing with the same pair of phonemes, the utterance /b//i//l/ means that it's going to cost you but /p//i//l/ means something you need to swallow. The /b/ and the /p/ trigger meaning differences but there

is no consistent meaning in the /b/ and the /b/ across contexts. Case in point: there's nothing that is similar about the concepts captured by /b//a//t/ and /b//i//l/ that puts them in a distinct category from the concepts marked by /p//a//t/ and /p//i//l/. The various uses of /b/ and /p/ are completely arbitrary in the sense that /p/ doesn't systematically mean bigger or yellower or softer or more maternal the /b/.

Each language has its own phoneme set. (Even different dialects of the same language have different phoneme sets; that's how you spontaneously recognize a "Texas" or an "Ausie" accent). One major category of evidence that humans are adapted for language is that human infants learn their "native" phoneme set in the first six or seven months of life. Of course, their parents don't "teach" them their phonemes in any ordinary sense of the word teach. Parents just talk and the infants "figure out" their phoneme set. Fascinatingly, infants learn their phonemes by *learning to ignore* all the speech sounds (potential phonemes) that don't happen to be actual phonemes in their patents' language. And, once ignored, they are very difficult to recover—hence your difficulty in speaking French; *tant pis*! The phonemes of any given language can be combined in essentially infinite ways to convey a similarly vast array of meanings—which is the next level in the linguistic hierarchy: morphemes. But of course infants don't create (many) morphemes; they listen and learn the current morphemes in their local population.

Unlike phonemes, morphemes do carry meaning. Many morphemes like "dog" and "cat" are what you would call words, but many morphemes aren't words. For example "cats" consists of two morphemes; one meaning an independent, barely domesticated member of the feline family, and another meaning more than one of those beasts (i.e., the plural morpheme). Thus /s/ is both a phoneme and a morpheme. "Cat" is a free morpheme, meaning it can stand on its own, but the pluralizing "s" morpheme is a bound morpheme, meaning it can do its work only when attached to a free morpheme. Other bound morphemes in English would be "mis-", and "un-", and "-ness". Tricky stuff.

Moving up another level we have *morpho-phonemic* rules. The pluralizing morpheme "s" behaves differently in different contexts. "Cat" + "s" is /k//a//t//s/; no problem. But "dog" + "s" is /d//o//g//z/; yes it is. Say them both and listen carefully; you're using different phonemes to make the plurals. Did you know that you "knew" that morpho-phonemic rule? How about *un*cooperative but *im*probable? Some part of your brain does know this stuff because it sounds right to you; and you "know" many more of these rules, applying them perfectly in everything you say. You were a *very* smart toddler—thanks to a long history of natural selection for language-learning abilities!

At the next level up we have what linguists call *syntax* which consists of rules for combining morphemes in a way that expresses unambiguous relationships among them. "Your neighbor ate the pig" and "The pig ate your neighbor" both consist of the same five morphemes, but you presumably have different responses to those two statements. In English we largely handle these syntax issues with word order, but that's not the only way to do it, as speakers of Russian can tell you. No matter; different languages have different syntactic rules, but they all have them, and they all work to clarify the relationship among the various morphemes in an utterance.

The take-away message is that all known human languages have this identical hierarchical organization. They have different phonemes, different morphemes, different morpho-phonemic rules, and different syntax. But all languages have these same levels, that interdigitate with each other in the same ways. Infants *must* bring to the world an *expectation* about this kind of interlocked hierarchical structure; otherwise they could not learn whatever language they encounter. In other words, human language adaptations must consist of a system of linked "slots," plus evolved preprogrammed modules that can "deduce" how those slots should be filled and used, based on early linguistic input. I contend that human language adaptations are among the most complex of human adaptations that we currently understand in this detail. But not everyone agrees. And it's not that they disagree about the complexity; bizarrely from my perspective, they disagree about whether language is an adaptation at all.

WHERE DOES ALL THIS INTEGRATED COMPLEXITY COME FROM?

Where does rich, layered, functional integration always come from? The only scientifically demonstrable natural force that can create anti-entropic (organized) structure is natural selection. Without selection everything is soon randomness—chaos. My friend Steven Pinker (2003) has eloquently defended the view that, based on the kinds of integrated complexity I have just described, language *must* be an evolved adaptation. Remember that an adaptation is a trait that exists because of a history of selection: It has been shaped by selection to accomplish a particular fitness-relevant function. How can we know if language—or any trait—is an adaptation? There are several ways of addressing this question. First, we could ask whether or not the trait shows a good fit to the hypothesized function; do its various features match what would be needed to accomplish that function? This kind of match could be called *design specificity*. Second, we could look for evidence that the trait has been favored by selection. (You learned a third general method—cross-species comparison—in Chapter 8. Can you see why that approach won't be very helpful in considering the evolution of language?) Let's examine the underpinnings of these two new methods.

REVERSE ENGINEERING

One way to understand how evolutionists answer the adaptation question is to think about how you might examine a mysterious artifact—an unknown tool or device of human design. Like natural selection, people design artifacts for specific functions. A laptop makes a miserable can-opener, and vice versa. You already know what laptops and can-openers look like, but here is an example that I trust is new to you (Figure 17-1). It's called a Curta and I bought one of them in 1966 and used it for its intended purpose. What do you think that purpose was? Try to formulate some guesses before you read any further. Take a look at Figure 17-2 which shows a partially disassembled Curta; does seeing more of its working parts help? It should.

The Curta, made in Liechtenstein, was the last of the pre-electronic,

Figure 17-1 A Curta. What is its function?

hand-held calculators. It can do addition, subtraction, multiplication, division, and even (with some effort) square roots. Perhaps you guessed this function by noticing the registers, dials, sliding buttons, and cranks. Figure 17-2 was probably more helpful; it's the individual components and, especially, the way they mesh together that lets any device—or adaptation—accomplish its function. The more times you disassembled and reassembled a Curta,

Figure 17-2 Its components make its function more obvious.

sliding its buttons and turning its cranks, the more obvious its function would become. This is what we mean by design specificity.

A Curta *could* be a paperweight or a peppermill. But those hypotheses would not match the type and organization of its features. If a Curta were a paperweight, it would be hard to explain why it has so many finely machined internal components that make it no better at fighting stray breezes than a solid lump of metal would be. And if it were a peppermill, it would be puzzling that it lacks a reservoir for peppercorns and suitable grinding blades, but has seemingly irrelevant parts like counters, buttons, and dials. Neither proposal—peppermill or paperweight—fits the Curta's detailed organization as well as the hypothesis that it's a calculator.

Of course, selection also refines designs to accomplish specific ends, and we can use the same kinds of scrutiny to test hypotheses about the evolved function of traits. The features of language strongly suggest that it is *not* a paperweight, peppermill, pogo stick, pineapple corer, piñata, or anything other than a highly organized acoustical system for the transmission of complex ideas from one hominin to another.

In case this argument seems absurdly obvious, you should know that some relatively well-known biologists and psychologists have argued against it (one could, of course, be well known for being wrong). The various kinds of objections to the functional view of language boil down to one main theme: Language is an incidental byproduct of something that *is* an adaptation, and language simply got dragged along. Let's be careful; this *kind* of argument is not absurd. Some traits of organisms certainly *are* byproducts of something else. The white color of bone is an uncontroversial example of a byproduct. Let's work through

that example to make sure we understand what a byproduct is.

An internal skeleton should be both as lightweight and as strong as possible. Selection has hit on the solution of building skeletons out of calcium, which is both present in an array of potential foods and able to form strong-for-their-weight structures. Our question is, did selection favor calcium as the building block of bone because it built white bones, or because it built lightweight and strong bones? It is not at all clear how whiteness might make a better skeleton, but it is obvious how a high strength/weight ratio might. So why is bone white? Because calcium is white. Thus, the whiteness of bone *is a byproduct* of selection for a bone-building material that is both lightweight and strong. Some traits of organisms absolutely are (mere) byproducts of natural selection for something else. But these byproducts are typically simple and don't have any demonstrable function. Why should they? They're just along for the ride.

So, returning to our main topic, could language be a byproduct of selection for something else? It could, but what would that other thing be? It's difficult to understand how anything with the obvious (communicative) function of language, and with its structural complexity and integration, which is repeated with different elements in all known languages, and—despite this complexity—is eminently learnable by "naïve" human infants all around the world (you get my point?); how could anything like that be a byproduct of something else? Something simple like "whiteness" could be a byproduct; but language?

I'm going to push this argument because my most important goal is to help my students think like 21st century Darwinists. To do that you will need to be able to distinguish between arguments that merely have the word "evolution" in them and arguments that are evolutionarily coherent. The specific argument I'm criticizing here is that language is a byproduct of large brains. OK, let's think about that. We know that brain enlargement is especially costly because brain tissue is very expensive to build and run. So, before language can be a byproduct of large brains, one needs an argument about why large, costly brains were favored in the first place. OK, maybe the byproduct advocates can do that, but it's not a step they can just skip. Here's a bigger problem for them: It's been known for more than a century that there are specific brain regions—specific, sizable chunks of neural tissue—that are dedicated to language. In other words, holding all other abilities constant, a "large brain" that had no language capacity could be smaller than a "large brain" that did have language capacities. Then, how is language a byproduct? It's an extra cost and if it's not functional—if it doesn't provide an adaptive benefit—selection won't favor the developmental mechanisms that build it. Selection did build it, despite its costs, so it must do something useful. Right: communication.

Remember, there is also a second category of evidence that language is an adaptation: evidence that there has been selection for language-related alleles. This evidence takes several forms. The first concerns specific language deficits that seem to have a genetic basis, because of how they are distributed within families or the pattern of their occurrence in twins. For example, if monozygotic (identical) twins are more likely to match on a trait—either both having it or both lacking it—than are dizygotic (fraternal) twins, this implies that there are genes for the trait, that the trait has significant *heritability*. (This is the same logic

we used in Chapter 11 in discussing allele differences between people who differ in sexual orientation.) A number of narrow language disabilities show moderate to high heritability. And in at least one case, the specific gene that is apparently responsible (FOXP2, on chromosome 7) has been identified.

Now, suppose (for simplicity) that there are two alleles at a locus and that one of those alleles disrupts normal language development. If language is a fitness-enhancing trait, what would you predict about the relative frequency of the two alleles? The one that disrupts language should be very rare, of course, because selection will be working against it. That prediction is generally confirmed: Alleles that derail language are extremely rare.

DRIFT AS A SPEEDOMETER OF EVOLUTIONARY CHANGE

The last kind of genetic evidence is subtle but worth understanding, in part because it exemplifies a class of argument that evolutionists are using more and more. This evidence involves a comparison between the effects of genetic drift and the effects of selection. Genetic drift, discussed towards the end of Chapter 6, is just random change in gene frequency. Under the influence of drift, an allele increases or decreases in frequency simply by chance. Here is a physical analogy I find useful.

Imagine a piece of driftwood floating on a large lake. Imagine also that there is no systematic current in the water of the lake, nor any consistent direction to the wind. Given these unsystematic forces, the driftwood is not especially likely to reach one shore or the other; it will just drift in one direction for a while and then in another. Now, let's think about its position on the lake—its distance from the shore—as a graphic representation of the frequency of two alternative alleles, *a* and *b*. When it is in the center of the lake, equidistant from both east and west shores, allele *a* and allele *b* are equally common in the population. If the wood drifts closer to the east shore and farther from the west, then allele *a* is more common, say 60%, and allele *b* is less common, say 40%. If it drifts the other direction, toward the west shore, then allele *b* is more common and allele *a* is less common. If, after drifting back and forth for a long time, it actually reached, say, the east shoreline, then allele *a* would be 100% and allele *b* would be completely lost.

Of course, the essence of drift is that the drifting object is just as likely to reach the west shoreline—with allele *a* being lost—as it is to reach the east shoreline, where allele *b* is lost. Moreover, either beaching is likely to take a long time precisely because nothing is propelling its motion in either direction. If it reaches a shoreline, that is because a series of chance drifting events moved it sufficiently far in one direction. Now, contrast drift with selection. In the case of drift, there is no consistent current or wind. But in the case of selection there is; that is the key difference. Selection for or against any particular allele (because of its positive or negative effects on fitness) will move it consistently toward one shore or the other—where it will be lost (0%, if it decreases fitness) or become the only allele at that locus (100%, if it increases fitness). Because selection is systematic and unrelenting—the wind may blow, generation after generation, in the same direction—it typically changes gene frequencies quickly. This contrasts with the slow rate of change when gene frequency merely drifts

up and down at random. OK, now we have our prediction: When selection has acted on a locus, allele frequencies change much more rapidly than if mere genetic drift has been at work. Once we know how fast random drift can change allele frequencies, we can compare that to the rates of genetic change in language-related alleles. When we make that comparison, it seems that selection has indeed been at work in pushing up the frequency of the alleles that support our linguistic ability (Pinker 2003).

The notion that we can see what natural selection has been favoring (or disfavoring) by examining the genome itself is very exciting because of the huge range of research questions it makes accessible. The next chapter explains one of the most innovative new methods for gauging selection's recent impact.

CHAPTER SUMMARY

Language has a hierarchical structure consisting of meaningless (but meaning-distinguishing) phonemes, combined together to make meaningful morphemes, linked by morpho-phonemic and syntactic rules to carry interpretable meanings. This shared structure allows infants to learn any language and strongly suggests that language abilities are a product of natural selection. Alleles related to language seem to have been targets of selection.

CITED REFERENCES

Steven Pinker (2003) Language as an adaptation to the cognitive niche. In *Language Evolution*, M. Christiansen & S. Kirby (eds.) pp 16–37. Oxford University Press.

FIGURE CREDITS

CHAPTER 18

DETECTING RECENT SELECTION

If I said that you can gaze into the recent past and see which alleles have been favored by selection, I would understand your skepticism; time machines don't exist. But this is another example where science is better than science fiction. Putting together our knowledge of selection and genetics we can fairly confidently identify the targets of recent selection. We have already seen a limited example of this kind of thinking in the previous chapter. That was the Jetta; here's the Ferrari.

Based on Chapter 6, one possible approach to this problem may come to mind: Common alleles must have been favored or they wouldn't now be common. That's a good insight, as far as it goes. As a review of Chapter 6, let's make sure we understand what's right about that insight. Consider a genetic locus with two alleles; call them j and k. When we say that selection is favoring allele j, we simply mean that individuals who carry allele j are producing more offspring on average than individuals who carry allele k. As the individuals who carry allele j continue to have higher reproductive success they will automatically increase the frequency of allele j (how common it is) in the population. Because individuals who carry allele k are having fewer offspring, its frequency will automatically decrease. This line of thinking suggests that alleles which have been favored by selection will have higher frequencies (be more common) than alleles that have been disfavored. The problem is that when you look at some particular common allele (one at high frequency), you can't tell if it was favored by *recent* selection or by selection at some time in the more distant past. It could have been favored by selection acting many millions of years ago; and that seems to be true for many common human genes, because we share those genes with species we're only distantly related to. So, just looking at how common (frequent) an allele is won't solve this problem *by itself*. A high frequency tells us that an allele has probably been favored, but we need another way of determining whether it was *recently* favored. This is going to be an interesting journey. Buckle your seatbelt; the Ferrari is growling.

LINKAGE

The key concept that we need in order to solve this problem is called *linkage disequilibrium*. I am truly sorry about how ugly and unapproachable this term is (and I will fix part of that for you). But understanding what linkage disequilibrium *is* and why it happens will serve as a useful review of what we've learned so far, and also provide a critical element of our recent-selection-detection device.

It's important to define new terms clearly so I'll do that now even though I know that we'll need to do some more work to unpack the definition. *Linkage disequilibrium is the elevated co-occurrence of alleles at different loci.* By now you know that I'm a dedicated fan of analogy, and I have several analogies that will help you understand this concept. But before I begin I need to confess that many people, myself included, find

the phrase "linkage disequilibrium" confusing. If I simply say "linkage" you will understand that I am talking about connections, about one thing affecting another, and that is a correct understanding. But if I say "linkage *dis*equilibrium" you won't know if I'm taking about connections or disconnections. That's the confusion that I want to avoid. I can't change the thousands of times this phrase has already been used in the scientific literature. In the interest of using a term that won't confuse my readers, but also makes clear that I am not talking about a new and different concept, I'm going to use this format: "linkage [disequilibrium]". I'm hoping that will let you read "linkage" (and get the correct "connection" meaning) and ignore the confusing add-on, without forgetting that the bulky two-word term is technically correct. OK, let's be done with the mere words and get back to the problem.

MEASURING LINKAGE

We need to begin with some basic probability theory. Let's flip both a quarter and a nickel. What is the chance of the quarter coming up heads and the nickel coming up tails? I'll answer and then explain. It's 0.5 X 0.5 = 0.25. This simple probability problem illustrates something called a "joint event"—a situation where two (or more) specified outcomes co-occur (occur together). Older child boy, younger child girl is a joint event involving co-occurrence in families. Monday cloudy, Tuesday rainy is a joint event involving a meteorological co-occurrence. You can think of many kinds of joint events, which are not limited to pairs. For example, A's in all your classes is a joint event.

Any time the component sub-events of a joint event are fully *independent* of each other (don't affect each other), the probability of their co-occurrence is just the product of the probabilities of the component sub-events. Just multiply. The probability of quarter-head is 0.5 and the probability of nickel-tail is 0.5 and multiplying the two gives us 0.25. That is a prediction. That's what probabilities are: predictions. If we wore out our thumbs performing many of these paired flips we would be very surprised if quarter-head and nickel-tail did co-occur more often than 25% of the time. If they did you would be entitled to think that the results were somehow connected—that there was some kind of *linkage* between them. Linkage would be strange in the realm of coin flips; what could cause the nickel outcome to depend on the quarter outcome? Nothing that I can think of; these two sub-events are likely to be independent, so the joint-event (multiplication) formula gives an accurate prediction of what happens when we actually flip the coins.

But, as you may have already realized, not all joint events are independent. For example, the weather of adjacent days is probably not independent and you would not be surprised to see linkage between these meteorological conditions. Even more to the point, if there were linkage, we would want to measure how strong that linkage was. To do that we begin by getting an independent prediction, just as we did with the coin flips. If we knew for example, that the frequency of cloudy days was 0.3 and the frequency of rainy days was 0.2, then we could calculate how likely the joint event "day 1-cloudy and day 2-rainy" *should be, if the two day's weather was independent.* Do you see how to do that? Just use the multiplication formula for independent joint events. In this case that

formula gives 0.3 X 0.2 = 0.06. In words rather than equations: if 30% of days are cloudy and 20% of days are rainy, then "day 1-cloudy and day 2-rainy" should co-occur only 6% of the time—as long as there's no linkage between these two outcomes. Now that we have our prediction, we can, by simple observation, determine how common "day 1-cloudy and day 2-rainy" co-occurrences *actually* are. The difference (by subtraction) between their actual co-occurrence and their predicted co-occurrence is a quantitative measure of their (you guessed it) *linkage*! As just shown, their predicted co-occurrence is 0.06. To finish this example let's say the actual co-occurrence is 0.11. Their linkage, as measured by the difference, is 0.11 - 0.06 = 0.05.

GENETIC LINKAGE

To close the circle, let's finally consider a genetic joint event: the co-occurrence in a single individual of allele *a* at locus 241 and allele *b* at locus 253 on the same chromosome. This is going to be like the weather example: The two loci are equivalent to the two days, and the alleles are equivalent to the weather conditions. Here I'm going to use variables (the letters p and q) instead of numbers for the frequencies; but you can substitute any numbers between 0 and 1 for p and q and it will all work fine. At locus 241 allele *a* has a frequency of p. At locus 253 allele *b* has a frequency of q. (Note: There is *no* required mathematical relationship between p and q like the one that obtains in the case of the Hardy-Weinberg Equilibrium, because here *a* and *b* are alleles at *different* loci, so p and q could both be close to 1, or both be close to zero, or anything in between.) Assuming that these alleles assort independently, what is the chance of having allele *a* at locus 241 *and* allele *b* at locus 253? Of course, the (independent) chance of this is simply *pq* (that is, *p* times *q*). If you have any doubt about this, please reread the preceding paragraphs; this is the same joint-event formula we used to solve the coin-flip joint event and the weather joint event. Now, the question is, does *pq* accurately predict how often the *a* and *b* alleles actually co-occur? If these alleles assort independently, it will. But if they don't assort independently—and instead are linked—the standard joint-event formula will underestimate their co-occurrence. Again, the difference between how often they are predicted to co-occur (by the simple joint-event formula) and how often they actually do co-occur measures how strongly linked they are—that statistic that geneticists call *linkage [disequilibrium]*. Hold onto that idea. We now need to build another part of the argument.

The weather on adjacent days tends to be linked because it is often influenced by the same weather system. Here's the important evolutionary question: What links alleles at different loci? The answer is even more direct than for weather: Two alleles at different loci can be linked because of their physical proximity on the same chromosome. Right; alleles on different chromosomes can't be linked, but those at different loci on the same chromosome can. Let's see how that works.

Remember that meiosis is the production of the sex cells (eggs or sperm) that carry your genes into the next generation. During meiosis your paternal and maternal copies of each chromosome cross over and exchange genes. (If you need a refresher, this is illustrated in Figure 3.3). When a crossover point occurs *between* two loci (for example between locus 241 and locus 253),

that crossover will "unlink" the alleles at those two loci, and they will assort independently, with their co-occurrence matching the simple joint-event formula. In that case, knowing what allele is present at locus 241 of the sex cell would give you no information about what allele will be present at locus 253, because they were separated—literally cut apart—by a crossover event. However, in the opposite case, where there is *no crossover point* between locus 241 and locus 253, alleles *a* and *b* will travel into the next generation together; and knowing that *a* is present at 241 lets you predict that *b* will be present at 253. In this case the two alleles would be "linked". As discussed above, we could recognize this statistically because the two alleles would co-occur more often than *pq* predicts. The *a* and *b* alleles would be in linkage [disequilibrium], and you know how to use the difference formula to calculate the strength of that linkage [disequilibrium].

LINKAGE AND POSITION

A human chromosome is a very long strand of DNA, containing roughly a thousand genes (I'm taking an average; some are longer than others). There are typically several, but not dozens of crossover points per chromosome per meiosis. The chance of a crossover occurring between any two loci depends on several factors. One of the most important is simply how far apart they are on the chromosome. The farther apart, the more likely it is that there will be a crossover point between them and hence the more likely their alleles will assort independently. The closer they are, the less likely a crossover point is to occur between them, and the more likely they are to assort together (be linked). This is a straight-forward prediction. Pick a "test" locus, say on chromosome 7. Now, select a series of other loci that lie at progressively greater distances away from our test locus. Distances on chromosomes are usually measured in kilobases—thousands of bases—and abbreviated as kb. So we'll choose a set of neighboring loci that are 20, 40, 60, 80, 100, 120, . . . out to 400 kb away from out test locus. This gives us a kind of scale, like mile markers on a highway. What we generally see is that linkage [disequilibrium] decreases steadily as we move farther from the test locus, eventually reaching the baseline of independent assortment. Put another way, the farther a locus is from the test locus, the less likely it is that their alleles will be linked—the less likely it is that their alleles will remain on the same chunk of chromosome. This is logical and it is exactly what we predicted at the beginning of the paragraph. Interestingly, this relationship—the farther away, the less strongly linked—is very clear if we repeat this set of observations using many different "test" loci. But it is variable: For some test loci, linkage [disequilibrium] falls off quickly as we move away from the test locus, and for others, it falls off much more slowly. Why should that be? As we answer this question our recent-selection-detection device (remember where we started?) will finally come into focus. We need just one more element.

LINKAGE AND TIME

Every time there is a meiotic event there is a chance that an allele at a test locus will be separated from an allele at a neighboring locus by a crossover between them. Remember that these meiotic events occur only in your gonads—creating the eggs or sperm which carry your genetic information to the next generation—and thus they occur at a generational time scale. So, how vulnerable is a given allele to being separated from alleles at neighboring loci? That depends on how long (how many generations) that particular allele has existed. Here's an example at one end of the spectrum. Suppose allele *s* just arose by mutation one generation ago on a chromosome that (at that time) had allele *m* at a nearby locus. Since there has only been one generation of meiosis (from the original *s*-mutant parent to its current offspring), there has been little opportunity for a crossover between them and the offspring will probably also carry the *s-m* co-occurrence that its parent had. If, on the other hand, we suppose that allele *t* arose 1000 generations ago on a chromosome that (at that time) had allele *n* at a nearby locus, we see that there have been many, many opportunities for a crossover between them. As a result, many of the great, great, great, etc. grandchildren of the original *t*-mutant individual will *no longer* carry the same *t-n* co-occurrence. Why? Because, at some point during those 1000 generations, *t* and *n* were separated by an intervening crossover event. More generations simply means more opportunities to be separated.

So, the "age" of an allele is important. For old alleles (that arose many generations ago) linkage [disequilibrium] will fall off sharply as we move away (along our 20, 40, 60, 80, etc. kb highway markers); as a result we will see independent assortment closer to an old allele. For young alleles (that have arisen recently) high levels of linkage [disequilibrium] will extend to considerably more distant loci.

Here's a quick summary of our two principles of linkage: 1) the farther apart on a chromosome two alleles are, the less likely they are to be linked, and 2) the more generations those alleles have existed, the less likely they are to be linked. If we don't expect too much precision from it, I can give you a simple analogy that will capture both of these ideas. Imagine once again two large decks of cards, one deck with blue backs and one with red backs. This time we're going to shuffle the decks together. For the limited purposes of this analogy I only need you to pay attention to one of those decks (say, the one with red backs), and I need you to imagine that it starts out in some kind of order, so you can see if that order has been disrupted. So let's put all the clubs in numerical order, then all the hearts in numerical order, etc. The shuffling is my loose analogy for the recombination that occurs during meiosis: If a blue-backed card has come between two red-backed cards, we'll say there was a crossover event between them. And each shuffle is one "generation" of meiotic recombination. Now it's easy to analogize the two principles of linkage summarized at the beginning of this paragraph. Principle 1: After the first shuffle, red-backed cards that are farther apart (the two of hearts and the ten of hearts) are more likely to end up with a blue-backed card between them than red-backed cards that are close together (the two of hearts and the four of hearts). Principle 2: The more *times* I shuffle the deck the more likely *any* pair of red-backed cards is to have a blue-backed card between them. Shall I translate back into gene language? The farther apart two genes are on a chromosome, the more likely they are to be separated by a crossover event. And, the more generations of meiosis two genes have been exposed to, the more likely they are to have been separated by a crossover event.

THE JOINT CRITERIA OF RECENT SELECTION

With these two principles in mind, the finish line is in sight! All we need to do is circle back to our very first idea: Alleles that have been favored by selection will be at high frequency. Now add what we have just learned: For new alleles, linkage [disequilibrium] extends to more distant loci—exhibits a broader plateau before independent assortment is reached. Thus, *a new allele that was favored by selection would rise to a high frequency before recombination would sever it from its neighbors.* Therefore, alleles recently favored by selection: *will be at high frequency and will exhibit linkage that extends to relatively distant loci.*

Congratulations! This is a fairly advanced aspect of evolutionary theory; it was first figured out in the 21st Century—in your lifetime. Now let's get our hands dirty with the method: How are we going to *measure* the rate at which linkage [disequilibrium] falls off?

HAPLOTYPE LENGTH

At this point it will be helpful to introduce a new but related concept. A *haplotype* is a set of *linked* genes that occur relatively close together on a single chromosome and are typically inherited as a unit. Right, they're linked because there hasn't been a crossover event between them. A haplotype would be recognizable as a set of SNP's (single-nucleotide polymorphisms; see Chapter 6) that regularly co-occur. Why do we need to pay attention to SNP's? Because SNP's are the only variable elements in the human genome (for the other 99.9% of nucleotides we're all the same), and we need things that vary to determine if those variable elements are assorting independently or systematically co-occurring. In other words, the SNP's are just markers or tokens that let us track what pieces of the chromosome are breaking apart or hanging together.

Thinking about what you have already learned in this chapter should make it clear that recombination can and does break up haplotypes (into smaller haplotypes), and mutation can make new ones (by creating a new allele). Let's take a closer look at this. Figure 3-3 shows the recombination that occurs in a single generation. Of course the mixed chromosomes that you see in panel 5 of Figure 3-3 will be passed to offspring where they will go through the same recombination process again, before being passed to the next generation where there will be yet another round of recombination, and so on. The result is that, across the generations, the *unrecombined* bits of chromosomes—the

haplotypes—get shorter and shorter (Figure 18-1). For reasons already discussed, if recent selection has been favoring an allele, the haplotype containing it should quickly increase in frequency—before recombination or mutation breaks it up (creates new, shorter haplotypes out of it). That rapid increase will have two consequences: First, such haplotypes should be long (their nearest crossover point should be far away); and second, the population should contain many identical (unrecombined) copies of it. Thus geneticists can assess whether an allele has been favored by recent selection by examining copies of the haplotype containing it. If those haplotypes are long and a large proportion of those copies are identical (because they haven't been disrupted by mutation or recombination events), that allele has probably been recently (and may still be) favored by selection.

This clever method for detecting the recent force of selection was developed and used to examine a variety of human alleles by Pardis Sabeti (Sabeti et al. 2005, 2007). Dr. Sabeti, in addition to her academic, educational, and athletic accomplishments, is the lead singer and song writer for the rock band, 1000 Days.

RESULTS OF THE METHOD

Sabeti has aimed her method at two alleles thought to provide resistance to the mosquito-transmitted malarial parasite, *Plasmodium falciparum*. The alleles in

Figure 18-1. This figure shows that haplotypes grow shorter with each generation.

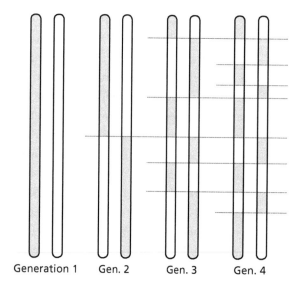

Generation 1   Gen. 2   Gen. 3   Gen. 4

question are called G6PD-202A and TNFSF5-726C, and both strongly exhibit the pattern of elevated haplotype frequency and long length predicted by her method. Relevant to our discussion of human skin color (Chapter 5), Sabeti has also used her method to identify two derived alleles (SLC24A5 A111T and SLC45A2 L374F) that are both at high frequency in Europeans but not in Africans (Sabeti et al. 2007). Her method has been used by others to produce many interesting and important findings; here are just two examples. Our ability to digest milk in adulthood (a derived trait) is the result of different mutations arising on different haplotypes in Europe and Africa. Each of these alleles is associated with long haplotypes that exist in many identical copies in their respective local populations (Tishkoff et al. 2007). Perhaps even more interesting, many of the alleles that modern humans (like us) got when they interbred with archaic humans such as Neanderthals and Denisovans (see Chapter 16) apparently provided adaptive benefits, since they bear the "common + long-haplotype" stamp of recent positive selection (Racimo et al. 2015).

For closure let's remember that this is a method for detecting *recent* selection. Why would the various alleles mentioned above have been recently favored? We think that the transition from hunting and gathering to farming and herding—beginning less than 10,000 years ago—changed many features of the human environment. For example, the domestication of dairy animals (cows, sheep, goats, etc.) created a new opportunity for adults to drink milk. Likewise the invention of irrigation systems greatly expanded the range of breeding sites for the mosquitoes that transmit malarial parasites to humans. Somewhat farther in the past

but still relatively recently in human evolution, anatomically modern humans left Africa and began to colonize Europe and Asia, where they experienced a significant reduction in UVb radiation. That environmental change reduced the risk of skin cancer and increased the risk of vitamin D deficiency. Your reading of Chapter 5 should lead you to expect that this new selective regime would strongly favor genes for less melanin production, and you'd be right. That same African exodus also brought anatomically modern humans into contact with other forms of *Homo*, members of at least two lineages that had diverged from our own several hundreds of thousands of years earlier, but which had not completed the process of allopatric speciation (see Chapter 7). Thus the ancestors of modern Europeans and Asians interbred with these archaic humans and, in the process, acquired alleles that were already well-adapted to these more temperate regions. These alleles were strongly favored in our ancestors and still can be found in us!

It seems that intelligently combining the insights of Darwin and Mendel can unravel many deep mysteries. Stay tuned for more.

CHAPTER SUMMARY

Alleles favored by selection should be at high frequency but high frequency alone can't reveal *when* an allele was favored. Alleles on the same chromosome tend to be linked (passed together to a sex cell) if they occur at nearby loci, but any alleles at different loci can eventually be unlinked when a recombinatorial crossover occurs between them. Alleles are exposed to the possibility of being unlinked every generation so, other things being equal, new alleles will have a broader band of neighbors to which they are still linked; they will sit on long haplotypes. Thus, strongly favored new alleles would rise to high frequency while their haplotypes were still long. The combination of high frequency plus long haplotype length is a signal of recent positive natural selection.

CITED REFERENCES

Fernando Racimo, Sriram Sankararaman, Rasmus Nielsen & Emilia Huerta-Sánchez (2015) "Evidence for archaic adaptive introgression in humans." Nature Reviews Genetics 16: 359–371.

Pardis C. Sabeti, David E. Reich, John M. Higgins, Haninah Z. P. Levine, Daniel J. Richter, Stephen F. Schaffner, Stacey B. Gabriel, Jill V. Platko, Nick J. Patterson, Gavin J. McDonald, Hans C. Ackerman, Sarah J. Campbell, David Altshuler, Richard Cooperk, Dominic Kwiatkowski, Ryk Ward & Eric S. Lander (2005). "Detecting recent positive selection in the human genome from haplotype structure." *Nature 419*: 832–837.

Pardis C. Sabeti, Patrick Varilly, Ben Fry, Jason Lohmueller, Elizabeth Hostetter, Chris Cotsapas, Xiaohui Xie, Elizabeth H. Byrne, Steven A. McCarroll, Rachelle Gaudet, Stephen F. Schaffner, Eric S. Lander & The International HapMap Consortium (2007) "Genome-wide detection and characterization of positive selection in human populations." Nature 449: 913–919.

Sarah A Tishkoff, Floyd A Reed, Alessia Ranciaro, Benjamin F Voight, Courtney C Babbitt, Jesse S Silverman, Kweli Powell, Holly M Mortensen, Jibril B Hirbo, Maha Osman, Muntaser Ibrahim, Sabah A Omar, Godfrey Lema, Thomas B Nyambo, Jilur Ghori, Suzannah Bumpstead, Jonathan K Pritchard, Gregory A Wray & Panos Deloukas (2007) "Convergent adaptation of human lactase persistence in Africa and Europe." Nature Genetics 39: 31–40.

FIGURE CREDIT

18-1: Image created by Judith Geiger.

CHAPTER 19

WHAT'S WRONG WITH US?

This book takes a strong "selectionist" stance, arguing that the traits of organisms are best understood as *designs for reproduction* that have been shaped by selection pressures operating in particular environments. Remembering the insistence of entropy—constantly eroding order in the universe—the adaptive precision of organisms is especially impressive. Yet it is also possible to see that the glass is not entirely full, that organisms—ourselves included—are not *perfectly* adapted. Why not? And should any imperfection that we see make us question the power of natural selection? Properly understood, the evolutionary processes you already understand actually predicts certain kinds of imperfection. Let me show you.

EVOLVED ENEMIES

Natural selection shapes human adaptations but, no matter how important we might think we are, we're not evolution's favorite child. Selection is an emotionless filter and it operates constantly, in *every* species. Unfortunately for us, some of those species are not our friends; they make their living by exploiting us. And it's often a zero-sum game between us and these evolving enemies, meaning that their gains are our losses. When a bacterium or virus is using you as a tool to jump to other hosts—by causing coughing, sneezing, or diarrhea—these discomforts may not be for your benefit but for the pathogen's. (There is a growing field of evolutionary medicine [Nesse and Williams, 1995] that explores these issues in more detail.) In such cases, any apparent human imperfection would not indicate selection's impotence; it would indicate that selection was working more intensely in the pathogen population than in ours. Why might that be? In Chapter 2 we discussed the evolution of antibiotic resistant bacteria—and that it happened in a just a few decades—in part because these pathogens reproduce so rapidly. The deck is stacked against organisms with long generations. I'm going to leave this first reason for human imperfection for now; but it will play a very important role in Chapter 20, where we try to explain the evolution of sexual reproduction.

GENES, NOT INDIVIDUALS

We've also previously met another cause of apparent human imperfect: selection works at the level of the gene more potently than it works at the level of the individual. Kin selected altruism is maladaptive for the individual (because the altruist is getting fitness costs), but it is beneficial for the underlying allele. Likewise, homosexuality does not promote the reproductive success of the average homosexual man, but at least one of the contributing alleles may raise the fitness of female carriers. No one benefits by having sickle-cell anemia, but the responsible allele provides malarial resistance in other genetic contexts (i.e., in heterozygotes). Finally, each gene codes for proteins which interact with proteins coded by genes at other loci. Selection obviously favors alleles that are "good mixers" in the sense that they

work with the other alleles that are currently common in the population. But with more than 19,500 protein-coding loci, unfavorable combinations may sometimes occur. To summarize all of these examples, if, *averaged over all the bodies that carry it*, an allele confers an evolutionary benefit, that allele will spread in the population. That situation may often entail fitness costs in *some* bodies that are balanced by fitness benefits in others. When we focus on the bodies experiencing the costs it looks like imperfection, but a more global perspective suggests that selection is indeed optimizing.

PROTECTIVE BIASES

Some apparent imperfections may actually be optimal for individuals—especially in the realm of mental adaptations. For example, people are fairly accurate at estimating horizontal distances. However they systematically *over*-estimate vertical distances. Do you see that this "error" could easily be adaptive? Horizontal distances are not inherently dangerous but, for a wingless creature like a human, vertical distances are. Vertical over-estimation could be a useful self-protective feature rather than a bug. Its "imperfect" as far as pure accuracy is concerned, but it may be optimal in terms of reproductive success.

EVOLUTIONARY LAGS PRODUCE MISMATCHES

Finally, as we discussed in Chapter 6, selection cannot summon up useful mutations. Mutations are random occurrences whose effects are unrelated to the needs of the organism. That means that there will often be a significant time lag between an environmental change and the emergence of new mutations that address it. The clear exception to this statement is when it's an environmental shift that has been common over the species' evolutionary history; in such cases we expect facultative responses that are quite rapid compared to large-scale changes in gene frequency. For example, most people exhibit facultative traits such as sweating if exposed to temperatures of 100° because that is a challenge that our ancestors regularly faced and our genes have thus been selected to mount such responses. On the other hand, a change in the average human environment to 140° F would trigger significant selection for new adaptations that our ancestors did not previously need. That would take time. The reason this issue of adaptive time-lags is especially important for anthropologists is that we humans have triggered extensive environmental change. That means that our adaptations will be imperfect in these new circumstances— ironically, circumstances we ourselves have created. Evolutionists use the word *mismatch* to refer to situations where adaptation has not caught up to recent environmental change.

Seven thousand years may sound like a long time. But, compared to the seven million years since our lineage diverged from the one that leads to chimpanzees, seven thousand years is just an evolutionary eye blink. To be precise, it's 0.1%. I mention seven thousand years because it is roughly the length of time that humans have been practicing agriculture—farming crops and tending domesticated animals. We were not fully dependent on agriculture seven thousand years ago; there was a slow ramping-up period. And the process started a bit later in some parts of the world than in others. But, before that time, all humans got all of their food from wild plants and animals. Thus, our ancestors were pre-agricultural hunters and gatherers for 99.9% of the time our lineage has existed.

DIETARY MISMATCHES

That does not mean there has been no evolution in the last seven thousand years. There has demonstrably been some. For example, as mentioned towards the end of the previous chapter, most mammals cannot digest milk as adults. The gene that codes for *lactase*—the enzyme that breaks down lact*ose* (milk sugar)—turns off after they have been weaned by their mothers. Lactose became available to adult humans after the domestication of milk-producing animals. As you might expect, this created a new selection pressure for adults to continue producing lactase. In fact, there is a clear statistical relationship showing an evolutionary response: The longer any given human population has kept dairy animals, the larger the percentage of adults who produce lactase. In other words, mutations that prevented a shutting down of the lactase locus spread where milk was available as a food for adults. But this is not a very big or very fancy evolutionary change: It's just the continued production of an enzyme that selection had already designed for milk digestion. Also note that even this minor innovation has not spread across the entire species: Many people are still lactose-intolerant, being unable to extend their lactase production past infancy. More elaborate adaptations to our new agricultural diet will probably take considerably longer than a few thousand years.

In fact, we still bear the stamp of many selection pressures that predominated during our species' long hunter-gatherer period. Our dietary preferences are good examples. Hunter-gatherers must harvest (find, process, detoxify, run down, kill, butcher, etc.) every calorie they consume. Getting this food was not free; in other words, to avoid starvation, they had to consume more calories than they expended in getting it. Hence, we prefer foods that are calorically dense (that is, foods that have a lot of calories per unit weight). Sugars and fats are calorically dense. Need I say more? These are tastes we love. When humans domesticated plants, they used artificial selection to increase the sugar content of numerous plant species, and they did the same to elevate fat levels in their domesticated animals. Wild animals of the type hunter-gatherers would have eaten have body fat levels between 2% and 4%, whereas domestic cattle or swine can have body fat levels over 25%. When you pay more for "USDA Prime" meat, you are paying for more fat. Salt is another example. It provides essential electrolytes, and insufficient salt intake can result in death. If they do not live in a seaside habitat, hunter-gatherers would generally find that salt was quite scarce. Hunter-gatherers travel long distances to collect it—sometimes eating soil to satisfy their needs. And salt is one of the first items hunter-gatherers trade for when they come into contact with agricultural peoples.

The bottom line is that we have strong taste preferences for the nutrients that were both essential and scarce during our hunter-gatherer past. Sometimes those ancestral taste preferences cause problems for us, precisely because fat, sugar, and salt are no longer scarce. In fact, in many parts of the world they are cheap and abundant. Thus, recent overconsumption of fat and sugar is correlated with heart (cardiovascular) disease and diabetes, and overconsumption

of salt is correlated with high blood pressure (hypertension), which can cause brain-damaging or fatal strokes. To put it simply, we are suffering from too much of what was, for our ancestors, a good thing. We're experiencing a mismatch; our evolved adaptations are not working as they were designed to work because they are operating in a novel environment.

That part of the story is relatively well known, and you may have read about it elsewhere. But I want to dig more deeply into one less well known aspect of these dietary shifts. Just as we're getting too much of some nutrients, we're getting too little of others. You may be surprised to learn that one of the most critical missing nutrients is a kind of fat. How could that be? We drizzle cheese on our French fries. We deep-fry everything. The simple fact is that there are many different kinds of fats. Some of them are greatly oversupplied in our contemporary diet, but one essential type is seriously undersupplied.

FATTY ACID MISMATCHES

Let's begin by laying out the various kinds of fats (technically, chemists call them fatty acids). You surely know some of them: Saturated fats, monounsaturated fats, polyunsaturated fats, and trans-fats are all names you will have seen on standard nutrition labels. All of these fatty acids share the same basic molecular composition. They are medium to long molecular chains consisting mostly of carbon and hydrogen atoms. Most of their carbon atoms are bonded to two hydrogen atoms (except the first carbon, which is bonded to three). When a carbon is bonded to two (or three) hydrogen atoms, the bond is "saturated." When a carbon is bonded to only one hydrogen atom, it forms a special double bond with its neighboring carbon atom (to make up for the missing hydrogen), and the resulting bond is said to be "unsaturated."

OK, now things are simple. If all the bonds in a fatty acid molecule are saturated bonds (with two or three hydrogens on each carbon), you have a saturated fat. If just one of the bonds is unsaturated (having one rather than two or three hydrogens), you are looking at a *mono*unsaturated fat. If more than one of the bonds is unsaturated (you guessed it), you have a *poly*unsaturated fat. How many bonds could be unsaturated? In the longest and most polyunsaturated fatty acid (the one that is most missing from our modern diets), there are six unsaturated bonds.

Unsaturated bonds make a fatty acid molecule floppy and flexible, as opposed to stiff and rigid. Thus, saturated fats are quite stiff, which you can see with your eyes because they tend to be solid at room temperature (e.g., butter). Monounsaturated fats are somewhat more flexible, for example, liquid at room temperature but solid in your refrigerator (e.g., real olive oil). Polyunsaturated fats are still more flexible—liquid even in the refrigerator—and they become progressively more flexible the more unsaturated bonds they have (e.g., canola oil). The one with six unsaturated bonds is still a liquid in the freezer.

Polyunsaturated fatty acids come in two major types, depending on where in the chain the first unsaturated bond occurs. They are called omega-3 and omega-6 fatty acids, denoting fatty acids whose first unsaturated bond occurs at the third or sixth carbon, respectively. Despite such seemingly small molecular differences, these various omega fats do very different jobs in the body; they cannot substitute for one another, and even significantly compete with each other (get in each other's way).

There is one more important dimension along which fatty acids differ. In principle, any monounsaturated or polyunsaturated fatty acid could be a trans-fat or a cis-fat. Trans- (and its opposite, cis-) refer to the geometric orientation of the two carbon atoms participating in an unsaturated bond: whether they lie on the same or opposite sides of the bond. (Note that this orientation issue is irrelevant to saturated fat because they have no unsaturated bonds.) As a result of this orientation difference, trans-fats are more rigid and stable and tend to be solid at body temperature. These differences in turn make them less prone to spoilage but at the same time interfere with one of their essential roles in the body, which I will explain below. You already know that the flexibility of a mono- or polyunsaturated fatty acid depends on how many double bonds it has. What I am saying now is that unsaturated cis-bonds are more flexible than unsaturated trans-bonds. So, there are two factors that jointly determine the flexibility of a fatty acid. The more unsaturated bonds it has, the more flexible it will be, and the more of those unsaturated bonds are cis-bonds, the more flexible it will be. For the record, trans-fats are rare in nature; most naturally occurring mono- and polyunsaturated fats are cis-fats. Food producers have developed techniques for turning cis-bonds into trans-bonds because it improves the shelf life of their products. What it does for *your* life is more dubious.

Fatty acids perform several important functions in the body. One well-known function is energy storage. Many kinds of fat can be made from sugar. And that is precisely what the body does when it has more sugar than it needs at the moment; it converts that excess sugar to fat. Then, that stored fat can be burned at some future date when calories are in short supply.

This energy-storage function was critical for our hunter-gatherer ancestors because their natural food supply had inevitable ups and downs. Our bodies are, of course, still anticipating that next bad season. Do you see the consequence of that? This, of course, is a topic on the "too much" side of our modern diet; let's return to the more surprising "too little" side.

Another very important role of fatty acids is to facilitate processes at cell membranes. Each kind of cell has an enclosing membrane made mostly out of fat, and much of the cell's biological activity depends on what happens in and across that membrane. The "queen" of the membrane fats is that very long, polyunsaturated fatty acid with 6 unsaturated bonds that we briefly mentioned above. Its name is DHA (docosahexaenoic acid). This omega-3 fatty acid cannot be made from sugar and is generally far too valuable to be burned for calories. It is super-floppy and flexible and it makes everything that happens in membranes happen more quickly and efficiently. Shortly, I will make painfully obvious why this is a big deal.

There are a variety of omega-3 fatty acids (those with their first unsaturated bond at the third carbon). Of these, DHA is the longest and has more unsaturated bonds than any of the others, making it, as I have said, the best membrane fat. Our bodies can make DHA from the shorter omega-3 fats. But—and this is a big but—there are two problems with our contemporary diet: 1) *all* of the omega-3's, both the shorter and the longer ones, are seriously *under*supplied, and 2) the omega-6's interfere with the process of converting shorter omega-3's into the longer membrane-critical DHA. And, guess what: The omega-6's are wildly *over*supplied in our present diet. The

current US diet has more than twenty times as much omega-6 as omega-3.

The reason for this omega-6/omega-3 imbalance is simple. Omega-6 fats are concentrated in plant seeds. You think you don't eat many seeds? Think again. Much of what Americans eat comes from two seeds: corn and soybeans. We eat plenty of corn and soybean oil directly because they are standard frying agents, and they are also components of salad dressings, mayonnaise, etc. But, just as importantly, corn and soybeans are what cattle, swine, and poultry are raised on, so all the meat, chicken, milk, cheese, and eggs are also loaded with omega-6. Fish—as long as it is not breaded and fried with corn or soybean oil—is a good source of omega-3; unless it is farmed! Guess what farmed fish are fed.

Here's something that will shock you: Heart disease was virtually unknown as recently as 1910. But, in less than a century, it became one of the two leading causes of death (each year it is a close contest between heart disease and all cancers combined). The rise in heart disease (and a variety of other health problems such as obesity) closely parallels the narrowing of our diet to corn and soybeans (O'Keefe and Cordain, 2004). By the way, Cordain is one of the originators of the so-called "paleo-diet" so you might like to see some of the science behind that movement. If we eat the diet we were designed by natural selection to eat, perhaps our bodies would function better.

FATTY ACIDS AND THE BRAIN

Omega-3's, especially DHA, also play a very important role in *brain* health. At any given moment, half of all the DHA in your body is in your brain.

Remembering that your brain is only about 2% of your total body weight makes it clear that the brain is a DHA hog. The brain is even more of a DHA hog than it is a calorie hog, since it uses 20% of your calories but 50% of your DHA. There are two reasons the brain needs so much DHA. First, brain cells—neurons—are very long and skinny and hence have proportionately large membranes. And fats are concentrated in membranes because their job is to conduct—to facilitate—membrane transactions. Second, neurons—more than any other cell type—need to perform very rapid membrane transactions in order to do their job of carrying information. Omega-3-starved brains do not work very well. Comparing across nations, the amount of omega-3 versus omega-6 in the diet predicts how well teens perform on standardized mental tests. In fact, the amount of these two fats in the diet predicts test scores better than how wealthy the nation is or how much it spends on public education (Lassek and Gaulin 2014).

This is another demonstration that, when we make dramatic changes to our circumstances—as we clearly have with our modern diets—our evolved adaptations may not operate in the way they were designed. I began this chapter by asserting that "the traits of organisms are best understood as designs for reproduction that have been shaped by selection pressures operating in particular environments." I still believe that to be true; this chapter simply emphasizes the word "particular."

CHAPTER SUMMARY

Adaptation will often look imperfect. Some of that apparent imperfection is illusory because the adaptations of one organism will invariably be compromised by the adaptations of its coevolving enemies. Also, many alleles are favored not because they confer benefits on all carriers in all contexts, but because they confer benefits on the average carrier in the average context, or because they confer advantages on the alleles themselves (as in kin-selected altruism). Moreover, because selection cannot create the mutations that would solve new adaptive challenges, recent environmental change will cause organisms to be out-of-synch with their new environments. For millions of years, hunting and gathering of wild foods was the only mode of subsistence our ancestors knew. The human body is thus adapted to live on that diet. We are reaping a harvest of health problems because of the various ways in which our modern diet differs from our ancestral one.

CITED REFERENCES

William D. Lassek, & Steven J. C. Gaulin (2014) "Linoleic and docosahexaenoic acids have opposite relationships with cognitive test performance in a sample of 28 countries. *Prostaglandins, Leukotrienes, and Essential Fatty Acids 91*: 195–201.

James H. O'Keefe & Loren Cordain (2004) "Cardiovascular disease resulting from a diet and lifestyle at odds with our Paleolithic genome: How to become a 21st-century hunter-gatherer" *Mayo Clinic Proceedings 79*: 101–108.

Randolph M. Nesse & George C. Williams (1995) *Why We Get Sick*. Time Books; New York.

CHAPTER 20

SEX WITH THE RED QUEEN

The observation that organisms reproduce does not surprise an evolutionist. What's around today is here only because it was good at getting into the next generation. Reproduction makes sense as the core adaptation—in fact all other adaptations exist to serve reproduction. But sex is just one way of reproducing. Asexual reproduction is another widespread way, and it is presumably the primitive condition (in the sense of "primitive" you met in Chapter 12). In other words sexual reproduction evolved from asexual reproduction. What selection pressures favored those early sexual individuals; and, if it's advantageous, why hasn't sexual reproduction completely replaced asexual reproduction in all species? The best answer we have to these questions is called the Red Queen model, and it is one of the cleverest evolutionary ideas of the twentieth century.

SEXUAL REPRODUCTION IS AN EVOLUTIONARY PUZZLE

To appreciate the cleverness of the Red Queen model, you first need to understand that there is a problem to be solved. When I ask students why sex exists, some shake their heads sadly and wonder just how naive professors can be. But what they're thinking has causation reversed. Of course sex is pleasurable; selection made it pleasurable (more precisely, favored individuals who found it pleasurable), as a way of getting them to pass on their genes. It's an "internal reward" designed by selection to get you to engage in sex. As a general consequence of this kind of selection pressure, we experience fitness-promoting situations as pleasurable and fitness-harming situations as unpleasant. So hedonism isn't the reason sex (or anything else) exists; what is the reason?

To realize the magnitude of the challenge posed by this question, it's important to specify what we mean by sexual reproduction and then to tally the costs associated with it. Full-blown sexual reproduction—the kind humans use—has three principal features: meiosis, recombination, and outcrossing. The first two are covered in Chapter 3, but here's a quick review. *Meiosis* is the reduction from a diploid to a haploid state. Your body cells are diploid, but your mature sex cells are haploid. Put another way, you pass only half of your genes to each of your offspring (your mate also gives half of his or hers, so the two of you together provide a full diploid set; two haploids make a diploid). *Recombination* (Figure 3-3) refers to the stage of meiosis when you shuffle your mom's and your dad's genes together in the process of determining exactly which half of your genes to put into your egg or sperm. *Outcrossing* is the step of seeking and recruiting haploid gametes from other members of the population. The reason I said that "full-blown sex" has three key features is that some creatures have what you might think of as "semi-sex" with just some of these features. For example, they might use meiosis and recombination to make haploid sex cells but then self-fertilize by mixing their own haploid sex cells together. This kind of semi-sex would make a new diploid genotype (because of the reshuffling of recombination), but all its genes would have come from a single parent. This is called "selfing" and you might find it helpful to map out chromosomally how it would work. Hold onto the idea of selfing; we'll be coming back to it.

To understand why sexual reproduction poses an evolutionary puzzle, we need to notice that each of the three components of sex—meiosis, recombination, and outcrossing—involves costs, costs that could be completely avoided by being asexual! Meiosis is costly because it reduces your genetic contribution to the next generation. An asexual organism puts all its genes in each of its offspring, whereas a sexual organism puts only half. The genes that are around today are the ones that were good at getting into the next generation, and asexual reproduction is *twice as good* as sexual reproduction at getting genes into the next generation. I can say it another way. Let's measure reproductive success as the rate at which a parent puts genes in the next generation. OK, then to keep up with the reproductive success of an asexual parent, a sexual parent would have to produce twice and many offspring! That's a big deal and places sexual parents at a significant competitive disadvantage.

Recombination adds a second cost. In principle an organism could use meiosis without recombination, producing haploid gametes but skipping the step of shuffling paternal and maternal genes. The reshuffling of recombination is costly because it produces novel genotypes. In our technology-driven culture we tend to think that novelty is good but, in the realm of organisms that have been refined by many millions of years of natural selection, novelty is quite likely to mess things up (that's why mutations are usually harmful; Figure 6-2). Think of it this way: Your genotype was good enough to survive to reproductive age; why try something new? Many new combinations will not be as good as what selection has already pre-screened. Finally, outcrossing piles on a third cost because mates must be located and cajoled into fusing their haploid gametes with ours. Many members of our population will be the wrong sex, not reproductively ready, already engaged in a mating venture (e.g., pregnant), or find us unsuitable (sigh!).

So, each of the three key features of sexual reproduction entails a separate and additive cost. Asexual reproduction seems pretty efficient because it avoids all of these costs. Now that we've sketched the magnitude of the problem, we're ready to seriously consider what benefits sex might offer that could compensate for all these costs. If it can't provide benefits that more than outweigh these costs, selection should get rid of it. Just in case you think deleting sex is impossible, let me tell you that there are asexual species, all of whose close relatives are sexual. That tells you that they are descended from species that were sexual. Right; it's just like the eyeless cave-dwelling species, all of whose close relatives have eyes. And guys, pay close attention: When a species reverts to asexuality, it's the males who disappear. So let's find those compensatory benefits!

BENEFITS OF OUTCROSSING

Instead of putting all their genes in each offspring, sexual reproducers put only 50% and recruit the other 50% from a mate. What might be the advantage of this arrangement? Here's an idea: What if the genes you recruit are much better than the genes you would have put there yourself? That way the 50% of your genes you do get to include could "surf" on the wave of great genes your mate provides. This could let your genes "hitchhike" into many more grandchildren than they would have if you were asexual and didn't recruit such excellent genes from a mate. This is, at least at the outset, a pretty plausible idea. The average member of the population is by definition, well, average. So, by reproducing *asexually* she would produce average offspring. But by reproducing *sexually*, and seeking mates who have the very best genes in the entire population, she could give her own genes a big boost by pairing them with genes that are destined to be very successful. Got that? You could insist on putting all of your genes in each offspring (asexual reproduction) in which case your genes are on their own with little chance of hitting it big. Or you could be content to put only 50% of your genes in each offspring (sexual reproduction) but buy them a first-class ticket into the evolutionary future by mating with an individual who has better genes than you do.

This will work—will favor sexual over asexual reproduction—*for a while*. But the problem is that it uses up the existing genetic variation. In plain words, when everybody chooses the best mates for several generations, the best genes get spread through the population. Soon everybody has the best genes and there's no longer any reason to recruit genes from a mate; you too have the best genes and you might as well revert to asexuality! So the "good-genes benefit" seems not to last. Can this idea be salvaged? Is there some reason or situation where the benefits of recruiting the best genes would continue indefinitely? There is, but we need to develop a parallel argument to see it.

CO-EVOLUTIONARY ARMS RACES

Let's think about the kinds of selection pressures that act on organisms. Some selection pressures come from inanimate (non-living) features of the environment, like the climate. Climate does generate selection pressures on organisms, for example favoring efficient adaptations for heating, cooling, or hydration. And sometimes the climate changes, thus demanding new adaptations. But climate and other inanimate selection pressures are not *hostile*; they do not change simply because the organism has finally evolved an effective suite of climatic adaptations. Simply put, the climate is not out to get you. But some sources of selection pressures *are* out to get you. That's because some sources of selection are both living—and hence evolving—and dependent on using you for their own reproductive goals. They are evolutionarily hostile.

A classic example is a predator–prey relationship. Cheetahs make more cheetahs out of gazelle meat. Of course a gazelle's reproductive career ends at the cheetah's lips, so there is a fundamental conflict of interest here. These situations, where multiple species generate selection pressures on each other, are called coevolutionary. When a new mutation that improves vision or hearing or acceleration arises and spreads in a gazelle population, more cheetahs will starve to death. When a new mutation that improves camouflage or stealth or stamina arises and spreads in a cheetah population, more gazelles will be converted to cheetah milk. The point is that every improvement in gazelles is an immediate evolutionary challenge to cheetahs, and vice versa. The two are locked into an inescapable *evolutionary arms race*, which neither is likely to win but neither can escape!

I'm guessing that neither will win, but it's an informed guess. Here's what informs it. Cheetahs and gazelles grow up and reproduce at similar rates; they have similar generation times. The pace of evolution is governed by the pace at which new individuals are offered up for selection to evaluate. If that pace is slow, adaptations are formed slowly; if is rapid, they can be formed rapidly. Because of their similar generation times cheetahs and gazelles can evolve new adaptations (to each other!) at the same rate. It's a *fair* contest because they make babies at the same rate. That's why I think neither is likely to win. And so far I'm right, since they're both still here.

Can you think of creatures that might evolve more rapidly than cheetahs and gazelles? Of course they would need to have short generation times. A good place to look would be small organisms. As we have mentioned several times, some species of bacteria have generation times of less than half an hour. This means that if a gazelle (or a human) was in an evolutionary arms race with a bacterium you would expect the bacterium to win. Of course we *are* in evolutionary arms races with bacteria, viruses, and other such parasites. They are like mini-predators that eat us from the inside out. Why didn't these parasites win the arms race millions of years ago. According to the Red Queen Model, the answer is "sex!"

THE RED QUEEN

Remember the "good-genes benefit"? It pays to be sexual if you can recruit the best available genes to mix with your own. We concluded that this benefit seems to dry up as it spreads the best genes throughout the population, thus negating the imperative to recruit genes from a mate. But what if the best genes in this generation are *different* from the best genes in the previous generation? That is guaranteed to be the case in the context of evolutionary arms races with parasites. These parasites evolve so rapidly that they are constantly posing new adaptive challenges. Here; a thought experiment will make this clear.

You're an asexual (so sorry) with your current generation time of 25 years. In the 25 years it takes you to mature, your parasites go through hundreds of thousands of generations, evolving better and better adaptations to exploiting the unique physiology defined by your genotype. It's hard for organisms to reach adaptive perfection because their environments keep changing. But that's not so true for your pathogens, because your genotype—whose various proteins they need to foil—is fixed and unchanging, so they do get better at exploiting you. When you reproduce asexually you will give your offspring the same genotype you have, and hence give them a huge burden of parasites that are better at exploiting them than they were at exploiting you when you were born. You stood still, evolutionarily speaking, but your parasites have gotten much more sophisticated. And what they are especially good at is exploiting your genotype, the same genotype you just gave to your kid. Bad, bad asexual mother! But is there anything else she can do? The Red Queen says there is: sex. The machinery of sex is designed to give your offspring a completely novel genotype, one that never existed before and hence one that these parasites have never been selected to exploit. Your sexually reproduced offspring are going to slap those parasites with a mismatch (Chapter 19)!

TESTING THE RED QUEEN MODEL

That's the essence of the Red Queen model: Sex evolved to give slowly reproducing organisms like ourselves a fighting chance in our evolutionary arms races against small, rapidly evolving parasites. In case you're curious, the model gets its name from an episode in Chapter 2 of Lewis Carroll's *Through the Looking Glass*. Alice and the Red Queen are running. Here is the passage:

> "Well, in our country," said Alice, still panting a little, "you'd generally get to somewhere else—if you run very fast for a long time, as we've been doing." "A slow sort of country!" said the Queen. "Now, here, you see, it takes all the running you can do, to keep in the same place. If you want to get somewhere else, you must run at least twice as fast as that!"

The literary background is fun, but we'd better be able to test the Red Queen model. What does it predict? How about this? The more pressure from parasites, the more important it is reproduce sexually. I want to feature an elegant experimental test of this prediction (Brockhurst 2011; Moran et al, 2011). In the experiment the parasite is a bacterium, *Serratia marchescens*, and the host (the stand-in for us) is a nematode worm, *Caenorhabditis elegans*, known colloquially as the glass worm. In nature, glass worm populations include males (who can reproduce only sexually), and individuals who have reproductive options; they can reproduce by selfing (see above) or they can outcross (see above) with a male. Selfing is "less sex" and outcrossing is "more sex." Review the earlier parts of this chapter if you don't understand that last sentence.

The experiment was designed to simulate evolution under different circumstances and it lasted for 30 glass-worm generations. (Why did I say it that way? Because glass worm generations are longer than bacterial generations, so I have to specify whose generations I'm talking about). Various strains of glass worms were allowed to evolve in three different kinds of environments. Environment 1 had no bacteria; environment 2 had bacteria but it was a fixed strain of bacteria that was not allowed to evolve during the experiment; and environment 3 started out with the same strain of bacteria as environment 2 but the bacterial strain was allowed to evolve to be more effective at attacking and killing glass worms. Environment 3 is most like the world we and glass worms actually live in. (Try to explain why.) The key finding is that Environment 3 selected for increasing outcrossing (more sex). Environment 2 did also, but only for a while, presumably until the glass worms had evolved a good solution to their non-evolving bacterial predators. After they did, there was no reason to recruit genes from mates any more—just as we suggested (under Benefits of Outcrossing), so they quit outcrossing. There are many additional predictions of the Red Queen model that were tested by Moran et al. (2011) and virtually all are supported. The model also makes predictions that could be tested by the comparative method. It would help you to firm up your understanding of both the Red Queen model and the comparative method to work on formulating some comparative predictions.

One more very important and far-reaching insight comes out of Red-Queen thinking. If sex exists to acquire benefit "X", then *mating preferences* should evolve so as to maximize the recruitment of "X". Since the Red Queen suggests that "X" is parasite resistance, then signs of health and vigor should be major dimensions of mate choice, across many sexual species. And, individuals should evolve to conspicuously display such signs of health and vigor during courtship or mating competition.

CHAPTER SUMMARY

Sex is an evolutionary puzzle because it imposes three substantial costs—meiosis, recombination, and outcrossing. Recruiting the best available genes could provide short-term advantages to sex but, unless environments are extremely unstable, mate choice will cause the best genes to become common in the population and thus reduce the benefits of further mate choice. Rapid coevolution of hostile parasites could cause significant generation-to-generation change in what host genes are most resistant, and could thus favor continued outcrossing. The Red Queen model also suggests the kinds of mating competition and courtship that are likely to evolve.

CITED REFERENCES

Lewis Carroll (1872) Through the Looking Glass, and What Alice Found There. MacMillan.

Michael A. Brockhurst (2011) "Sex, death, and the Red Queen." *Science 333*: 166–167.

Levi T. Morran, Olivia G. Schmidt, Ian A. Gelarden, Raymond C. Parrish II & Curtis M. Lively (2011) "Running with the Red Queen: Host-parasite coevolution selects for biparental sex." Science 333: 216-218.

CHAPTER 21

SEXUAL SELECTION: WHY FEMALES AND MALES SOMETIMES DIFFER

Now we know why sex exists, but what's the story on females and males? This is another fascinating evolutionary puzzle, and its answer makes many predictions about the nature of sexual relationships. It's always good to begin by sketching the puzzle.

We know that selection crafts the adaptations of a species to meet the challenges of its environment. This perspective seems to suggest that, within each population, organisms will become very similar to each other as their phenotypes converge on whatever best meets the local challenges. To a large degree this is what we see in the nature. We all have the same numbers of hands and feet, noses and eyes; our hearts are in the same place and have the same arrangement of parts. But there is a conspicuous class of exceptions. Many species reveal not one but *two* typical "plans," one for males and one for females. This could happen only if selection were favoring different traits in the two sexes; but why would it? Why would there be two different optima instead of one?

Twelve years after he published *On the Origin of Species*, Darwin (1871) published another large work, one volume of which—*Selection in Relation to Sex*—was dedicated to answering this question. His touchstone example was the peacock, or more precisely, the peacock's tail. Does the resplendent train of a male peafowl help him find food? Avoid predators? Fight off parasites and pathogens? No, it actually hinders all of these fitness-serving goals. Then how have the alleles that build this seemingly worse-than-useless tail been preserved? Darwin's simple answer was: The tail is attractive to females. That's clearly true, but it's not the whole answer. Why don't peahens have fancy tails to similarly attract peacocks? That's the deeper puzzle.

COMPETITION FOR MATES

Think about how selection works. Mere survival gets precisely zero genes into the next generation. To be evolutionarily successful, an individual must survive to adulthood *and then mate*. Even if a trait *decreased* the chances of survival—as a large, heavy, flashy tail probably would—it could still be favored by selection, as long as it provided a big enough mating boost during one's (admittedly shorter) lifetime. Sexual selection, as defined by Darwin (and as still understood today), is selection for traits that increase mating success. Live fast, die young—and leave plenty of offspring! (Once you have assimilated the ideas in this chapter, you could try to explain why men's lives average four to five years shorter than women's.)

There are several broad categories of sexually selected traits. The two categories that will most concern us in this course are courtship traits and aggressive traits: The phrase "make love or make war" may help you grasp the dichotomy. Let's stick with the male perspective for the moment (and then we'll throw that open for evaluation). Selection could favor traits that allow a male to entice—to dazzle—females so that other males essentially disappear. Or, selection could favor traits that allow a male to beat up or so thoroughly intimidate his competitors that they do not even dare to approach the females. Either kind of trait—dazzling or dominating—would be favored by sexual selection as long as it increased mating success sufficiently to make up for its costs in reduced survival. There have been some interesting suggestions (e.g., Puts 2010) about factors that might favor one kind of mating competition (courting or fighting) over the other, but this seems to be unsettled science at the moment. I'm not going to address that issue further in this chapter. Instead, I'll take up the equally challenging and interesting question of *which sex* will evolve these mate-monopolizing traits—which sex will compete more intensely for mates.

What is your intuition? Which sex will evolve the courtship and/or fighting traits that help it get mates? The peacock example or your broader experience may lead you to suspect that the answer is "always the male." Alternatively, if you think it through from first principles, you may come to a different conclusion: In any sexual species, males and females are equally dependent on getting a mate (because a male cannot reproduce without a female, and a female cannot reproduce without a male). Given that, shouldn't the two sexes compete with equal intensity for mates? Since we can't seem to resolve this just by thinking about it, what does nature tell us; what do we actually see in the world?

WHICH SEX COMPETES, AND WHY

In reality, all possible patterns occur. In other words, there are many species where males have either courtship or aggressive traits that females completely lack. There are also many species in which these sexually selected traits—bright coloration or weapons—are present to approximately the same degree in both sexes. And, though such cases are rare, there clearly are species where *only the females* are flamboyant or aggressive. The point is not that some females are aggressive. The point is that there are entire species where the females are consistently more aggressive (or more adorned) than the males. What can explain these patterns? In other words, what would we have to know about a species in order to predict which sex—males, females, or both—will be the target(s) of sexual selection? Put simply, which sex will compete more intensely for mates?

Both Charles Darwin (1871) and Robert Trivers (1972), the developer of the reciprocal altruism theory, made attempts to answer this question. All the answers, including the most recent one offered by Tim Clutton-Brock and Amanda Vincent (1991) have a certain logical framework in common, so let's try to understand that general framework, and then we can explore how each theory uses that framework. Darwin knew that, when only one sex had sexually competitive traits (courtship or aggressive structures), it was almost always the male. He suggested that an unbalanced sex ratio could be the cause. In particular, he argued that if males were common and females were scare, competition for mates would be asymmetrical. Females would find an abundance of mates and would gain no advantage from competing for them; but males would find few females and could benefit by competing for them. Darwin was both a good theorist and a good observer. Thus he was able to discover that his hypothesis was wrong; sex ratios are not generally unbalanced in nature. Females are not scarce,

so this is not the reason that males compete for mates more often than females do.

One hundred years later, Robert Trivers (1972) made another suggestion: It's not the *numbers* of males and females that is unbalanced; it's the *reproductive work* they do in forming the offspring. Let's take a typical mammalian example. What does a female deer do in the course of reproducing? Besides producing the egg, she gestates the fetus for about six months and lactates for her fawn through another five. And what does her mate do? He contributes a tiny sperm cell, and then walks away. This, too, is an imbalance. But on this view it is not females themselves who are scarce; it is female reproductive work. Sperm are cheap and abundant compared to eggs, uteruses, and milk. Following the core Darwinian logic, that imbalance in reproductive work means that sperm makers will need to compete for access to the nurturing capacities of uteruses and mammary glands.

Trivers' theory was a plausible theory because it predicted the full range of observed possibilities. It predicted sexually competitive males in species where females do most of the reproductive work. It predicted that both sexes would have sexually competitive traits in species where males and females share the reproductive work equally. And, importantly, it predicted *sexually competitive females* in species where males do most of the reproductive work. As a mammal you might have a hard time imagining such a case, but consider birds. A male could build the nest, incubate the eggs, and tend the young after they hatch, all by himself; phalaropes are a good example. Trivers argued that in such cases females should be more brightly colored and more aggressive, and they typically are.

Thus, for the vast majority of species, Trivers' predictions were accurate. That's the mark of a good explanation and, as a result, his theory held sway for two decades. But the few exceptions continued to bother people. Specifically, the exceptions were cases where males appear to perform *all* the parental care but nevertheless still compete for mating access more than females do. Do you see that such cases seem to contradict Trivers' theory?

All good scientists care disproportionately about the (sometimes) tiny percentage of cases where a theory does not fit. That is how Einstein was able to improve on Newton's ideas. And that's what Clutton-Brock and Vincent did. They concentrated on a small set of critical test cases: those species in which only males provide parental care. According to Trivers' theory, females should be the sexual competitors in *all* of these species. In actuality, they are in some, but not all. What factor explains when males compete for mates and when females compete for mates in these species where males provide all the parental care? It seems to be *relative reproductive rate*. Of course, I'll explain. To begin, let's return to our deer example.

THE KEY VARIABLE: SEX DIFFERENCES IN REPRODUCTIVE RATE

How many offspring might a female deer produce in a year? Deer occasionally twin, so two per year would be her maximum reproductive rate. The key comparison is the number of offspring a male deer could produce in a year. The answer depends on how many fertile females he mates with. Maybe five, ten, fifteen per year; what might the limit be? Here's the point. Once a female copulates and is fertilized,

if that "reproductive venture" is to bear fruit, she can't begin another such venture for a year (until that offspring is weaned). In contrast, once a male fertilizes a female, launching one reproductive venture, how long before he can fertilize a different female and launch a second, and a third, etc.? I think the contrast is clear: Male deer *can* have higher reproductive rates than female deer. I italicized "can" because not all males *will* have higher reproductive rates than females. Why? Because Darwin was right that sex ratios are generally balanced. If one male fertilizes 15 females, that automatically means that 14 males will fertilize none. Now you see what Clutton-Brock and Vincent saw: If one sex *can* achieve higher reproductive success by excluding other members of it sex from mating, *then selection will favor traits that help them do so*. Since, in deer, males can reap this benefit and females can't, sexual selection has acted more strongly on males. That's right; that's why female deer don't have antlers.

MALES CAN CARE AND STILL BE FASTER

In deer, females seem to have slower reproductive rates because they invest more in each offspring than males do. Wouldn't the sex that invests more in offspring *always* have slower reproductive rates? I think that was an implicit assumption in Trivers' model. And that question highlights the reason that Clutton-Brock and Vincent focused on species that have only paternal care (Figure 21-1). Fortunately, reproductive rate is an *empirical question*. That simply means that reproductive rate can be measured, and that's "game on" for scientists. The interesting cases are the ones where males do all of the parental care but where males nevertheless

Reproductive Rate		Competition for mates more intense in males	Competition for mates more intense in females
Males faster	Fish	Cottus (2 spp) Oxylebius pictus Chromis notata Chrysiptera cyanea Badis badis Pimephales Promelas Etheostoma olmstedi Gasterosteus aculeatus Forsterygion varium	
	Frogs	Alytes obstetricans Hyla rosenbergii Eleutherodactylus coqui	
Females faster	Fish	Hippocampus spp	Apogon notatus Nerophis ophidion Syngnathus typhle
	Birds	(Rhea americana?)	Actitis macularia Phalaropus (2 spp) Eudromias morinellus Jacana (5 spp) Rostrathula benghalensis Turnix sylvaticus

Figure 21-1. In species that have parental care by males alone, the relative reproductive rate of males and females predicts which which sex will compete for mates.

compete for mates more than females do. Why do they compete? Is it because they have higher reproductive rates, despite being caring dads?

Let's take *Gasterosteus aculeatus*, the three-spined stickleback (a fish), as an example. In this species, the male builds a nest of algae and other aquatic vegetation where females lay their eggs, which he fertilizes by ejaculating over them. After fertilization he nourishes the developing eggs by oxygenating them with his fins, and he protects them and the resulting hatchlings from predators. The female departs immediately after egg laying and begins maturing a new batch of eggs (which she typically lays for a different male). The relevant question would appear to be, how long it takes a female to mature a new batch of eggs *compared* to how long it takes a male to finish

rearing the eggs she has just laid for him. If you came to that conclusion, great; you are following the logic perfectly. But nature often has more tricks up her elaborate sleeve. Male sticklebacks who are tending a nest that already contains the eggs of one female continue to use it as a courtship device to entice additional females to also contribute their eggs! OK, the math is still straight forward. We just need to have the egg number and egg-maturation rate on the "female" side of the equation, and the rearing rate and number of laying females on the "male" side. Whichever product is bigger, that's the sex with the higher reproductive rate. Cranking through that calculation suggests that, despite doing all the parental care, male sticklebacks can still reproduce at a higher rate than females. Hence it's the females (actually, their eggs) that are in short supply and males thus evolved sexually competitive traits in this species.

The test cases that let us decided between Trivers' theory and Clutton Brock and Vincent's theory are species where males provide all the parental care (Figure 21-1). Trivers' theory predicts that females should compete more intensely for mates in all of these species. Clutton-Brock and Vincent (1991) found that that prediction is incorrect. Even though they do all the parental care, males compete for mates in all of these species where they can reproduce at higher rates than females. In other words, the reproductive-rate model most accurately predicts which sex will be shaped by of sexual selection.

A simple summary will make sense if you've followed the argument. In many species, one sex will be quicker to complete a reproductive venture and thus return to the pool of available mating partners. Whichever sex returns to the mate pool more quickly will find members of the slower-to-return sex scarce, and hence worth competing for. Selection will therefore favor sexually competitive traits in the "fast" sex. Try to see what general principle Clutton-Brock and Vincent's theory has in common with the ideas of both Darwin and Trivers. Once you understand how sexual selection works in general, try to say how it has acted in humans. Do men or women manifest more sexually competitive traits and, in terms of the reproductive-rate theory, why?

CHAPTER SUMMARY

Sexual selection is natural selection for mating success. In many species sexual selection impacts males and females in similar ways; but in many others it produces dramatic sex differences, with one sex evolving strong sexually competitive traits, of either the courtship or aggressive type. Several theories have been advanced to explain the pattern of sexual competition across species. The most successful theory suggests that the sex that completes reproductive ventures (and hence returns to the mate pool) more quickly will evolve more sexually competitive traits. This perspective could be used to explain various sex differences in humans.

CITED REFERENCES

Timothy H. Clutton-Brock and Amanda J. C. Vincent (1991). "Sexual selection and the potential reproductive rates of males and females." *Nature 351*: 58-60.

Charles R. Darwin (1871) Sexual Selection and the Descent of Man. Vol II Selection in Relation to Sex. John Murray; London.

David Puts (2010) "Beauty and the beast: Mechanisms of sexual selection in humans." Evolution and Human Behavior 31: 157-175.

Robert L. Trivers (1972) "Parental investment and sexual selection." *In Sexual Selection and the Descent of Man, 1871-1971*. (B. Campbell, Ed.) pp 136–179. Aldine; Chicago.

FIGURE CREDIT

21-1: Image created by Judith Geiger.

CHAPTER 22

OF HUMAN BONDING

In the previous chapter you learned that the force of sexual selection is driven by the relative reproductive rates of females and males. At the end of that chapter, I asked you to try to place our own species in the framework of the reproductive-rate model. If you did that you would see that because men do not gestate or lactate, they could have much higher reproductive rates than women have. In fact we know that some individual men have had thousands of offspring—something a woman could not possibly do. So men are the fast sex, and how fast they can be will depend on just how many partners they can recruit to produce offspring for them. This perspective leads to a set of interlocking puzzles: Why should a man pair up with one woman when there are so many other options for increasing his reproductive success? Why should a woman put all her eggs in one genetic basket and produce all her offspring with the same man? In short, why do humans form long-term pair bonds?

LOVE IS NOT THE ANSWER; IT'S PART OF THE PUZZLE

When I pose such questions I often get this kind of response: "Because they're in love!" Sweet and romantic as this answer might be, it's not very coherent because it starts in the middle of the problem and dodges the difficult part. Love—the capacity to feel love and to be motivated by it, to allow it close our eyes to other reproductive opportunities—is part of what we're trying to explain. It's the motivational machinery of that keeps the man and woman together. Saying "they're in love" is just highlighting the emotional component of the pair-bonding adaptation. Here's the way an evolutionist would ask the question: Why are humans the kind of creatures that are susceptible to falling in love and thus truncating their mating opportunities? If love were not good for fitness, selection would not have created the neural and hormonal circuitry that permits it! (For more on that circuitry see the second half of this chapter.) So, asking why we pair bond is really the same as asking why we fall in love.

PAIR-BONDING IS DERIVED IN THE HUMAN LINEAGE

Putting this problem in phylogenetic context, pair bonding is not very common in mammals; about 4% of mammal species form durable bonds between one male and one female. Virtually all the rest have mating systems that are either *promiscuous* (where there are no stable mating relationships at all) or *polygynous* (where successful males have harems and unsuccessful males are excluded from mating). Among our closest living relatives, chimpanzees are promiscuous and gorillas have harems. For comparison you might be interested to know that birds show the reverse pattern: About 90% of bird species form monogamous breeding units; most of the remaining 10% are polygynous or promiscuous, but about 0.5% are *polyandrous* (where a successful female will have a "harem" of males who mate with her and rear her young without her help; the phalaropes briefly mentioned in the previous chapter are examples). What would you need to know to predict which sex will evolve sexually competitive traits in these polyandrous bird species? If you absorbed the key message of the last chapter you should be able to answer that question.

To return to the central theme of this chapter, why are humans such odd mammals in terms of their mating relationships? Why do males hang around with one female instead of trying to fertilize as many as they can? Do you see why I'm phrasing the question from the male point of view? It should be obvious that a male's reproductive success will be proportionate to the number of females he can fertilize—because many females can be producing offspring for him simultaneously. (I invite you to check the Guinness Book of Records on this topic.)

This statement is not obviously reversible by sex. Having a dozen mates won't give a woman twelve times the reproductive success of a monogamous woman, because she can only gestate one baby at a time, regardless of how many sex partners she has. So, a woman probably wouldn't gain as much by playing the field as a man would, but she might reap some benefits. For example, she might end up with more grandchildren if her own children are more genetically diverse as a result of having different fathers. Remembering that sex may have evolved as a novelty-generating counterstrategy to parasites, you could think of promiscuity (producing offspring with many different partners) as "ultrasex." (Put that together with the comparative method and what do you get? The prediction that human mating systems will be less monogamous in parts of the world where the parasite burden is high, a prediction that turns out to be true.) Women might also gain other benefits from having multiple mates. Men might provide resources such as food or protection for their mates. From a woman's perspective, mating with an array of men may encourage all of them to provision and protect her and her offspring.

ALTRICIAL YOUNG BENEFIT FROM ADDED CARE

Thus we see that, for both women and men, there are reasons *not* to form stable pair bonds. Then why do we do it? This is a key question about human nature, one that we first mentioned in Chapter 15. There we suggested that helpless offspring need more parenting. You'll recall that members of the genus *Homo* need to birth their brainy infants early enough in their development so that the infant's head can fit through a bipedally constricted birth canal. This "pre-emptive" birth pattern means that human infants are quite helpless—*altricial* is the scientific term—and therefore able to benefit from additional parental care.

There is reasonable support for the idea that helpless young generate natural selection for biparental care. Where could you look for relevant evidence? Remember that the comparative method is a powerful tool for testing the function of adaptations. Bird species show a wide spectrum of developmental patterns. In many species the altricial nestlings are naked and quite helpless, relying on the parent for food, warmth and protection for weeks or even months. In others, the young are more *precocial*; for example they are feathered and can walk around soon after they hatch. As you should predict, the species with altricial young generally have biparental care, but the species with precocial young tend to have uniparental care, typically by the female alone but, in polyandrous species, by the male alone. One of the aspects of biology that gives me endless pleasure is its diversity. Here's what I mean. Suppose I told you that there are some species of birds where the young are super-precocial? These are the *megapodes*, including birds like the Australian Brushturkey and the Malleefowl. They don't even need to be incubated while developing in the egg because the eggs are laid in a big compost heap that generates heat. When they hatch, the strong and highly coordinated young dig their way out and begin feeding themselves; most species have fully feathered wings and can fly the day they hatch. They never know who their parents are because there is *no parental care* at all! So there is a very neat continuum, from species with no parental care, through species with uniparental care, to species with biparental care. And the bird species with the most altricial young are precisely the species most likely to have biparental care.

The greater needs of altricial human infants recalibrate the relative payoffs of monogamy versus promiscuity. When considering a new problem it can be useful to first analyze the most extreme (or limit) case. For example, let's imagine a species where no offspring can survive without extended biparental care. This would mean that any male who pursued the strategy of fertilizing females and then abandoning them to seek additional matings would have a lifetime reproductive success of zero—because all his (possibly numerous) offspring would die. That's clearly a losing strategy. We admitted that this is a limit case, but it's still informative. The more a species approached that limit situation, the more selection would favor males who did *not* abandon their mates, but instead hung around to help ensure the survival and eventual reproductive success of their offspring. The female perspective is equally important. If biparental care is essential, females who mate with males who subsequently abandon them also lose big in the Darwinian game. So selection should begin to favor females who are choosy and refuse to mate except with males who show credible evidence that they are going to hang around and help with the kids.

Humans are clearly not the limit case; at least in the modern world, many offspring do survive with uniparental care. But we're also not a species with young who can independently move about, run away from predators, and find their own food. Our offspring are very helpless and benefit greatly from parental care, protection, and support. Many studies suggest that, even with an extensive social safety net, children raised in single-parent homes tend to suffer life-long costs. How much greater would those costs have been for ancestral humans living a hunting-and-gathering way of life? In other words, how would the reproductive costs and benefits of pair bonding versus promiscuity have played out over the big sweep of human evolution?

A CASE STUDY OF PATERNAL PROVISIONING IN HUNTER-GATHERERS

Drawing on his extensive field work with the Hadza in northwest Tanzania, Frank Marlowe (2003) has generated some data that helps us answer this question. The Hadza are of great interest to anthropologists because they are contemporary hunters-and-gatherers, among the very last humans still living a lifestyle that characterized our ancestors for hundreds of thousands of years. As their various governments settle people like the Hadza on reservations (as North American colonists did with indigenous populations here), an irreplaceable window on ancient human lifeways is closing forever. Thanks to the efforts of dedicated anthropologists like Marlowe, we've learned a lot about these hunting-and-gathering lifeways.

In all described hunter-gatherers, there is a sexual division of labor: Men hunt and women gather. There is a little variation among populations when it comes to who does the fishing and honey collecting, but men bring home almost all of the meat that people eat and women bring home most of the plant foods. Unlike wild roots, fruits, and seeds, meat sometimes comes in pretty big packets (e.g., a giraffe!) that would spoil before a family could eat it all. We've already seen (Chapters 10 and 15) that such situations are ripe for reciprocity: I give you the extra meat I can't eat this week, and you do the same for me when you make your next big kill. That is absolutely what happens in hunter-gatherer populations. Men's meat gets shared around the camp but a woman's gathered foods are much more likely to stay at her family's hearth. Because meat gets shared around, some anthropologists think that men don't hunt to provision their kids. Instead they argue that hunting is primarily "showing off." According to this view men hunt to advertise their genetic quality and thereby get more mating opportunities. The debate about whether hunting is primarily provisioning or primarily showing off is not going to be settled here. But Marlowe has some relevant evidence that certainly bears on the evolution of human pair bonding.

Marlowe pursued this question by, over a period of time, measuring all the food that men and women brought back to camp and computing the foods' value in the common currency of kilocalories (Kcal) per day. In this way we can fairly compare the daily contributions of women and men (Table 22-1). Let's first compare all adult women with all adult men. The average adult woman brings home 3,076 kcal per day while the average adult man bags 2,792 kcal per day. Making a few simple calculations we can see that these two averages add up to 5,868 kcal, of which women are contributing (3,076/5,868 = 52.4%) and men are contributing (2,792/5,868 = 47.6%): fairly similar but the guys are slacking a bit. Now, to see if parenting makes any difference to men's and women's contributions we want to make similar comparisons for men and women at various stages of parenting: those with any children under 8 years of age, those with children under 3 years of age, and finally those with children under 1 year of age.

The first thing to notice is that the total stays pretty constant, more than 5,500 and less than 6,000 across all these categories. But having kids lowers women's contributions and it increases men's. Notice the consistent pattern:

The younger the children, the less food women bring home and the more food men bring home. In families with the youngest children—in their most helpless stage—men are contributing nearly 70% of the Kcals. Hadza men are stepping up to the plate precisely when it's most difficult for mothers to address all the needs of their very altricial infants. I'll mention also that Marlowe highlights an important exception to this pattern: Men raise their foraging effort (as shown in Table 22-1) only for their *own* offspring, not for stepchildren. How does that observation bear on our argument about the evolution of pair bonding?

These observations—with men's provisioning peaking when their offspring are most helpless—accord well with the idea that human pair bonding helps to address the challenges posed by highly altricial young. By remaining with his partner, at least through the period of high infant vulnerability, a man can increase his own reproductive success. And by selecting and bonding with a man who will help her when she most needs it, a woman can reap similar evolutionary benefits. If you understand these arguments and data, perhaps you can suggest some non-human species that you predict might fall in love.

Table 22-1. Caloric contributions by women and men.

	women	men	total	% by women	% by men
all adults	3076	2792	5868	52.4%	47.6%
children < 8 years	2697	3049	5746	46.9%	53.1%
children < 3 years	2346	3227	5573	42.1%	57.9%
children < 1 year	1713	3851	5564	30.8%	69.2%

ALLELES FOR LOVE?

As we approach the end of the course, you should notice that your knowledge about human evolution becomes more unified, and that you are able to connect theories, data, and methods from different areas of study. In closing my journey with you, I want to unite ideas from genetics with theories about pair bonding, and explore them with the comparative method. My presentation is based on research by Hasse Walum and his colleagues at the Karolinska Institute in Stockholm. The research has some technical aspects but I think you're up to it at this point in the course.

As you know, when a gene is expressed, the result is a protein. These proteins interact with other proteins (specified by other genes) and with the environment in shaping our traits. Note that we have never drawn a strict line between anatomical traits, like the shape of the pelvis or the size of the brain, and behavioral traits such as tool-using abilities, or pair-bonding inclinations, or language abilities. We have not drawn a line because there isn't one. In both the anatomical and the behavioral arena, alleles are favored if and only if they build adaptive traits—traits that work well in the prevailing environment. Arguments about selection shaping hominin tool use (Chapter 13), arguments about the evolution of altruism (Chapter 9 and 10) and Marlowe's arguments about selection for human pair bonds (this chapter) all assume that selection works on behavior as well as anatomy. This is not as big a leap as it seems on the surface, because selection for behavior *is* selection for anatomy—for example, for the neuroanatomy, hormones, and the like that produce the behavior. The neurobiology and genetics underlying pair bonding provide an example. Let's take a tour of love.

OF MICE (OK, VOLES) AND MEN

The story starts with voles (field mice) of the genus *Microtus*. I have a special fondness for voles because I studied them for more than a decade, for essentially the same reason they are discussed here: In a single genus, different species of *Microtus* exhibit a wide range of mating systems. For example, *M. pennsylvanicus* (meadow voles) and *M. montanus* (montane voles) are highly promiscuous, whereas *M. ochrogaster* (prairie voles) and *M. pinetorum* (pine voles) are monogamous. The promiscuous species show little or no pair-bonding behavior, but the monogamous ones form strong pair bonds. That is very handy for researchers: It gives us a clear case of evolutionary divergence among closely related species (members of a single genus). We could use that divergence to test theories about the functions of pair-bonds (and some researchers have), but here we want to understand the genetic and neurobiological differences between the monogamous and promiscuous vole species. We want to do that to find out if there are parallel differences within our own species—but I am getting ahead of the story.

Of course the system is more complicated than what we can cover here, but to give you an appreciation for what we can learn about these kinds of adaptations we're going to focus on just two genes. One of these genes codes for a neuropeptide that allows certain kinds of neurons (brain cells) to communicate with each other. This neuropeptide is called arginine vasopressin (AVP is its nickname); you should think of it as a message carrier. The other gene, *avpr1a*, codes for a receptor protein called V1aR. (Genes generally have logically abbreviated names; "<u>A</u><u>V</u><u>P</u> receptor <u>one-a</u>" is shortened to *avpr1a*.) Gene products cannot do their work unless they have a way to be "heard." Just as you need a radio to receive radio waves and a television to receive TV waves, the body needs many specific kinds of receptors to interpret the messages carried by specific gene products. You can think of the V1aR protein as a specialized catcher's mitt for AVP. If a neuron lacks V1aR (for example, if its *avpr1a* gene is turned off or mutated), that neuron will not be able to receive the AVP message.

What do the proteins AVP and V1aR have to do with pair bonding? Experiments show that if you increase the amount of AVP in their brains, voles will more readily form pair bonds. Conversely, if you give them a substance that interferes with the ability of V1aR to catch the AVP message, they will be less likely to pair bond. Thus, these two proteins have important effects on key aspects of mating behavior.

Now, remember that monogamous vole species spontaneously form pair bonds, whereas promiscuous vole species do not. As would be expected if these differences had been shaped by natural selection, they seem to have a genetic basis: When we measure their natural levels we find that the promiscuous vole species have less V1aR in their brains, because they have fewer neurons that express the *avpr1a* gene. When scientists experimentally increase the density of cells that express the *avpr1a* gene in the brains of promiscuous vole species, they pair bond more than they do otherwise. Not only do the monogamous species have more brain cells that express the *avpr1a* gene, they also have a different version of the gene, with an extra 428-base "tail." If you transfer this elongated version of the *avpr1a* gene from the monogamous species to the promiscuous species, the behavior of the promiscuous voles changes, becoming more like

that of the monogamous voles. Finally, there is some allelic variation in the *avpr1a* gene in monogamous vole species (for example, not all prairie voles have the same *avpr1a* genotype); and the strength of their pair bonds correlates with which *avpr1a* alleles they have.

Cool stuff. We can think of the loci that code for the AVP and V1aR proteins as genes that shape pair bonding. In other words, when selection is building stronger (or weaker) pair bonds, perhaps it is accomplishing that by favoring certain alleles of these genes that affect how much of these proteins are made. At this point, you probably want to know if humans have these same genes. Given your understanding of evolution, do you think that would be likely? Remember that evolution is a tinkerer. Much is conserved and reused; for example, whales have a forelimb—a flipper—that has most of the same bones as your arm.

OK, no more waiting: The answer is yes. Humans have the gene that codes for AVP, as do most mammals. Humans also have several genes that code for receptors of AVP, including a 1A type receptor, the *AVPR1A* gene, which is homologous to the *avpr1a* vole gene (note that the gene names are the same except that the human gene is capitalized). In the case of genes, "homologous" means that the base sequences are similar enough in the vole *avpr1a* gene and the human *AVPR1A* gene that they seem likely to be derived from the same ancestral sequence—which would have to be at least 65 million years old in this case. In humans, both the gene coding for AVP and the APRR1A gene are actual genes not pseudogenes (as so many of our olfactory receptor genes are). Not only does human *AVPR1A* share a common ancestor with vole *avpr1a*, but the human gene also has a "tail," as do the AVP receptor genes of monogamous (but not promiscuous) vole species. And, finally, there are different alleles of the human *AVPR1A* gene. The question you probably want to ask is, do people who have certain *AVPR1A* alleles form stronger (or weaker) pair bonds than individuals with different alleles? So sorry, but the jury is still out on this final point; we have one study that says "yes" and one (not yet published but reported at a conference) that says "no."

Of course we know that AVP is not the only protein affecting bonding behavior in animals. For example, there is another neuropeptide called *oxytocin* (OT) that of course has its own specialized receptor, and that is also known to be related to both pair-bonding and parent-offspring bonding in various species of voles and primates. Recent work has shown that there are different alleles of the human oxytocin receptor gene (*OXTR*), and that one allele is particular is associated with weaker pair-bonding (Walum et al. 2012).

Love is, must be, chemical. Some species are capable of it because selection has tweaked particular proteins. I do hope that realization doesn't make love less romantic for you. Personally I find it much richer knowing that I was *designed* to feel, and enjoy, love's rewards.

CODA

No one thinks we currently have this all worked out. That is absolutely *not* my claim. Science is the ongoing process of testing (and often rejecting) hypotheses to push back the ocean of our ignorance and establish islands of understanding. But after more than a century and a half of rigorous testing, we see the theory of evolution by natural selection sitting on one of the higher of those islands. Scientists have reached the consensus that natural selection has—without the slightest foresight, and in consistent opposition to entropy—designed all organisms to match their environments. That happened because, generation after generation, selection was sorting through the fitness effects of alternative Mendelian alleles that were originally the products of mutation. Thus we, and all creatures, are the cumulative effects of mere genetic junk, tossed into the hopper of natural selection and retained or rejected on the basis of its suitability to immediate environmental demands. Trash winnowed for function. That's what all organisms are: beautiful trash—the best trash ever.

"There is grandeur in this view of life . . ." Darwin wrote in the last paragraph of *The Origin of Species*. Yes, without a doubt; grandeur in the view that you and I are the current standard bearers of genes that for billions of generations—without a single interruption—have built creatures that survived and reproduced, despite impossible odds. I congratulate you! May you put your legacy to good use.

CHAPTER SUMMARY

Human pair-bonding is highly derived, being absent in all the great apes. Cross-species comparisons (especially with birds) suggest that pair-bonding may have evolved to provide additional parental care for our highly altricial infants—which itself is an evolutionary result of the conjunction of large brains and bipedality. The observation that males in a hunter-gatherer population increase their provisioning when they have young children supports the "extra-care hypothesis" for the evolution of human pair-bonding. Comparative studies of bonding and non-bonding vole species suggest that genes specifying certain neuropeptides and their receptor proteins play a role in pair-bonding behavior. Based on studies of individual variation in the strength of human pair-bonds, the very same genes may to play a similar role in human bonding behavior.

CITED REFERENCES

Frank W. Marlowe (2003) "A critical period for provisioning by Hadza men: Implications for pair bonding." Evolution and Human Behavior 24: 217–229.

Hasse Walum, Lars Westberg, Susanne Henningsson, Jenae M. Neiderhiser, David Reiss, Wilmar Igl, Jody M. Ganiban, Erica L. Spotts, Nancy L. Pedersen, Elias Eriksson & Paul Lichtenstein (2008) "Genetic variation in the vasopressin receptor 1a gene (AVPR1A) associates with pair-bonding behavior in humans." Proceedings of the National Academy of Sciences, USA 105: 14153–14156.

Hasse Walum, Paul Lichtenstein, Jenae M. Neiderhiser, David Reiss, Jody M. Ganiban, Erica L. Spotts, Nancy L. Pedersen, Henrik Anckarsäter, Henrik Larsson, and Lars Westberg (2012). "Variation in the Oxytocin Receptor Gene Is Associated with Pair-Bonding and Social Behavior." Biological Psychiatry, 71: 419-426.

FIGURE CREDIT

22-1: Image created by Judith Geiger.

GLOSSARY

acetabular width: The acetabulum is the socket in the hip where the head of the femur rests. The width is simply a measure of the size of this socket. Its size is thought to give information about the nature of an animal's gait—the way it walks. This is useful for extinct animals whose gait we cannot observe directly. A larger acetabulum suggest the joint bore more weight, which in turn suggests bipedality.

Ache: A tribe of South American hunter-gatherers.

Acheulean: Stone tools that are more sophisticated than Oldowan tools; Acheulean tools first appear about 1.75 million years ago (MYA) and are bifacial—having flakes removed on both sides.

adaptation: A trait preserved by natural selection because it improved the fit between the organism and its environment.

admixture events: A hyper-clinical phrase for interbreeding between taxa; for example, interbreeding between *H. sapiens sapiens* and *H. sapiens neanderthalensis*.

agemate: Similar-aged members of a social group. A set of agemates comprise a cohort.

allele: A version of a gene; variants (alternatives) that can occur at the same locus.

allelo-chemicals: Toxic compounds that do not enter the metabolic pathways of a plant but inflict costs on animals that consume the plant; defensive compounds; also sometimes called secondary compounds because they are secondary to the plant's metabolism.

allopatry: Geographic separation. The allopatric model of speciation posits that geographic separation, combined with divergent selection pressures (and drift), can cause one species to split into two.

altriciality: The state of being born (or hatched) at an early stage of development; altricial young are relatively helpless and need extra care. (See precociality).

antagonist: A chemical that interferes with biochemical activity of a gene product.

anterior: Front, first; the opposite of posterior.

apes: Our group of primates; living (non-extinct) apes include the lesser apes in the genus *Hylobates* (the gibbons), as well as the four great ape genera: *Pongo* (the orangutans), *Pan* (the chimpanzees), *Gorilla* (you guessed it!), and *Homo* (folks you might date).

Arborealism, arboreal: A mode of life that depends on spending a lot of time in trees as opposed to on the ground.

atherosclerosis: Thickening of the blood vessel walls due to a build-up of fatty materials; these build-ups are called plaques. Remember the phrase "solid at body temperature."

autapomorphy: A completely unique derived trait; a trait not shared with any other taxon and therefore useless for determining cladistic relationships. For example, as far as we can tell, language seems to be an autapomorphy.

autoimmune disease: An array of diseases that have one thing in common: Some of the body's own cells are being mistakenly attacked by its immune system, whose normal function is to attack invading pathogens.

callitrichid: The marmosets and tamarins; the smallest New World monkeys.

cardiovascular disease: Diseases of the heart or blood vessels; atherosclerosis is the most common type.

carrier: A person who has a particular allele but does not express it. For example, a female carrier of

Xq28 ordinarily does not manifest homosexual tendencies.

cecal valves: Valves that divide the cecum, a part of the intestine, into a series of smaller compartments.

cellulose: A carbohydrate that is the principal component of plant (but not animal) cell walls. It is tough, fibrous, and indigestible by any animal with a backbone, but it can be digested by some invertebrates, and cooking degrades it making the plant cell contents more available.

cheek teeth: Chewing teeth as opposed to biting teeth. Molars and premolars are cheek teeth; incisors and canines are not. Large chewing surface area is thought to reflect a high-fiber diet.

cladistics: A set of methodological tools used to classify organisms phylogenetically.

coalitionary support: In many primate species, individuals do not contest resources alone, but form alliances and "friendships" and support each other in squabbles over resources.

coevolution: The joint evolution of two or more species, each exerting selection pressures on the other.

commensal: Literally means sharing food. Commensal invertebrates often live in the digestive system of plant-eating vertebrates and do the cellulose-digesting work for their vertebrate hosts.

congener: A member of the same genus. *Anolis carolinensis* and *Anolis sagrei* are congeners, as are *Homo sapiens* and *Homo erectus*.

convergence: Adaptive similarity that results when different populations experience similar selection pressures.

cost of males: Another way of stating the cost of meiosis, because males generally don't bear offspring.

costly signaling: Advertising genetic quality by accepting costs. Members of the slow sex should evolve to ignore the displays of the fast sex unless they honestly reveal some aspect of mate value. A prevailing view is that unless these signals are costly (for example, energetically costly) they could be faked and hence would not convey useful information. According to some anthropologists, male hunting might have evolved primarily as a costly signal rather than to provision a woman and her offspring.

cranial: Relating to the cranium or skull.

cuckoldry: Any case where a man is fooled into provisioning children whom he mistakenly believes to be his genetic offspring.

DEE: Daily energy expenditure; higher than resting metabolic rate (RMR); how much higher will depend on activity levels.

derived: A trait that arose since the common ancestor of the taxonomic group under study. Language is derived in apes (only one ape has it).

diabetes: Disorder resulting from abnormally high levels of blood sugar. The kind of diabetes affected by diet is called "Type 2 diabetes" and is a consequence of high insulin resistance in which the body responds poorly to the blood-sugar-reducing effects of the hormone insulin.

divergence: Adaptive dissimilarity that results when initially similar populations experience different selection pressures.

DNA: The hereditary molecule on this planet. A long molecule consisting twin phosphate-sugar backbones linked by pairs of chemical bases. Base-pairing rules allow DNA's extremely accurate replication. DNA directs the assembly of proteins.

dominant: An allele that is expressed even in heterozygotes.

drift: More precisely, genetic drift. Random fluctuations in gene frequency due solely to chance rather than to natural selection. See Chapter 6's section on Natural Selection's Limitations.

duality of patterning: Refers to the fact that two separate tiers of rules govern language: a set of (phonological) rules for combining meaningless sounds into meaningful words, overlaid by a different set of (grammatical) rules for combining words to convey ideas (the relationships among the words).

dysarthria: A speech impairment (in the lips, tongue, vocal chords, etc.) as opposed to a language impairment (in the mental machinery for learning and using language).

ectotherm: A cold-blooded animal; one that does not regulate its body temperature chemically.

emigrate: To leave the natal group (see "natal group").

endotherm: A warm-blooded animal; one that maintains a relatively constant body temperature by chemical means.

entropy: The natural tendency of the universe to disorder and chaos, a force that organisms massively resist.

evolutionary game theory: A branch of applied mathematics that looks for a "strategy" (trait) that is immune to invasion; in other words, a trait that is better than all its alternatives, and would therefore be perpetuated over evolutionary time.

expensive tissue hypothesis (ETH): The idea that evolution can increase the size of one expensive kind of tissue (e.g., the brain) only if it reduces the size of some other kind of expensive tissue (e.g., the gut).

femur: The upper leg bone.

femoral head: The rounded end of the femur that meshes with the acetabulum. The head tends to be larger in bipeds than in quadrupeds.

femoral neck: The part of the femur between the head and the greater trochanter. The part that sits at a right angle to the shaft. The neck tends to be longer in bipedal than in quadrupedal apes.

fMRI: Functional Magnetic Resonance Imaging; a technique that allows researchers to see what areas of the brain are most active when a particular task is being performed.

glacial-interglacial cycles: The alternating pulses of colder and warmer climate phases that punctuate the Pleistocene. Taking a broad view of the earth's climate we are now in an interglacial period. During glacial phases more of the earth's water was locked up in glaciers producing substantially lower sea levels (and hence larger continents) than we see today. Interglacial phases have the opposite effect, raising sea levels and shrinking continents. Because of these changes, coastal sites that were inhabited during a glacial period would now lay hundreds of feet below sea level.

grooming: Removal of ectoparasites (ticks, fleas, lice) from the body of a companion. Grooming occupies a lot of social time in many species of monkeys and apes.

H-Y antibodies: Molecules produced by a mother to protect her against the foreign Y-chromosome proteins produced by her gestating sons.

H-Y antigen: (Originally *antibody generator*) Any molecule (e.g., protein) resulting from genes on the human Y-chromosome that stimulates the production of antibodies.

haplogroup: A group of phylogenetically connected haplotypes that share a common ancestor. For example, in our Figure 16-9, bearers of the M, G, N, and I genes all belong to the L3 haplogroup, because they are all descendants of an L3 bearer. As we mentioned, all these mitochondrial lineages have more descendants than are shown in Figure 16-9; so M, for example, comprises a haplogroup with all of its many descendants. Likewise G, N, and I are the roots of three haplogroups with all of their descendants. In other words, haplogroups can be recognized at any level of the hierarchy, as long as all of the descendants are included.

haplotype: A set of alleles that get passed down together because there has been no recombination between them (and no mutation within them). It's haplotypes that scientists are tabulating when they build trees like our Figure 16-9. Because mt-DNA and (most) Y-DNA don't recombine, their haplotypes are modified only by mutation, and thus remain intact and recognizable for long periods of evolutionary time.

Hardy-Weinberg equilibrium: An equation that gives the expected genotype frequencies in a population based on the allele frequencies.

HDL/LDL: So-called good and bad cholesterol. HDL reduces and LDL promotes atherosclerotic plaques.

herbivore: A plant eater.

heritability: a population-based statistic that assesses how much of the variation in a trait is caused by individuals having different alleles affecting the trait

Hiwi: A tribe of South American hunter-gatherers.

hominid: Correctly applied, this term refers to all the great apes. In older usage it referred to species on the human line after the divergence from the line that leads to chimpanzees—what we now call hominins.

homoplasy: A fancy term for evolutionary convergence; when relatively distantly related forms evolve similar phenotypes as a result of experiencing similar selection pressures.

hypertension: High blood pressure in the arterial system. The reason high blood pressure is a medical problem is that it forces the heart to work harder to circulate blood.

intragroup aggression: Fighting among the members of a social group, usually over access to resources such as food or mates.

IU: International unit. The size of an international unit varies depending on the substance. One IU of vitamin D3 is 0.025 micrograms. A microgram is one millionth of a gram, so an IU of vitamin D3 is just one fortieth of one millionth of a gram.

KYA: Thousand(s) of years ago (e.g., 27 KYA means 27,000 years ago).

Kcal/day: depending on the study, a measure of the daily foraging returns of an individual, or the daily energy needs of an individual.

Kcal: A standard measure of the energetic content of a food.

kin selection: Evolutionary force that spreads genes via their actor-mediated fitness effects on other carriers of the same gene. A form of selection that can favor altruism because of altruism's favorable effects on the alleles causing the altruism.

Kinsey scale: (Named for the famous sex researcher who devised it) A simple tool used to assess sexual orientation. Participants are asked to report, separately, their attraction, behavior, fantasy, etc., on a 7-point scale where "0" means "always the opposite sex" and "6" means "always my own sex," with 1 to 5 representing various gradations in between.

lacertid lizard, scleroglossan lizard, agamid lizard, iguanid lizard: Various kinds of lizards more and less closely related to the study species in Herrel's study; see Figure 2-1.

lamella (plural, lamellae): Adhesive scales on the toes of many lizard species. Figure 2-3.

life-history: The scheduling of the phases of the lifespan (e.g., gestation, infancy, childhood, maturity, old age). Species differ in the pace at which individuals move through these phases. For example, chimpanzees grow up more quickly and have shorter lifespans than humans.

linkage [disequilibrium]: The statistically elevated tendency for two alleles at different loci on the same chromosome to co-occur.

locus (plural, loci): The "address" on a particular chromosome where genes coding for a particular protein regularly occur.

mandibular robusticity: The mandible is the jaw bone (technically two bones fused at the chin) that hold the lower teeth. Megadonty is associated with mandibular robusticity because heavy chewing requires both large chewing teeth and a large mandible to bear the pressures generated.

masticatory apparatus: The functionally linked set of anatomical traits involved in chewing, including the teeth, the jaws in which they sit, and the muscles that operate those jaws.

mate-guarding: Male behaviors that focus on preventing cuckoldry (i.e., on making sure their partner's offspring are theirs).

megadonty: The condition of having large molars and premolars—large chewing teeth. Having large incisors and canines—large biting teeth—is *not* called megadonty. Megadonty is believed to be associated with a diet based on course, fibrous plant material.

meiosis: The reduction from a diploid state to a haploid state; part of the process of sex cell (egg and sperm) production.

melanin: A dark pigment; a gene product deposited in the surface layers of the skin that blocks deeper penetration of UVb radiation.

metabolic syndrome: A combination of medical disorders that increase the risk of both cardiovascular disease and diabetes.

Miocene: A geologic epoch lasting from about 23.0 million years ago (MYA) to about 5.3 MYA. The Miocene precedes the Pliocene.

mitochondrial DNA: mt-DNA. Genetic information passed only by mothers to both sexes of offspring.

monkeys: Many species of mostly quadrupedal primates; monkeys include the genera *Ateles*, *Nasalis*, *Macaca*, *Papio* and many others.

morpheme: An arbitrary set of phonemes used to designate some meaning.

morphology: Anatomy, structure.

morphometrics: Measurements of anatomical traits, e.g., how wide is the lizard's head?

mutation: An error in gene copying; the source of all new alleles.

MYA: Million(s) of years ago.

natural selection: Differential reproduction arising from better versus worse fit with the prevailing environment.

neuropeptide: A protein that brain cells use to communicate with each other.

nursling: A young offspring dependent for its nutrition on its mother's milk production.

occiput: The back of the skull.

Oldowan: Mode 1 stone tools. They first appear about 2.6 MYA.

operational sex ratio: The ratio of females ready and able to begin a reproductive venture to males in the same position. This is not automatically equal to the raw sex ratio because females (or males) may be unavailable because of commitments to ongoing reproductive ventures (e.g., because of pregnancy).

opsin: Retinal pigment allowing nerve cells to fire when they are struck by light; different opsins respond to different wavelengths of light.

osteomalacia: A medical problem characterized by softening of the bones due to defects of mineral metabolism, especially calcium metabolism. Vitamin D is a key agent in mineral metabolism, so vitamin D deficiency is a primary cause of osteomalacia. Osteomalacia, when it occurs in children, is also known as rickets.

outcrossing: The process of joining a haploid sex cell from one individual with a haploid sex cell from some other individual. One of three components of sexual reproduction. The other two are meiosis and recombination.

pair bond: This word refers to both relatively long-term and stable associations between a breeding male and a breeding female as well as the emotional ties that maintain these associations.

parasite: An organism that benefits at the expense of another, its host. Parasites are generally much smaller than and live in or on their hosts.

parental investment: Anything done or contributed by a parent that increases the survival or reproductive prospects of a particular offspring at a cost to the parent's future reproductive capacity. Parental investment is what economists call a "cost function"; this means that what is spent on one offspring is unavailable to be spent on another.

partial penetrance: The situation when an allele is neither fully dominant nor fully recessive; when an allele is partially expressed.

paternity confidence: The probability that a man's wife's children are his own genetic progeny. When paternity confidence is low, men tend not to provision; hence selection may favor female traits that help to keep paternity confidence high.

pathogen: A microscopic, typically uni-cellular parasite. Parasites can be pathogens if they cause disease in their hosts.

pelvis: the bony girdle that joins the legs to the trunk. It tends to be short and broad in bipeds.

phalanx (plural, phalanges): The bones comprising the fingers and toes. Curved phalanges are common in species that do a lot of tree climbing.

phenotypic gambit: An analytical assumption used by students of both animal and human social behavior. The assumption that if a given social interaction produces some apparent short-term advantage (e.g., procurement of a food item), such interactions will be favored because they will result in higher reproductive success.

phoneme: The unique set of meaningless sounds that are used to distinguish meaning in any particular language.

phylogenetic: Pertaining to the ancestor–descendant relationships among species. An approach to classifying organisms based on those ancestor–descendant relationships.

pleiotropic: an adjective meaning a gene or gene product that has multiple effects on the phenotype. This is an important concept. Unlike the genes that Mendel studied, most genes are significantly pleiotropic.

Pleistocene: A geologic epoch lasting from about 2.6 million years ago (MYA) to about 11,700 years ago. The Pleistocene is marked by dramatic climatic shifts between colder (glacial) and warmer (interglacial) phases. The Pleistocene was preceded by the Pliocene and followed by the Holocene, which includes the present. The end of the Pleistocene (and beginning of the Holocene) is defined by the end of the most recent glacial period.

Plio-Pleistocene: The period straddling the boundary between the Pliocene and the Pleistocene. Roughly 2.8 to 2.4 MYA.

Pliocene: A geologic epoch lasting from about 5.3 million years ago (MYA) to about 2.6 MYA. The Pliocene was preceded by the Miocene and followed by the Pleistocene.

Podarcis sicula: Genus and species name (like *Homo sapiens*) of the lizard whose evolution was studied by Herrel's team.

polygenic: Shaped by genes at more than one locus.

posterior: Back, last; the opposite of anterior.

precociality: The state of being born (or hatched) at an advanced stage of development; precocial young are relatively independent and need less care.

preeclampsia: A condition of pregnancy associated with abnormally high blood pressure and protein in the urine. It is associated with potentially serious health risks for both mother and infant.

primates: The order of mammals to which humans, other apes, monkeys, and prosimians belong.

primitive: A trait that evolved prior to the common ancestor of the group of interest. Grasping hands are primitive for apes. All apes have them.

proxy: An estimate.

pseudogene: A gene that has been turned off as a result of changes in its A,T,C,G coding sequence. A gene that no longer causes a protein to be produced.

reciprocity, reciprocal altruism: Accepting costs in order to benefit those neighbors who behave the same way toward you.

recessive: An allele that is expressed only in homozygotes.

recombination: The exchange of genetic material between paternally- and maternally-derived chromosomes during sex cell formation. One of three components of sexual reproduction. The other two are meiosis and outcrossing.

rhizome: Underground storage organ of a plant; a rootstock from which the plant can send up new green shoots after lying dormant during a cold or dry season; usually grows horizontally. Ginger is a rhizome still used in a variety of human cuisines.

RMR: Resting metabolic rate; the "fuel efficiency" of an organism, measured in calories per unit time.

sagittal crest: A bony ridge the extends from the top of the skull and increases the area for temporalis muscle attachment.

secondary altriciality: Altriciality in a species whose close relatives have precocial young; derived altriciality, as in humans, since our close relatives (e.g., chimps, gorillas) are much more precocial.

selfing: The opposite of outcrossing: Creating offspring by joining haploid sex cells from the same individual.

sexual reproduction: Reproduction involving meiosis, recombination and outcrossing.

sexual selection: Selection for traits that increase mating success.

sexually antagonistic gene: A gene that increases fitness in one sex and decreases it in another. Except for genes on the Y-chromosome, all genes occur in both sexes. Such genes are favored by selection if their average effect on fitness is positive, regardless of how the pluses and minuses are distributed across males and females.

social-brain hypothesis: Robin Dunbar's proposal that evolution favors increases in brain size when the complexities of social life demand it.

squamates: Members of the Squamata, including all scaled reptiles.

subspecies: A taxon below the level of the species. Named biological units within a single species.

symbolic behavior: Behavior can only be inferred from the material remains that hominins leave behind. Oldowan and Acheulean tools look very pragmatic. They seem designed to address basic survival tasks. But the drilled shell ornaments and cave paintings of animals that arise after the evolution of *H. sapiens* suggest different kinds of motivations and goals. These are early manifestations of "art for art's sake."

syntax: rules for combining morphemes to convey ideas.

tit-for-tat: A "nice" strategy that is largely immune to invasion by less-nice strategies; tit-for-tat plays altruistically on the first round and thereafter does whatever its partner did on the previous round.

trichromatic vision: The ability to see in full color as humans do; requires three different opsins.

tuber: Underground storage organ of a plant; similar to rhizome (some tubers are thickened rhizomes). Potatoes are tubers you have almost certainly eaten.

ungulate: Any hoofed mammal.

uniformitarianism: A core principle of science stipulating that the forces we posit in our explanations must be observable and constant (or vary in ways that are themselves explainable in terms of higher-level constants). OK, that was pretty philosophical but I wanted to be precise. In the realm of evolutionary science, uniformitarianism requires that we explain all of the observable facts of biology (adaptation, speciation, biogeography, homology, extinction, etc.) in terms of the same set of forces, namely natural selection in Mendelian populations. See Chapter 7.

vitamin D3: The biologically active form of vitamin D, cholecalciferol.

voiced/unvoiced: Two kinds of "consonants;" the vocal chords vibrate when a voiced consonant (for example, /b/, /d/, or /g/) is being produced, but they do not vibrate when an unvoiced consonant is being produced (for example, /p/, /t/, or /k/). Put your hand on your throat to verify the difference.

wean: Terminate an infant or child's dependence on breast milk by providing alternate foods.

wild-type population: A population living in nature and characterized by the genotypes and adaptations that have been favored by natural selection. Wild-type populations (e.g., the wolves of Alaska) stand in contrast to strains or breeds (e.g., Italian greyhounds) that have been created by humans through selective breeding.

X-linked genetic factor: An allele on the X-chromosome.

Xq28: A small region of the X-chromosome that appears to carry one or more alleles affecting sexual orientation in humans.